Shattered Dreams

Outward Odyssey
A People's History of Spaceflight

Series editor
Colin Burgess

Shattered
Dreams

The Lost and Canceled Space Missions

Colin Burgess

Foreword by Don Thomas

UNIVERSITY OF NEBRASKA PRESS • LINCOLN

Library of Congress Cataloging-in-
Publication Data
Names: Burgess, Colin, 1947– author.
| Thomas, Don, 1955– writer of
foreword.
Title: Shattered dreams: the lost
and canceled space missions / Colin
Burgess; foreword by Don Thomas.
Description: Lincoln: University
of Nebraska Press, [2019] | Series:
Outward odyssey: a people's
history of spaceflight | Includes
bibliographical references and index.
Identifiers: LCCN 2018028072
ISBN 9781496206756 (cloth: alk. paper)
ISBN 9781496214201 (epub)
ISBN 9781496214218 (mobi)
ISBN 9781496214225 (pdf)
Subjects: LCSH: Astronauts—
Biography. | Manned space
flight—History. | Outer space—
Exploration—History.
Classification: LCC TL789.85.A1 B866
2019 | DDC 629.450092/2—dc23
LC record available at https://lccn.loc
.gov/2018028072

Set in Adobe Garamond Pro by
Mikala R. Kolander.

Frontispiece courtesy NASA.

This book is dedicated to the fond memory of
Kim Poor (1952–2017), celebrated space artist, founder
of Novaspace Galleries and Astronaut Central, and
creator with his beloved wife Sally of the annual and
phenomenally successful Spacefest shows, many of which
I attended. In recent years, Kim was diagnosed with MJD
Ataxia, a progressive neurological disease that confined
him to a wheelchair and increasingly limited his ability
to speak. Despite these profound challenges and with the
loving support of Sally and their children Kelsey
and Nathan, Kim continued to the end to take an active
role in ventures that have done much to promote
space activities and space art.

Picking up the pieces of a shattered dream is better than having no pieces to pick up at all.

—Matshona Dhliwayo

Contents

Illustrations

Tables

Foreword

For some, they are lessons learned early in life. For others it may take decades. But eventually everyone, through their own personal life experiences or from those close to them, either learns or comes to the realization that life can be unfair. Do everything right and follow every rule, and you can still come up short. Similarly, we all learn that there are no guarantees in life except paying taxes and dying. These life lessons are always difficult to learn, but eventually we all experience them to various degrees.

These lessons can be extraordinarily painful for hardworking, hard-charging, goal-oriented individuals like astronauts and astronaut candidates. Nearly every one of the astronauts I have met had long dreamed of becoming an astronaut from an early age. Some, like myself, first dreamed of going into space while in elementary school as we watched the first Mercury astronauts launch into space. For others it was when they were in high school watching Neil Armstrong's first step on the surface of the moon in 1969 or in college watching Sally Ride become the first American female astronaut to reach space. But for nearly all the astronauts, once the decision was made that they wanted to venture into space to be a part of the journey of exploration, they pursued that dream, that goal, with laser-sharp focus. It became their life mission.

For me it took thirty-three years from dream to reality, and that time was seldom spent daydreaming. Once the fire was lit inside, it was full throttle and full speed ahead. For most of us the journey was not an easy one, with most experiencing various forms of setback, delays, and failure along the way. Through hard work, persistence, and good fortune, many individuals were successful in achieving their dream of flying in space.

But events in life can change the best laid plans in an instant. Sometimes personal events can lead to change. A birth, a marriage, a divorce.

Sometimes medical issues pop up suddenly that can change your eligibility. Sometimes individuals change their plans. Sometimes the change is unwelcomingly thrust on to them. For example, following the space shuttle *Challenger* accident, wide-ranging program changes were implemented, including the cancellation of plans to launch shuttles from Vandenberg and, for a time, the cancellation of the payload specialist program.

As a young boy, I dreamed of walking on the moon one day. When the Apollo lunar program came to an end in 1972 with *Apollo 17* completing the final lunar landing mission, my plan necessarily changed to visiting a space station one day or to orbiting the earth in a yet-to-be-designed space shuttle. I went on to fly four flights aboard the space shuttle; but while training for a fifth mission, which was to take me to the International Space Station, an arbitrary and political medical decision emanating from high up the bureaucratic tower in NASA Headquarters had me removed from that flight only two months before the then-scheduled launch and after more than three years of training and months and years of time spent away from my home and family. It was a most difficult pill to swallow at the time.

As you read through these stories of shattered dreams and missed opportunities, I think it is important not to view them as highlighting failure of not accomplishing personal goals but to instead marvel and focus on the human drive to achieve dreams in life. The dreams, the determination, the hard work, and the dedication in each of these stories is no different from those of the astronauts who successfully made it to space. In most cases, these individuals did nothing wrong and, in fact, did everything right. Sometimes in life you are dealt a bad hand that is beyond your control. Sometimes you end up at the right spot but at the wrong time. And sometimes you are just plain unlucky.

So let these stories be a tribute to those who had cosmic dreams but whose time was not quite right. May their spirits soar and remind us of how fragile life can be, encouraging our future explorers to never give up on their dreams.

Don Thomas
NASA *mission specialist,* STS-65, STS-70, STS-83, *and* STS-94

Preface

During a recent interview with a radio journalist, I was asked where my ideas for new books came from. I responded by saying that on many occasions in the past they had their origins in something as simple as a casual conversation or subjects that people had suggested I might pursue. The important thing, I emphasized, was to recognize these prompts and then act on them as soon as possible. It was equally important for me to know that I would enjoy the research, that the book was a viable product for a potential publisher, and that people who later put their hands in their pockets to buy the book would find it interesting.

I must admit, however, that the entire concept of the Outward Odyssey series—now celebrating over a decade and a half of achievement—was not mine to begin with and came from a far more traditional source.

It all began in March 2003, when I received a message from my new-found publisher, the University of Nebraska Press (UNP), and specifically their then editor-in-chief Gary Dunham. A self-confessed spaceflight enthusiast, he said that he had enjoyed publishing my books *Teacher in Space: Christa McAuliffe and the Challenger Legacy* and *Fallen Astronauts* and that he was exploring the possibility of UNP putting together a series of hard-cover books detailing the story of our exploration of space and the men and women who were, and are, part of that history. It was not envisaged as a series that trod overly familiar paths, but one along the lines of a universal "people's history" that did not cover technical advances or offer a manifest destiny approach to the subject. Instead, it would relate over several volumes the social or human history of space exploration and its impact on people. He felt eight volumes might be a good starting point and asked me if I would consider taking on the role of series editor.

Although this was well beyond anything I had ever attempted, after due consideration I rather boldly replied that I felt I was up to the challenge. Bold, as I had no previous experience or qualifications as an editor and would be working from my home near Sydney, Australia—far removed from UNP headquarters in Lincoln, Nebraska.

The plan involved finding suitable authors and having them prepare proposals based on a book outline I conceived and allocated to them, as well as bringing them up to speed on the social mandate of the series and of their book in particular. I would also emphasize their contractual obligations and offer information on the fixed style guide they had to employ in whatever they wrote. Once their proposal was found acceptable by the university's editorial board, I would then guide the author through the writing, editing, and publication process on behalf of UNP. In basic terms, I became a go-between, constantly communicating with all the potential authors and the publisher. The series needed a name, and after some deliberation I suggested Outward Odyssey. This found a ready acceptance at the press, and work could begin.

Initially, I started looking at authors of previously published books on space exploration, but then I realized I should be trying to unearth a whole new generation of authors for the series. And with the approval of the press this somewhat radical concept was adopted.

Around five years later Gary Dunham left UNP for other publishing pastures. In the years since, I have been aided, guided, and greatly supported by senior editor Robert Taylor and his talented team at UNP. He has been of especial and enthusiastic help to me in moving the series along. The original-concept target of eight volumes was eventually reached—not without a few problems along the way—but UNP wanted the series to continue beyond that number, and I was agreeable. The long-running nature of the series is a remarkable achievement for everyone concerned and, unlike the title of this book, a dream that truly became a stunning and ongoing reality.

This latest volume in the Outward Odyssey series, *Shattered Dreams: The Lost and Canceled Space Missions*, tells the very human and remarkable story of a number of people who held a cherished dream of flying into space and how those plans unraveled through flight cancellations or other, often tragic, reasons. Some came agonizingly close to achieving their goal of looking down on the earth from space or travelling to the moon. While most of the subjects of this book are generally familiar names in spaceflight history, others will be having their stories told for the very first time in book form.

Some of the stories contained in this series volume date back several years as articles originally written for different publications such as the British Interplanetary Society's *Spaceflight* magazine or *Quest: The History of Spaceflight Quarterly* or even as biographical summaries in books published elsewhere (such as *The First Soviet Cosmonaut Team*, written with Rex Hall). These stories have been rewritten and expanded with a host of fresh information, while others were researched and compiled with the assistance of many people, chiefly with the families of each person whose story is related in this book.

Colin Burgess
Series editor, Outward Odyssey

Acknowledgments

As always, there are numerous people to whom I owe bouquets of sincere thanks for their assistance and support. Mostly, I want to thank those who are very close to the stories told in this book and kindly gave much-needed assistance and information, not only in the compilation of each chapter, but in checking that what I wrote was completely accurate. They would then give me their final approval. This wonderful support has enabled me to bring to the pages of this book the dreams, ambitions, and accomplishments of some truly amazing people. I could not have done this without them, and their willingness to help and guide me is appreciated far more than I can say.

Many of those who assisted in bringing this book to fruition have been valued friends and helpers over many years. These include Francis French, Bert Vis, Michael Cassutt, David Shomper, and David Shayler, who have always been willing to assist by reading through my story drafts and offering suggestions to ensure that it is both authoritative and free of errors. Any blunders that do remain are solely my responsibility.

As well, for their continuing efforts in offering additional information, quality data, and photographs, I am once again indebted to other overseas friends and fellow space researchers Ed Hengeveld, Robert Pearlman (www.collectspace.com), Joachim Becker (www.spacefacts.de), and Gordon Hooper.

The following people were contacted in the course of researching this book, and I am indebted to each and every one of them for the information they have supplied. I hope they enjoy this book, and though for many it may bring back some melancholy or even bitter memories, it is also a respectful tribute to the lives and achievements of a number of very special people. Given that, I would like to say a sincere thank you to Diane

Allen, Ana (Caldeiro) Badillio, Nancy and Scott Bull, Steve Coester, Irene Cummins, Richard Farrimond, Jack Ferrell, Dominic Gorie, Suzanne Graveline, David Harland, Charles Jennings, John Kaneshige, Wes Lineberry, Frank (Bill) Murcham, Dee O'Hara, Damion Planchon (Damion Lloyd Photography), Tony Quine, Scott Robertson, Rick Schwarting, Sue (Thorne) Schwarting, Melanie Thorne, Paul Scully-Power, Robert K. Stevenson, Robert (Bob) Stumpf, Pratiwi Sudarmono, Harry Swenson, Kevin Taylor, Pierre Thuot, Joseph Totah, Leslie Tuttle, Charlie Walker, Dorothy Wood, Lucas Wood, Nigel Wood, and Al Worden.

My sincere thanks also go to Svetlana Omelchenko for her kindness in sending me several long letters outlining her story, which were translated into English by friends.

Many thanks also to shuttle astronaut and author Don Thomas for preparing such a wonderfully appropriate and empathetic foreword to this book.

As with several previous publications in the Outward Odyssey series, freelance copy editor Jeremy Hall has applied his considerable skills and sharp eyes in editing this book and giving it that final polish, while project editor Sara Springsteen and the entire team at UNP thoroughly deserve my ongoing gratitude for their support and enthusiasm. And last, but certainly not least, profuse thanks to all those readers of the Outward Odyssey series who have taken the time to send me and the series authors messages saying how much they have enjoyed a particular book or the series as a whole.

As the old saying suggests, appreciation can make a day—or even change a life. Writing a book such as this is time consuming and definitely never easy, but knowing that people are actually reading it—and caring enough to respond—makes it well worth the effort.

Thank you.

Prologue

End of a Spaceflight Dream

The step that we are on is only a step to the next place, and no step
regardless of how massive is ever a destination.

—Craig D. Lounsbrough

The history of human space exploration is replete with scores of dedicated, highly motivated people whose lofty ambitions of flying into the cosmos were, for any number of reasons, never realized. Some, such as Mercury astronaut Donald (Deke) Slayton, managed through sheer determination to overcome illnesses that had seen them grounded for several years and subsequently journey into space. Slayton had suffered from a common ailment known as atrial fibrillation but finally achieved orbit on the momentous Apollo-Soyuz Test Project mission in 1975.

While Slayton regained his flight status, several of the Soviet Union's first cosmonaut team of twenty would-be spacefarers did not share the same good fortune. Eight of their number would never fly into space, through illness, accidents, misbehavior, and even death.

Valentin Bondarenko died in hospital from terrible burns he suffered after an oxygen-fueled fire erupted during a test in an isolation chamber on 23 March 1961.

Grigori Nelyubov had been backup pilot for Yuri Gagarin and Gherman Titov on their epic missions but was summarily dismissed from the cosmonaut team for drunken behavior and arrogance on 27 March 1963, for which he had refused to apologize. He departed the training center on 4 May, and after an ensuing life filled with sorrow and regret, it is believed he deliberately stepped in front of a train and was killed while drunk on 18 February 1966.

Valentin Filatyev was dismissed from the team as an example to the other cosmonauts for simply being with Grigori Nelyubov on the night of the latter's drunken escapade at a railway station. He left the cosmonaut corps on 17 April 1963.

Ivan Anikeyev was likewise sacked from the cosmonaut corps for nothing more than being with Grigori Nelyubov on the night he was involved in a drunken altercation.

After a test ride in a centrifuge, Anatoly Kartashov was found to be suffering from a minor physical ailment and was stood down indefinitely. He resigned from the cosmonaut team on 7 April 1962.

Valentin Varlarmov badly injured his neck when he dove into a shallow lake on 24 July 1960. As a result, he was removed from the cosmonaut team on 6 March 1961.

Mars Rafikov was dismissed from the group on 24 March 1962 for continuing instances of drunkenness and reported domestic issues leading to a divorce.

Dmitri Zaikin was a backup pilot on *Voskhod 2* and lost a flight assignment in the Soyuz program when he developed an ulcer in April 1968, which led to his medical disqualification. He stayed on for several years as a trainer of cosmonauts.

Following the two highly successful orbital missions of cosmonauts Yuri Gagarin and Gherman Titov in the Soviet Union's space program, there was now a need to select additional pilots for future flights. On New Year's Eve 1961, the Central Committee of the Communist Party in the Soviet Union approved the selection of this new group of cosmonauts. The committee members had also heeded the recommendation of the director of cosmonaut training, Gen. Nikolai Kamanin, that five of those selected be women. It was widely known that a number of female pilots in the United States were being medically tested—albeit unofficially—as potential astronauts. "We cannot allow that the first woman in space will be an American," Kamanin wrote in his diary. "This would be an insult to the patriotic feelings of Soviet women."

Although the recruitment process demanded the selection of a number of suitably qualified male jet pilots from the Soviet air force, the main difference in choosing the five women was that they did not need to have any piloting experience, although military, aerobatic, or sport flying would obviously provide considerable advantage. The main prerequisite was an advanced parachuting qualification. This was determined by the fact that they would be required to eject from their Vostok spacecraft prior to landing, as a satisfactory rocket braking system was still under development. The selection process began in earnest on 15 January when the files of fifty-eight women were dumped on Kamanin's desk.

Following a long and exhaustive process, the selection of five women was finally approved. They were Tatyana Kuznetsova, Valentina Ponomareva, Irina Solovyeva, Zhanna Yorkina, and Valentina Tereshkova. At the end of an intensive training program, Tereshkova was the one chosen to fly on the *Vostok 6* mission, with Solovyeva and Ponomareva acting as her first and second backup pilots.

Although there were difficulties with nausea and physical discomfort experienced by Tereshkova during her *Vostok 6* mission, the final flight in the Vostok series, it became a historic and propagandistic triumph for the Soviet Union. Meanwhile, the women continued to train for further spaceflights as the Voskhod program began, with two successful missions. The first carried three cosmonauts into space, while on the flight of the two-man *Voskhod 2* cosmonaut Alexei Leonov carried out the first human space walk. Further space spectaculars were soon under development, with one planned mission being an all-women crew operating a ten-day orbital flight of *Voskhod 4*. By this time, Tereshkova had married fellow cosmonaut Andrian Nikolayev, and they were the parents of a daughter. As a new mother, Tereshkova would no longer be considered. For this new venture, General Kamanin selected Valentina Ponomareva as mission commander, along with pilot Irina Solovyeva. Zhanna Yorkina and Tatyana Kuznetsova were assigned to serve as their backups. As well as achieving what would have been the third-longest spaceflight to that time, Solovyeva was scheduled to perform a space walk during the mission.

Then, in January 1966, the chief designer of the Soviet space program, Sergei Korolev, died in the hospital following what is said to have been a poorly performed operation, although the exact details have never been released. Thereafter, the space program abandoned work on any future Voskhod missions and instead moved ahead with the new spacecraft design known as Soyuz. The four women had been in general training for the

Voskhod 4 mission, but their flight was canceled before any mission-specific training had been conducted. To their disappointment, they would never receive another spaceflight assignment, and though they remained cosmonaut candidates for a while, their chances of this happening were gone. They all resigned from the cosmonaut detachment in October 1969, and their names remained a state secret until 1987.

The list of Soviet and Commonwealth of Nations (CIS) cosmonauts selected after the initial group of twenty jet pilots from the Soviet air force in 1960 is a long one, but so too is a list of those who were selected but never flew, containing far too many names to mention in this chapter but certainly numbering in their dozens—men and women alike. The story of Svetlana Omelchenko, one of those who qualified as a cosmonaut candidate, is recounted in this book as representative of those disappointed souls who were selected to fly but never made it to the launchpad.

The Interkosmos program of flying Soviet Bloc cosmonauts on week-long missions to the *Mir* space station gave a flight opportunity to test pilots from several participating nations, but each of them also had a backup pilot, most of whom returned to their regular duties postflight, never having achieved their goal.

For many others, however, those long-held dreams of flying into space would also remain unfulfilled, and this shared disappointment was not confined to the ranks of American astronauts and Soviet and CIS cosmonauts. Tragically, one of the major influences on who would fly and who would not was the catastrophic loss of the space shuttle *Challenger* on a freezing-cold morning in January 1986, which not only took the lives of seven spacefarers but ended the plans for so many others who might have followed. Prior to the *Challenger* tragedy, NASA had announced a lengthy roster of shuttle missions, most of them nominating only partial crews, as flight payloads and mission objectives were still waiting to be finalized.

Many potential crewmembers—including non-NASA personnel from private industry, overseas payload specialists, and U.S. military services—were well into mission training. This last group, almost exclusively composed of U.S. Air Force personnel, were known collectively as manned spaceflight engineers, or MSEs, training to operate as payload specialists on several deeply classified space missions under the auspices of the U.S. Department of Defense. Only two MSE astronauts would eventually be carried on shuttle missions prior to the *Challenger* accident—Gary Payton and William Pailes. Thereafter, the loss of the veteran space shuttle and its crew, which included two payload specialists on their first and only space mission, teacher Christa McAuliffe and Hughes engineer Greg Jarvis, caused the immediate suspension of NASA's human spaceflight program. During the thirty-two-month hiatus that ensued, there was a reevaluation of exactly who should be launched on shuttle missions once the program resumed. Consequently, the payload specialist program was temporarily suspended, which for most of those in mission training meant the end of their chance to fly.

Indonesian payload specialist Pratiwi Sudarmono (and backup Taufik Akbar) were scheduled to fly in June 1986 aboard the shuttle *Columbia*, chiefly in order to supervise the launch of the Indonesian communications satellite Palapa B.

On that same STS-61H mission, Britain's Sqn. Ldr. Nigel Wood (RAF) was assigned to the Skynet 4A mission, with fellow RAF officer Richard Farrimond serving as his backup payload specialist.

Edward (Pete) Aldridge Jr., then secretary of the U.S. Air Force, was a designated payload specialist on STS-62A, the first space shuttle mission scheduled to be launched from Vandenberg Air Force Base in California. MSE Brett Watterson was also a member of that crew.

Nagapathi Chidamabar Bhat and his backup payload specialist Paramaswaren Radhakrishnan from the Indian Space Research Organization (ISRO) were training for the STS-61I mission, which was to have included the launch of the Indian satellite INSAT-IC.

There was an even deeper, later tragedy in store for MSE Charles Edward (Chuck) Jones, who had been slated to fly aboard the shuttle *Challenger* on STS-71B in December 1986. On Tuesday, 11 September 2001, the former U.S. Air Force officer was on a routine business trip aboard American Airlines Flight 11 when it was hijacked by terrorists and deliberately flown into the north tower of New York's World Trade Center.

Table 1 is a list of scheduled spaceflights that were undergoing development and crewing prior to the loss of *Challenger* in January 1986, which would have included any non-NASA personnel in their crews.

Table 1. Space shuttle flight manifest prior to loss of *Challenger* orbiter

Mission	Space shuttle	Launch date	Non-NASA crew	Backup crew
STS-61E	*Columbia*	6 March 1986	Samuel Durrance* Ronald Parise*	Kenneth Nordsieck
STS-61H	*Columbia*	24 June 1986	Pratiwi Sudarmono Nigel Wood	Taufik Akbar Richard Farrimond
STS-62A	*Discovery*	1 July 1986	Edward Aldridge Brett Watterson (MSE)	Randy Odle (MSE)
STS-61M	*Challenger*	22 July 1986	Robert Wood	Charles Walker*
STS-61N	*Discovery*	4 September 1986	Frank Casserino (MSE)	Daryl Joseph (MSE)
STS-61I	*Challenger*	27 September 1986	Nagapathi Bhat	P. Radhakrishnan
STS-62B	*Discovery*	29 September 1986	Katherine Roberts (MSE)	
STS-61K	*Columbia*	1 October 1986	Byron Lichtenberg* Michael Lampton* Robert Stevenson	Dirk Frimout* Charles Chappell
STS-61L	*Atlantis*	1 November 1986	John Konrad	Stephen Cunningham
STS-71B	*Challenger*	6 December 1986	Charles Jones (MSE)	
STS-71A	*Columbia*	1 January 1987	Kenneth Nordsieck	Ronald Parise*
STS-71C	*Atlantis*	1 January 1987	Peter Longhurst	Christopher Holmes
STS-71D	*Columbia*	1 February 1987	Robert Wood	Charles Walker*
STS-71E	*Challenger*	1 March 1987	Drew Gaffney* Robert Phillips	Millie Hughes-Fulford*
STS-71F	*Atlantis*	1 March 1987	Steven MacLean*	Bjarni Tryggvason*
STS-71M	*Columbia*	1 August 1987	Kenneth Nordsieck	
STS-81G	*Challenger*	23 February 1988	Mamoru Mohri* Chiaki Mukai*	Takao Doi*
STS-81M	*Atlantis*	1 July 1988	Millie Hughes-Fulford*	

* Achieved later spaceflight(s)

Source: NASA.

While offering an incorrect perception of safe, regular shuttle space missions prior to the *Challenger* tragedy, NASA was weighing numerous requests to fly payload specialists on future flights. The space agency had set something of a precedent by flying two politicians on separate missions, as well as a Saudi prince, and there was some speculation of flying poets and filmmakers on future flights. There was even talk of singer John Denver serenading the world with one of his songs from orbit.

Prior to the loss of *Challenger* there was one program that had already begun, with the intended goal of selecting a journalist to fly into space. A list of finalists had already been drawn up, including veteran broadcaster Walter Cronkite—the likely choice to take on the role. However, that was all before the *Challenger* crew was lost seventy-three seconds after liftoff from the Kennedy Space Center.

After an enforced post-*Challenger* hiatus, the payload specialist program would eventually resume, with a number of candidates operating as payload specialist backups and still others as alternate payload specialists. Several of those backups and alternates would never fly into space (see table 2). Then, following the loss of the shuttle *Columbia* on 1 February 2003, the payload specialist program was canceled, and no more candidates were manifested up to the time of the final space shuttle mission (STS-135) in July 2011.

Table 2. Unflown backup payload specialists

Mission	Unflown backup payload specialist	Unflown alternate payload specialist
STS-40	Bill Williams Robert Philips	
STS-44	Michael Belt	John Hawker
STS-42	Ken Money	
STS-45	Charles Chappell	Arrah Sue Simpson
STS-50		Brian Finley
STS-47	Stanley Koszelak	
STS-55	Renate Brümmer	
STS-58	Ford Collins Lawrence Young	
STS-55		Julie Sanchez
STS-67	Scott Vangen	Ricardo Rodriguez

STS-73	Glynn Holt
	Daniel Matthieson
STS-78	Luca Urbani
STS-83	Paul Ronney
	Alan Johnston
STS-94	Paul Ronney
	Alan Johnston
STS-87	Yaroslav Pustovyi
STS-90	Alexander Dunlap
STS-107	Itzhak Mayo

Source: NASA.

As previously mentioned, thirteen American women pilots underwent medical testing at the Lovelace Clinic in New Mexico, where the thirty-two Mercury astronaut finalists had earlier undergone similar supervised tests. Although many of them produced outstanding results, the tests had never been sanctioned by NASA; and despite the protestations of some of the women (who became known as the Mercury 13), their request to join NASA's astronaut corps was denied and set aside.

Since their first astronaut group was announced in 1983, the Canadian Space Agency (CSA) has recruited a total of fourteen astronauts—including two selected in 2009 (Jeremy Hansen and David Saint-Jacques) and another two named in 2017 (Joshua Kutryk and Jenni Sidey), all four of whom are yet to be assigned to a flight. Of the remaining ten, only two—Ken Money (in the 1983 group) and Michael McKay (in the 1992 group)—retired from the CSA without ever flying into space.

Several members of the NASA groups 4 and 6 scientist-astronauts resigned from the space agency because they did not wish to continue learning to fly jet aircraft or because they had a desire to return to their studies due to a frustrating lack of future flight opportunities. They were F. Curtis Michel (in group 4) and Philip Chapman, Donald Holmquest, John Llewellyn, and Brian O'Leary (in group 6). Since then, only three NASA astronauts have resigned from the space agency without ever flying into space: John Bull (group 5), who resigned for severe health reasons; Col. Christopher (Gus) Loria, with the U.S. Marine Corps (USMC) (group 16), who suffered a back injury that was eventually deemed inoperable and returned to operational duties with the Marine Corps; and Cmdr. Neil Woodward III, with the U.S. Navy (USN) (group 17), who moved on to detached duties with NASA before retiring from the space agency and the U.S. Navy in 2008. Medical doctor Yvonne Cagle, a colonel in the U.S. Air Force (USAF), moved into medical research with NASA following her selection as a group 16 astronaut and, while she is technically still on the astronaut list, is unlikely to ever transition back to flight status.

For those who could afford the extravagantly high cost, there was a new way into space. At the beginning of the new millennium, in a project first arranged by MirCorp (and later Space Adventures), business tycoons and celebrities were given the chance to purchase a seat on a Russian Soyuz spacecraft headed to the International Space Station (ISS). They could achieve this by handing over an eight-figure sum of money to the Russian Federal Space Agency and being prepared to undergo several months of training in Moscow, in addition to later ISS familiarization in Houston. Despite paying for the privilege, they were never guaranteed that Soyuz seat; if they were found to be lacking in general good health, their place would go to the next cashed-up customer. Naturally enough, those in the astronaut and cosmonaut corps were furious about the loss of a coveted couch on a Soyuz mission. They had trained many years to be eligible to fly, and now this new breed of "space tourist" was purchasing and claiming those precious seats with minimal training.

The first such space tourist was American businessman and multimillionaire Dennis Tito. Initially, NASA totally rejected the concept and refused to allow Tito to train alongside the NASA crews. They later relented, and in mid-2001 Tito flew to the ISS aboard the *Soyuz 32* spacecraft, spending eight days within the orbiting space laboratory. Having proved through Tito's experience that it could be done, other candidates began shelling out multimillions in order to spend a few days orbiting the earth. However, despite achieving true spaceflight, they were not permitted to call themselves astronauts, and as the initially used "space tourist" carried unwelcome connotations for them, the term was later revised to "spaceflight participant."

Mark Shuttleworth from South Africa became the second person to purchase a Soyuz seat and flew to the ISS in April 2002. Others would follow, including Gregory Olsen from the United States, Anousheh Ansari from

Iran, and Hungarian-born American Charles Simonyi. Simonyi flew to the ISS in 2007 and then made a second flight in 2009. Other flown participants of interest were Richard Garriott, son of Skylab astronaut Owen Garriott, and Guy Laliberté, cofounder of Cirque du Soleil. The governments of Malaysia and South Korea also seized the opportunity to purchase Soyuz seats and send one of their own nationals into space, with Sheikh Muzsaphar Shukor and Yi So-yeon representing their respective countries on these paid expeditions.

In the event of an unexpected illness or other difficulties, paid backups had also undergone training, and some were eventually successful in flying to the ISS. The last person to undergo training as a space participant was the renowned British singer Sarah Brightman. She was scheduled to fly aboard *Soyuz TMA-18M* in September 2015, but late in her training, she pulled out of the mission for undisclosed reasons. Her male backup, Japanese artist Satoshi Takamatsu, also withdrew from the flight, and since that time, there have been no further announcements of space participant flights. The current list of those who failed to achieve spaceflight in this program, either as the prime or backup candidate, reads as follows:

Lance Bass (USA), *Soyuz TMA-1*

Daisuke Enomoto (Japan), *Soyuz TMA-9*

Faiz Khaleed (Malaysia), *Soyuz TMA-11*

Ko San (South Korea), *Soyuz TMA-12*

Nik Halik (Australia), *Soyuz TMA-13*

Esther Dyson (USA), *Soyuz TMA-14*

Barbara Barrett (USA), *Soyuz TMA-16*

Sarah Brightman (UK), *Soyuz TMA-18M*

Satoshi Takamatsu (Japan), *Soyuz TMA-18M*

Today, there are 7.3 billion people who call this blue planet their home. Since 1961, only a comparatively small number have had the extraordinary privilege of viewing and marveling at our world from the vantage point of Earth orbit. Many others have had that elusive dream almost in their grasp but have never known the sensation of having a rocket ignite beneath them. For the rest of us, we can only vicariously share the experiences of those who did fly into space, through images and footage, although we are reminded that photographs taken from orbit can never quite match the awesome splendors that unfold before the human eye.

As we continue to reach out into the heavens, the numbers of space explorers will obviously grow commensurately, and so too will the number of potential spacefarers who will never live to see their dream fulfilled. This book tells the stories of a number of men and women who held that all-too-fleeting dream but lost their chance for reasons as simple as a slight health problem. Flights were also canceled following the tragic and far-reaching losses of the space shuttles *Challenger* and *Columbia*, as well as through fatal, earthbound accidents. Nevertheless, their very human stories still amaze and inspire us as we continue to move out into the wonders and mysteries of our universe.

As *Apollo 11* astronaut Michael Collins once said, "Exploration is not a choice, really, it's an imperative."

1. Losing the Moon

Apollo, the Abandoned Missions

To be sure, all this costs us all a good deal of money. This year's
space budget is three times what it was in January 1961, and it is
greater than the space budget of the previous eight years combined.
That budget now stands at 5 billion, 400 million dollars a year—a
staggering sum, though somewhat less than we pay for
cigarettes and cigars every year.

—President John F. Kennedy

Many readers will undoubtedly recall the fad era of the so-called mission
statements that adorned the walls of most company offices in the 1990s.
The words they contained were intended to inspire workers and managers to even greater heights of achievement, as well as provide a motivating
guide to the actions, decision making, and overall goals of an organization.
One could suggest, however, that the mission statement to end all mission
statements was delivered one late spring day on 25 May 1961, when President
John F. Kennedy—four days short of his forty-fourth birthday—made the
trip across Washington from the White House to Capitol Hill to deliver a
monumental undertaking before a joint session of Congress.

Tired of finishing second to the Soviet Union in spaceflight achievements, a resolute President Kennedy was literally ready to shoot for the
moon. Ignoring the recommendations of many of his closest advisers, he
had decided a bold promise of action was required. He also needed to
overcome the aftermath and political ramifications of the calamitous and
costly Bay of Pigs invasion of Cuba, which, in the eyes of many, had portrayed him in the infancy of his presidency as a poor and indecisive leader.

In one of the young president's most passionate and eloquent speeches, he told the joint session of Congress, "I believe that this nation should commit itself, before this decade is out, of landing a man on the moon and returning him safely to the earth. No single space project in this period will be more impressive to mankind, or more important for the long-range exploration of space. And none will be so difficult or expensive to accomplish."

"Difficult" was right, so too was "expensive." More than $20 billion later John Kennedy's dream of a manned lunar landing had become a spectacular reality, although an assassin's bullets meant he was never destined to see it achieved.

In retrospect, the president's national commitment was not only audacious but also delivered at considerable political risk. The United States had yet to orbit a man around the earth; in fact, the only human-tended space experience the nation could boast by mid-1961 was a fifteen-minute suborbital lob made by Alan Shepard earlier that month. Nevertheless, the Apollo program was now undergoing preliminary work and planning and, in time, would exemplify the spirited character of Kennedy's presidency.

As the Apollo program pressed on into the 1970s and as more and more astronauts left lingering footprints in the lunar soil, the once-enamored U.S. public was becoming increasingly apathetic, and many people of influence began to query NASA's mandate. They started asking their congressional representatives just why further millions were being spent—totally wasted in their opinion—pursuing what they deemed to be just an extra few miserable moon rocks, when more pressing earthbound social problems were being starved of finances. By now, many of the nation's citizens had become desensitized to the televised sight of playful astronauts bounding or driving across the lunar terrain. The once-formidable spaceflight fervor was now at a low ebb, and the writing was clearly on the wall for Project Apollo. The United States had beaten the Soviet Union to the moon, and the euphoria of conquest had rapidly abated. In the face of this mounting public apathy, the budgetary shears were about to be unsheathed.

In a 2010 article, "Exploding the Myth of Popular Support for Project Apollo," one-time NASA chief historian Roger Launius had a critical look at the prevailing statistics:

> *At the end of 1965, the* New York Times *reported that a poll conducted in six American cities showed five other public issues holding priority over*

efforts in outer space. Polls in the 1960s also consistently ranked spaceflight near the top of those programs to be cut in the federal budget. Most Americans seemingly preferred doing something about air and water pollution, job training for unskilled workers, national beautification, and poverty before spending federal funds on human spaceflight. The following year Newsweek *echoed the* Times *story, stating: "The U.S. space program is in decline. The Vietnam war and the desperate conditions of the nation's poor and its cities—which make space flight seem, in comparison, like an embarrassing national self-indulgence—have combined to drag down a program where the sky was no longer the limit."*

NASA's last three planned lunar missions were about to be expelled from history, along with the space agency's ambitious but unfulfilled plans for a range of farsighted and enterprising journeys beyond our planet, extending the glory that had once been Project Apollo.

Joe Henry Engle had led life in the fast lane as one of America's most respected and skillful pilots. By early 1971 he had just about done it all; he had ridden some of the hottest planes in the sky and, on no less than three occasions, had piloted the mighty rocket-powered x-15 research aircraft to an altitude greater than fifty miles, thereby qualifying him as a U.S. Air Force astronaut. In April 1966 NASA made it even better for thirty-three-year-old Captain Engle when he was one of those selected in their latest group of nineteen astronauts. After his acceptance, he paid his dues working hard in the astronaut corps. And now he was looking forward to what would undoubtedly be the pinnacle of his career and his life—he was going to walk on the moon on the lunar landing *Apollo 17* mission. Fate, however, still held a few sad ironies in store for the affable, young test pilot from Chapman, Kansas.

Two years earlier, in July 1969, Neil Armstrong and Edwin "Buzz" Aldrin had become the first humans to walk on the surface of the moon, and NASA had accomplished what is regarded as mankind's most sublime, intricate, and ambitious scientific enterprise ever. While it was hardly "the greatest week in the history of the world since the Creation," as President Richard Nixon declared to the crew and the world when he welcomed them back to Earth, the race to the moon had nevertheless brought America together

1. The original crew selected to fly the *Apollo 17* mission. *From left*: Joe Engle (LMP), Gene Cernan (CDR), and Ron Evans (CMP). Courtesy NASA.

like very few events in that century of achievement. Nevertheless, for all his public enthusiasm and slick hyperbole, the president cared little for spaceflight activity.

A Republican Party conservative, Richard Nixon did not believe his government should be spending massive sums of money on the space program, or even on social programs for that matter. Well before the first lunar landing, some Republicans were already calling for the scrapping of Project Apollo, but Nixon was shrewd and ignored these appeals. He had an ulterior motive; should the first lunar landing fail, he felt the blame would fall squarely on the preceding Democratic administrations of Kennedy and Johnson. To that end, NASA's administrator, Dr. Thomas Paine (appointed by President Lyndon Johnson), had not been replaced by a Republican appointee, as was the custom.

In June 1969 Nixon also appointed Vice President Spiro Agnew as head of a task force to determine what directions the space program should take during the seventies and eighties. Following the success of *Apollo 11*, the president then began to cut the NASA budget quite savagely, while a public once addicted to the achievements of Apollo grew ever more disenchanted and indifferent with each successive lunar mission.

Part of the problem, surprisingly, was NASA itself. In the space agency's public statements and literature, they had portrayed *Apollo 11* as the culmination of a grand effort to get to the moon ahead of the Soviet Union, rather than as the beginning of a new era of exploration and scientific discovery. Other reasons for the public disquiet were the increasing pressures of poverty, social change, and the Vietnam War—financial and moral issues that were dividing the nation. Both Congress and the White House noted an unmistakable shift in the public mood and kept it in mind when considering future space funding.

In summing up the public attitude in 1970, the U.S. representative and future mayor of New York City Edward Koch had a lot to say after NASA had boldly proposed flying human beings to Mars. "I just can't for the life of me see voting for monies to find out whether or not there is some microbe on Mars," he raged, "when in fact I know there are rats in Harlem apartments."

Originally, there were ten lunar missions planned—*Apollo 11* to *Apollo 20*—which would have placed twenty astronauts on the moon. When privately assessing which of them would fly on the coveted lunar missions, NASA's astronauts were well aware of the time-honored method of selection employed by astronaut chiefs Alan Shepard and Deke Slayton, both of whom had been grounded for medical reasons. This ordained that any crew serving as backups to another crew would then skip the two successive flights and be assigned to the following mission as the prime crew. Thus, in acting as backups to the *Apollo 10* crew, Mercury astronaut Gordon Cooper, Ed Mitchell, and Donn Eisele were favored to fly on *Apollo 13*. This began to unravel rapidly when NASA informed Eisele that he would likely never fly again after being part of the controversial *Apollo 7* crew under Wally Schirra, as well as his recent poor attitude toward training and a distracting rift in his marriage. Eisele subsequently resigned from the space agency. Then Alan Shepard himself would upset the proverbial apple cart.

America's first man in space had been desperate to get back into a spacecraft since his history-making but all-too-brief ballistic flight back in May 1961. With the winding down of the Mercury program, Shepard had tried for a second and long-duration flight in that series but, failing this, had been assigned as commander of the first two-man Gemini mission. Then he was unexpectedly struck down by Ménière's disease, a disorder of the inner ear that impairs balance and causes dizzying attacks of vertigo. When he could no longer pretend it was something he could somehow shake off, Shepard was removed from the active astronaut list, grounded, and barred from all forms of flying. Although devastated and bitterly disappointed by this turn of events, he nevertheless stayed on with NASA as he continued the fight to regain his flight status. In the interim, he was appointed head of the Astronaut Office.

By 1968 Shepard's condition had worsened, and he was becoming increasingly deaf in his left ear. Then he heard about an ear surgeon in Los Angeles who might be able to help through a radical but risky operation, and Shepard decided to give it a shot. During the delicate surgery, a small silicone tube was implanted in his ear to drain excess fluid from the semicircular canal through the mastoid bone to the top of the spinal column. Fortunately for the veteran astronaut, the risky operation was a complete success, and once he was given medical clearance, Shepard was placed back on flight status. All too soon, that was not good enough for the former U.S. Navy pilot; using his considerable administrative influence within NASA, he soon began canvassing for command of a lunar mission.

Much to the chagrin of his Mercury colleague Gordon Cooper, Shepard was gifted the command of *Apollo 13*. Having served as backup commander for *Apollo 10*, Cooper vehemently protested that the mission should rightfully be his, but he could muster very little support within NASA for his grievance. By now, he had become well known in the agency's corridors of power as a troublesome loner with a passion for racing cars and speedboats, with churlish public views (stating on one occasion, "I guess NASA wants astronauts to be tiddlywink players"), and with a casual attitude toward training. He had become a thorn in many people's sides because of his outspoken and recalcitrant views. Once he had lost command of *Apollo 13*, and with little backing, Cooper quickly got the message that he would never fly into space again and resigned from NASA in disgust. Shepard, together with rookie astronauts Ed Mitchell and Stu Roosa, was now scheduled to fly to the moon.

However, NASA prudently decided that Shepard needed some additional training time, and as a result, the crews of *Apollo 13* and *Apollo 14* were transposed. Jim Lovell's crew, which included Fred Haise as the lunar module pilot (LMP) and Ken Mattingly as the command module pilot (CMP), went up a peg in the order, and they set about readying themselves for an earlier flight to the moon on *Apollo 13*. Much to his annoyance, Mattingly would later be dropped from the mission after he was inadvertently exposed to German measles and replaced by his backup, Jack Swigert, just three days before the scheduled launch. Mattingly never did catch German measles and was subsequently reassigned as command module pilot on *Apollo 16* to compensate for his disappointment.

The production of Saturn V rockets was placed on hold in the spring of 1967. Then, during the formulation of the budget for fiscal year 1968, the U.S. Congress decided not to appropriate any money for the construction of any new Saturn V rockets. Following receipt of a NASA directive from administrator James Webb to limit Saturn V production to Vehicle SA-515, the Marshall Space Flight Center began terminating the manufacture of engine hardware for the Apollo and Apollo Applications programs. NASA now had to work out the optimal way to utilize the Saturn rockets that had survived the production cut.

The Apollo Applications Program (AAP) provided for a short-term, Earth-orbiting space station, fundamentally assembled using leftover hardware from the lunar landing program. Prior to the budgetary cuts, the AAP (later renamed *Skylab*) had called for a "wet lab" concept, in which two Saturn IB rockets would be launched, one placing the S-IVB stage into orbit, where it would then become an orbiting space laboratory. A second Saturn would follow, carrying the astronauts and docking module. After a thirty-day mission aboard the space laboratory, the first crew would return, and then another Saturn IB launch would carry a second crew of astronauts into orbit, docking with the station to begin a fifty-six-day occupancy.

Later, there would be yet another dual 1B launch—the first carrying the Apollo Telescope Mount (ATM) and the second carrying another crew on a subsequent fifty-six-day mission. Prior to fiscal year 1968, plans had called for up to three of these so-called wet labs, to be followed into space by three "dry labs." After fiscal year 1968, plans called for a follow-up dry lab, and there was an assumption that the production of the Saturn V would recommence.

In September 1968 Spiro Agnew's task force presented its report to Richard Nixon. Instead of taking any immediate action, the president allowed it to sit on his desk, without making any comment for four months. The report contained some interesting possible directions for the U.S. space program. The first option was a rapid program similar to Apollo, which involved a crewed journey to Mars in 1983 and would require funding of some $9 billion per year from 1980 onward. A final decision on this had to be made in 1974. The second choice was a Mars expedition to leave Earth in 1986. The cost of this venture was $8 billion per year from 1980 onward, and it required a commitment by 1977. The final option was to defer a Mars flight until the year 2000, with a decision needed by 1990.

One of the main elements in each of these plans was the development of a reusable space vehicle that could make routine flights to an Earth-orbiting space station, which was the genesis of the space shuttle program. Another requirement for any flight to Mars was a rocket powerful enough to send humans, their fuel, and food supplies on the journey. A team headed by Wernher von Braun had already drawn up plans for a rocket engine known as Nerva, which was nuclear powered and designed to provide sufficient thrust for both the space shuttle and a Mars vehicle.

Shortly after the *Apollo 11* launch and before the landing, NASA's newest administrator, Thomas O. Paine, signed off on the decision to switch Apollo Applications to a dry lab concept that would require a Saturn V launch.

In a 22 July 1969 news release, NASA formally announced the AAP reorientation to the dry workshop, or laboratory, configuration. Both the fully outfitted workshop and integrated ATM were to be launched aboard a single Saturn V in 1972. Once the laboratory had been placed in a secure circular orbit, it would be followed about a day later by the first three-man crew. They would launch aboard a Saturn 1B and link up in orbit with the laboratory-ATM cluster, thus beginning the manned portion of the mission.

A week later NASA issued a tentative launch and landing site schedule for the nine remaining Apollo missions (see table 3). For the first lunar flights, safety constraints dictated that they set down in areas of relatively flat terrain. However, there was agreement that if the crew of the forthcoming *Apollo 12* achieved their landing with a high degree of accuracy, then the later landing missions would be carried out with an increased confidence, allowing them to set down in regions of difficult terrain known to be of far greater scientific interest.

Table 3. Originally designated Apollo landing sites

Flight	Launch	Landing area
Apollo 12	November 1969	Oceanus Procellarum lowlands
Apollo 13	March 1970	Fra Mauro highlands
Apollo 14	July 1970	Crater Censorinus highlands
Apollo 15	November 1970	Littrow volcanic area
Apollo 16	April 1971	Crater Tycho (Surveyor VII impact area)
Apollo 17	September 1971	Marius Hills volcanic domes
Apollo 18	February 1972	Schroter's Valley, riverlike channel ways
Apollo 19	July 1972	Hyginus Rille region—Linear Rille crater area
Apollo 20	December 1972	Crater Copernicus, large crater impact area

Source: NASA Office of Manned Space Fight, "Manned Space Flight Weekly Report—July 28, 1969," quoted in Ertel and Newkirk, *The Apollo Spacecraft*, 4:311.

Then, in October 1969, a further revised launch schedule set the *Apollo 19* landing back to November 1972 and *Apollo 20* to May 1973. Between the *Apollo 18* mission (then planned for February 1972) and *Apollo 19*, three Earth-orbital flights were also tentatively on the manifest—training flights preparatory to the establishment of America's first space station in 1975. At the time, the director of flight operations—Chris Kraft, from Houston's Manned Spaceflight Center (later the Johnson Space Center)—expressed some concern at the busy schedule. "It's going to be difficult," he declared, "to handle both Apollo and Apollo Applications from an operational point of view as well as a people point of view in 1972."

A further reason for delaying the later Apollo landings was the possibility of the assigned crews attempting to set down in remote and difficult lunar areas such as the large, bright-rayed crater Copernicus, just south of Mare Imbrium. Another proposed destination (then planned for *Apollo 16*) was the rim of Tycho, also a relatively young crater, probably of impact origin, in the southern lunar highlands, which was rated by scientists as a top-priority landing site.

Meanwhile, the flight schedule continued. *Apollo 12*, under the command of Charles (Pete) Conrad, virtually mirrored the success of the first lunar landing flight, with a pinpoint touchdown in the Ocean of Storms on 14 November 1969, setting down as planned just two hundred yards from the Surveyor 3 spacecraft, which had soft-landed there two years earlier. Conrad and his lunar module pilot, Alan Bean, spent thirty-one hours on the moon's surface before blasting off to rendezvous with CMP Dick Gordon in lunar orbit and returning home with fifteen pounds of moon rock and soil.

By 1970, however, NASA was struggling. Nixon's administration had been relentlessly pouring billions of dollars into the yawning maw of the Vietnam conflict, and "soft" programs such as Apollo were rapidly plummeting down the preferred-funding list.

Following the first two Apollo lunar missions, it soon became abundantly clear to everyone that in all probability NASA was going to have to pare *Apollo 20* from the flight schedule due to budgetary constraints. President Kennedy had been right; landing men on another world was a very costly exercise. Enough Saturn Vs had already been budgeted to see out the lunar landing program through to *Apollo 20*, but Apollo Applications also needed a Saturn V to launch the massive space laboratory into orbit.

It was now becoming increasingly clear to Tom Paine that the production of the Saturn V would not recommence, and production of the smaller Saturn 1B had also been similarly halted. Ultimately, he had no other option; on 4 January 1970 *Apollo 20* was officially removed from the flight manifest. The Saturn rocket thus freed up was allocated to the Earth-orbiting space station program. Nevertheless, even *Apollo 18* and *Apollo 19* now began to look a little doubtful.

As space historian David Shayler observed of the cancellation of *Apollo 20*,

The decision had actually been made the previous month, looking to save costs, but with the main hardware already built and paid for, the cost savings would instead come from not having to train a lunar crew, pro-

vide wages for a team at the Cape to prepare the hardware, fund the three teams of flight controllers and support staff in mission control, or reimburse the U.S. Navy for recovery operations at the end of the mission. It also alleviated the need for an additional Saturn V to launch the unmanned workshop, which would have been difficult as the production line for the launch vehicle had long since been terminated, the decision being implemented during the summer of 1967.

It was all proving to be a real quandary for NASA administrator Tom Paine, who told a February press conference about the need to align space operations with the fiscal year 1971 budget.

We recognize the many important needs and urgent problems we face here on Earth. America's space achievements in the 1960s have rightly raised hopes that this country and all mankind can do more to overcome pressing problems of society. The space program should inspire bolder solutions and suggest new approaches. It has already provided many direct and indirect benefits and is creating new wealth and capabilities.

However we recognize that under current fiscal restraints NASA must find new ways to stretch out current programs and reduce our present operational base. [NASA will] press forward in 1971 at a reduced level, but in the right direction with the basic ingredients we need for major achievements in the 1970s and beyond. . . . We will not dissipate the strong teams that sent men to explore the moon and automated spacecraft to observe the planets.

In April of that year, the life-or-death flight of *Apollo 13* dramatically evinced the colossal risks inherent in manned spaceflight. Then, with the crew safely back on Earth, public apathy set in once again.

In the 17 August 1970 issue of *Aviation Week and Space Technology*, the following was reported:

In a notice to the National Academy of Sciences' Space Science Board and to his own advisory board on lunar and planetary missions, NASA Administrator Thomas O. Paine asked for a recommendation by Aug. 24 on the course of future lunar landings. Paine asked the two groups to decide between these alternatives: Continue with the Apollo manned lunar landing missions as now scheduled—Apollo 14 through 19 [or] delete two of

those missions—Apollo 15 and Apollo 19—for reasons of economy and to
preserve plans for a significant shift in emphasis of manned space explo-
ration away from the moon and back to earth-oriented areas of inter-
est by the mid-1970s.

According to the crewing procedure then in place, the crews for *Apollo 18* and *Apollo 19* were fairly well established, but there is a lingering uncertainty about the actual makeup of the crew of *Apollo 20*, had the mission not been scrubbed. Early speculation centered on Pete Conrad commanding the flight, even though Deke Slayton was not certain he wanted any astronaut who had already commanded a lunar landing mission to be offered the chance to lead a repeat mission. There were just too many qualified and prepared astronauts waiting for their chance at the gold ring.

Therefore, even though there was conjecture at the time that Conrad would head the *Apollo 20* mission, it is unlikely that he would have filled that position. Even before the flight was officially scrubbed, he had decided it was a long shot anyway and had thrown himself into training for the space station program. However, it does seem that Paul Weitz would have been the command module pilot on *Apollo 20*, along with LMP Jack Lousma. When asked if the crew had ever been officially named to the lunar flight, Lousma told the author, "It was understood informally but was not made official."

Furthermore, if *Apollo 20* had gone as planned and Pete Conrad had declined the role of mission commander, the speculation is that Stuart Roosa would have stepped in to fulfill that role, although other names raised as mission commander were those of Don Lind and Ed Mitchell. Whatever transpired, Jack Lousma and Paul Weitz were always going to be a part of the crew of *Apollo 20*.

With the expected cancellation of *Apollo 20*, Conrad now firmly set his sights on making his fourth spaceflight as part of the Skylab program. He implored his *Apollo 12* command module pilot, Dick Gordon, to join him, but Gordon was determined to walk on the moon this time, not just fly around it.

When Alan Shepard's crew was rescheduled to *Apollo 14*, Gene Cernan, Ron Evans, and Joe Engle were also named as their backups. Using the backup-skip-two formula, Joe Engle now realized the three of them were right in line for *Apollo 17*. Shortly after, the prime crew for *Apollo 15* was

2. The three astronauts who might have formed the crew for *Apollo 19*. *From left*: Stuart Roosa (CDR), Jack Lousma (LMP), and Paul Weitz (CMP). Courtesy NASA.

announced as Dave Scott (CDR), Jim Irwin (LMP), and Al Worden (CMP). As expected, the backup crew was made up of Dick Gordon (CDR), Vance Brand (CMP), and scientist-astronaut Dr. Harrison (Jack) Schmitt (LMP).

Original plans for *Apollo 18*, *Apollo 19*, and *Apollo 20* were for the lunar crew to visit a number of large impact craters, in the hope that the collected samples might include ancient rocks from deep inside the moon. Geologists and other scientists were hoping that these samples might prove to be essentially unchanged from when the moon was formed. On Earth, such primordial material is buried well beyond our reach, and studying the lunar samples could have provided a rich bonanza of data on the early solar system.

Then, in the summer of 1970, the ax finally dropped once again. On 2 September 1970 it was announced that *Apollo 15* and *Apollo 19* were officially canceled. Soon after, there would be no "pressing forward" for Paine. Although he may have rubber-stamped the decision, it seems he also had to accept the political realities behind making this savage cut to the Apollo program and resigned effective 15 September. He was a Democrat appointed to the role of NASA administrator by President Lyndon Johnson, and Richard Nixon's administration cared little for Paine's views on any long-term policies regarding the future of NASA's space program. His position as NASA administrator now fell into the capable hands of Dr. George M. Low.

Subsequently, in an enforced reshuffling of the flight manifest, *Apollo 16* retained its original lunar destination of the Descartes Plain, but the mission was renumbered and became the new *Apollo 15,* together with the original *Apollo 15* crew. *Apollo 17* now became *Apollo 16,* while *Apollo 18* was renamed *Apollo 17*—and was also announced as the final manned lunar flight.

At the same time, the recommendations of Vice President Agnew's task force were shelved. Following the enforced gutting of the space agency's manned and unmanned programs by the White House, one adverse result of the wind down in space activities was the human cost. From a peak nationwide employment of 400,000 people in 1965 to 180,000 in 1970, the decimation of the space program had a devastating effect in a number of states that had built up large aerospace industries around the Apollo program.

It was recognized in this latest crisis for the space effort that the states most affected were electorally important to Nixon for the upcoming 1972 election; therefore, California, Texas, Florida, and other southern states were being targeted by the White House in order to return the incumbent president to office. Realizing that these states were the ones being hit hardest by the space recession, it was decided to unveil another large space project. Thus, in January 1972, President Nixon proudly announced that he had given approval to NASA to begin development of a winged, reusable space shuttle, which was expected to fly in the mid to late seventies and provide America's pathway into space until the end of the century.

A deep gloom still prevailed at NASA over the savage cutbacks to the lunar program. With an abundance of astronauts hoping for their first or even a repeat space mission and with only a limited number of seats available for the upcoming Skylab missions, the future was looking decidedly bleak.

Tentative plans from 1969 had called for *Apollo 18* to launch and reach the moon in July 1973. Dick Gordon (CDR) and Harrison Schmitt (LMP) were scheduled to descend to a landing in the crater Gassendi on the northern edge of Mare Humorum. Meanwhile, Vance Brand (CMP) would remain behind, flying solo in lunar orbit.

Apollo 19 was penciled in for a December 1973 launch, with a planned landing site on the floor of the prominent crater Copernicus. The probable landing crew would have been Fred Haise (CDR)—the lunar module pilot from the failed *Apollo 13* mission—and rookie astronaut Jerry Carr (LMP). Bill Pogue was to have stayed in lunar orbit aboard their command module.

Once again, the crews had never been officially announced, but the author asked Fred Haise if he could confirm his likely role. In part, Haise replied,

When I was assigned after Apollo 13 as the backup commander to John Young [Apollo 16], it was the start of my training cycle to eventually fly Apollo 19. I had Bill Pogue assigned as the CMP and Jerry Carr as the LMP. However, in September of 1970, the last two missions were canceled, which was another disappointment for me [after Apollo 13]. At that time, Stuart Roosa and Ed Mitchell were assigned to join me in fulfilling the "deadhead" backup-crew assignment. That is a long way of saying that [neither] I nor anyone actually started the specific training on the Apollo 18 or 19 missions.

Furthermore, it was decided that a Saturn V would be used to launch the space station core module as originally scheduled, and plans called for this module to be occupied by three astronauts up until June 1973. Beyond that, according to an official statement by the associate administrator for manned space flight Dale Myers, spaceflight activities would remain "at a standstill as far as orbital operations are concerned until the shuttle comes on line, hopefully in the 1976–77 time period."

Unfortunately for the astronauts, there were just too few planned missions for too many candidates, and a lot had to miss out. The scientific community was also outraged. Why appoint a group of scientist-astronauts as NASA had done back in 1965, they argued, when the opportunity for any of them to fly to the moon was extremely remote?

Three lunar scientists expressed their concern about the cancellation of *Apollo 15* and *Apollo 19* in a September article in the *New York Times*. Dr. Thomas Gold from Cornell University said, "It's like buying a Rolls Royce and then not using it because you claim you can't afford the gas." Nobel Prize winner Dr. Harold Urey declared, "I think the American people and Congress should realize that the moon is an extremely old object. . . . This gives scientists a way of studying an object that goes back to the very beginning of the solar system." He added that saving $40 million in cancelling the two flights was "chicken feed" in light of the $25 billion already spent on the Apollo program. Finally, former scientist-astronaut Dr. Brian O'Leary weighed in: "The scientific community has become disenchanted with NASA. The present decision seems ridiculous."

The *New York Times* then offered its own solution to the situation. "Throughout the last decade this newspaper opposed the top priority then accorded Project Apollo on the ground that too much money was being diverted from urgent social needs," their editorial stated. "But now that these huge sums have been spent the need is to obtain the maximum yield, scientifically and otherwise, from that investment. Surely NASA, which has been able to reach the moon, can find a better solution than the one now afforded for adjusting to austerity in space research. One desirable alternative would be to enlist foreign resources in the exploitation of Apollo technology, perhaps by offering to send teams of British, French or Soviet astronauts on the journey pioneered by Apollo 11."

The heat was truly on for NASA, and they began to weigh the possibility of flying geologist Dr. Harrison (Jack) Schmitt on what was now the final lunar landing mission, *Apollo 17*. At that time, Schmitt was still assigned as backup lunar module pilot to the *Apollo 15* crew, along with Dick Gordon and Vance Brand, but with the cancellation of *Apollo 18*, this had now become a dead-end job.

According to an interview Schmitt conducted with space historian Robert Pearlman in 2012, once the *Apollo 18* mission had been canceled, NASA Headquarters began insisting on flying him on *Apollo 15*. "Slayton fought against that because he wanted Schmitt to serve on a backup crew first," Pearlman wrote. "Schmitt acknowledges that that was the right thing to do because serving as backup taught him how to fly Apollo. He would not have been [as] prepared to go if slipped directly into a prime crew. Given Slayton's reasoning, and Schmitt's experience, I think it would be dubious at best that Slayton would have agreed to putting another scientist on the prime crew without first a rotation on a backup crew."

When Dick Gordon got wind that NASA was considering sending Schmitt to the moon, he began jockeying to have his entire crew replace that of Gene Cernan on *Apollo 17*. There were no holds barred in this last-gasp effort to secure the final lunar flight, and it was left to chief astronaut Deke Slayton to make a decision, albeit with extreme pressure being exerted by NASA Headquarters, to get a scientist on the last flight. But his influence only extended so far, and his crewing recommendation was rejected, as recorded by Cernan in his 1999 memoir, *Last Man on the Moon*.

> *Unknown to me, Deke sent his recommendation to Washington: Cernan, Evans and Engle would fly the final mission. Headquarters shot that idea down immediately. Their own decision had already been made, and it*

3. The original backup crew for *Apollo 15* undergoing training for that mission. *From left*: Dick Gordon (CDR), Vance Brand (CMP), and Harrison (Jack) Schmitt (LMP). Schmitt would later be assigned to the *Apollo 17* crew in lieu of Joe Engle. Courtesy NASA.

snatched the choice out of Deke's hands. It was made very, very clear to the Godfather [Slayton] that the only name they absolutely demanded to be on the crew list for 17 was Dr. Harrison H. "Jack" Schmitt. . . . Deke fought it, but the handwriting was on the wall and he surrendered to the inevitable, accepting a compromise. Instead of Cernan-Evans-Engle, the crew became Cernan-Evans-Schmitt. Fine, said Washington. They didn't care, as long as Schmitt got the ride.

In the interim, both crews had trained hard, seeking to impress on everyone that they were the best available team for the job. Gene Cernan had certainly not helped matters for his crew when he crashed a helicopter into the Banana River during training, but he did not seem to suffer any injuries or aftereffects, so the intense rivalry continued anew.

By August 1971 it was time to announce the names of the crew chosen for *Apollo 17*, and Cernan's crew got the nod—with one exception. LMP Joe Engle had been dropped from the crew to make way for Jack Schmitt.

Schmitt felt that Gordon and Brand should have made the lunar flight, as they were already a crew in training, and jeopardized his own selection by making a personal appeal to Slayton. However, the decision had already been made and announced. Deke Slayton would not and could not change his mind, and Dick Gordon had to accept the call.

Joe Engle was visibly upset for some time and not a little bitter about the decision, but he finally came to accept the fact that he had been replaced in the *Apollo 17* crew for political reasons. When asked by a reporter how he felt about missing out on the flight, he said the toughest thing of all was telling his kids that daddy wasn't going to the moon.

When Cernan was officially notified of the final makeup of his *Apollo 17* crew, he accepted the news with acute disappointment and not a little anger.

> *I was crushed at the thought of my team being broken up. Joe had worked hard for the lunar module pilot job, and we had spent so many long months together in the* LM *simulator that we understood the nuances of each other's personality and the inflections of our voices. We could react instinctively to what the other man did in a critical situation, and I was very concerned that I could ever have that same kind of rapport with anyone for whom flying was not a first love. I was forced to risk my life on a choice mandated by Washington, one of my first bitter tastes of politics.*

For his part, Schmitt told one newspaper reporter that his experience as a "professional observer" and geologist will "contribute significantly to lunar observations." Asked about his selection over Engle, Schmitt said, "There's no question that Joe Engle is one of the most outstandingly qualified test pilots in the business. But as far as my qualifications to fly the spacecraft are concerned, I would attempt to compete with anybody in the program. Although we don't have that kind of competition, I wouldn't be a bit afraid of doing it."

Despite missing out on *Apollo 17*, Engle remained on active duty with

NASA and, from June to October 1977, commanded one of the two crews that flew the unpowered space shuttle approach and landing tests to confirm the craft's glide and landing characteristics. Then, in 1981 he commanded the second test flight of the shuttle orbiter *Columbia* on a two-day space mission along with fellow astronaut Dick Truly. He flew into space for the final time on shuttle mission STS-511 in August 1985, and when he retired from NASA, he held the rank of major general in the U.S. Air Force.

He may not have made it to the moon, but Joe Engle became the only person ever to have flown two different winged vehicles into space: the x-15 and the space shuttle. He also remains the only person to have manually flown a space shuttle through the phases of reentry and landing.

George Low would only serve a seven-month term as NASA administrator before being replaced by James Fletcher in April 1971. NASA was still not out of the financial woods, and the embattled space agency received yet another jolt that October when one of Nixon's deputy directors, Caspar Weinberger, told Fletcher that the president was giving serious thought to also scrubbing *Apollo 16* and *Apollo 17* from the lunar program. On 3 November Fletcher sent Weinberger a comprehensive ten-page report on why the missions should proceed as scheduled, explaining the impact such a move would have on national goals, science programs, and such vital issues as employment in NASA and across the aerospace industry:

> *From a scientific standpoint these final two missions are extremely import-*
> *ant, especially Apollo 17 which will be the only flight carrying some of*
> *the most advanced experiments originally planned for Apollo 18 and 19,*
> *cancelled last year. With what we have learned from Apollo 15 and pre-*
> *vious missions, we seem to be on the verge of discovering what the entire*
> *moon is like: its structure, its composition, its resources, and perhaps even*
> *its origin. If Apollo 16 and 17 lead to these discoveries, the Apollo pro-*
> *gram will go down in history not only as man's greatest adventure, but*
> *also his greatest scientific achievement. Recognizing the great scientific*
> *potential and the relatively small saving ($133 million) compared to the*
> *investment already made in Apollo ($24 billion), I must as Administra-*
> *tor of NASA strongly recommend that the program be carried to comple-*
> *tion as now planned.*

Nixon finally relented, and the last two Apollo missions went ahead. Jack Schmitt got to walk on the moon on *Apollo 17*, and his trained eye at the landing site of Taurus-Littrow caused many valuable discoveries to be made and some spectacular samples to be collected for return to Earth and later analysis. During his lunar expeditions, Schmitt described the landing area as "a geologist's paradise if I ever saw one."

On 14 December 1972 Gene Cernan became the last person to leave footprints in the lunar soil. As he took a final, lingering look around before climbing up into the lunar module, he commented, "And as we leave the moon at Taurus-Littrow, we leave as we came, and, God willing, as we shall return, with peace and hope for all mankind." The Apollo program was for all purposes at an end.

A final comment on the canceled Apollo flights came from an astronaut who would have walked on the moon had *Apollo 19* taken place. Jerry Carr, originally assigned to the mission as the lunar module pilot, was circumspect as he looked back on his lost opportunity. Carr recalled, "The Apollo era was, indeed, a dramatic and exciting time for all of us [and] it was a black day for me when the Apollo program was canceled. *Apollo 19* was to have been my mission, but when it was canceled, I was assigned as commander of the third Skylab mission. As it turned out, I feel very fortunate that I had the opportunity to participate in the effort to expand human knowledge in the area of long-duration spaceflight."

The final Apollo lunar landing mission ended successfully more than four decades ago, and though there is plenty of rhetoric being readily bandied around the NASA corridors, there are still no definite plans for human beings to return to the moon.

Despite the relative success (and ignominious end) of the *Skylab* space station in the 1970s, the United States still depends on the International Space Station, with NASA astronauts ferried to the gigantic orbiting space laboratory squeezed inside Russia's Soyuz spacecraft. At the very least, a crewed journey to Mars is at least fifteen years away.

Apollo is now a distant memory of a time when an ebullient and audacious NASA, backed by an equally enthusiastic Congress and White House, was able to turn the dreams of science fiction into the reality of twelve Americans walking on the surface of the moon.

Given the troubles NASA is currently having in obtaining funding for human and robotic space exploration, a return to the moon is not expected to occur for some years to come. The irony of where the United States could have been now was eloquently stated back in 1985, as a former Apollo astronaut was watching the launch of the first military space shuttle. "To think," he wistfully remarked, "we could have been going to Mars today."

The landing sites for those lost Apollo missions still remain physically unexplored but beckoning—targets perhaps for future generations of astronauts but, for the moment, well beyond our hopeful expectations.

2. Earthbound Astronaut

Scientist-Astronaut Duane "Doc" Graveline

All knowledge attains its ethical value and its human significance
only by the human sense with which it is employed.
Only a good man can be a great physician.

—Carl Wilhelm Hermann Nothnagel

Wednesday, 18 August 1965, was a day filled with utter devastation for research scientist and U.S. Air Force flight surgeon Duane Edgar Graveline. Just seven weeks earlier, on 28 June, he had been announced as a member of NASA's fourth group of astronauts. This group was markedly different to the previous three; rather than men plucked from the nation's services with aviation in their blood and a history of test-piloting the hottest jets in the air, it was comprised of six candidates drawn from diverse fields of science and medicine who would train to live and work in space under the new banner of scientist-astronauts.

Sadly for Duane Graveline, known to everyone as "Doc," he would also go down in spaceflight history as the shortest-serving NASA astronaut. Divorce proceedings instituted by his wife following the selection announcement caused the space agency to demand on principle his immediate resignation. Back then, the word *divorce* had no place in the squeaky-clean aura NASA was trying to maintain around its astronauts, even though many seemingly solid marriages were known to be floundering. The grim prospect of creating adverse publicity for the space agency and consequently missing out on a chance to fly into space was close to terrifying for the astronauts involved and, for many, was the sole incentive in maintaining a false pretense of stability in the astronaut's home.

Today, an astronaut divorce is not deemed a newsworthy subject—far from it—but in the early days of the highly publicized race to the moon with the Soviet Union, it was a completely different ball game. For Doc Graveline the reported end of his marriage also meant the end of a long-held dream.

As the news of his withdrawal from the astronaut corps spread and became public, it was a time of tumult and introspection for the thirty-four-year-old U.S. Air Force flight surgeon and physician. Although NASA released a bulletin suggesting that Dr. Graveline had resigned from the space agency "for personal reasons," investigative newspaper journalists had already seized on the reason behind his sudden resignation, unfairly citing certain bitter accusations contained in his wife's equally sudden and career-busting divorce petition.

"It was an abrupt and humiliating end to my career as an astronaut," Dr. Graveline told the author in 2006. "Suddenly all my dreams of flying into space and working there were gone. I was completely gutted. The day of my resignation [from NASA], I was also told that NASA wanted to take my official portrait photo for their files. If you look closely at that photo, you can see despair and confusion written all over my face. I knew I was dead."

Many sympathetic NASA insiders felt that their bosses had overreacted, and their decision was tainted by institutionalized hypocrisy. "It was really unfair," according to James S. Logan, a former chief of medical operations at the Johnson Space Center in Houston and the founder of the Space Enterprise Institute, a nonprofit educational foundation. "A lot of them were doing all kinds of extramarital stuff, and the agency knew about it. It shows how sensitive the American culture was at the time and how exqui-sitely sensitive NASA was to the idea that the astronauts were any less than perfection personified."

To many people, an unfortunate and public disappointment such as this would cause ongoing bitterness and a lifetime of regret, but for Doc Graveline it represented a sadly missed opportunity to apply all his med-ical and scientific training while working in the unique environment of space. He would, nevertheless, go on to achieve deserved acclaim in other arenas. Throughout his life, he continued to set and achieve new goals for himself in the medical profession, and in doing so he treated, helped, and guided many thousands of people, both directly and indirectly. As well, he touched the lives of countless others through his relentless determination

4. *Left*: Official portrait photo of Dr. Duane Graveline taken soon after his resignation from the astronaut corps. Courtesy NASA. *Right*: A far happier portrait in his later years. Courtesy Duane Graveline, spacedoc.com.

to educate them about detrimental medical fallacies created and exhorted by powerful statin drug companies. In signing autographs for space fans throughout his life, he normally appended the words "NASA astronaut" after his name, but he could so easily have written "a champion for humanity."

Duane Edgar Graveline (who preferred to be called "Doc") was born on 2 March 1931 in the small town of Newport, Vermont, situated on a southern tip of the tranquil Lake Memphremagog, ten miles south of the Canadian border. He grew up as a farm boy amid the lush wilderness and grandeur of the White Mountains. His parents, Edgar and Tina, imbued in their eldest son a strong, lifelong pride in his French Canadian heritage. Before they met, his mother Tina Lamere had been a renowned ski jumper, while Edgar became a sporting-goods store owner and marina operator with a passion for flying.

Young Duane spent much of his early childhood living with his grand-parents on their three-hundred-acre dairy farm and took his education at a nearby one-room schoolhouse, which his father had attended years before him. He still recalls with fondness the day he found his father's name etched deeply into one of the classroom seats.

He always credited his grandmother, affectionately known as Mamere, with giving him guidance on the road to becoming a doctor. "Even before I started school my Mamere always told me I would be a doctor," he remembered with a smile. "It did not seem to be a matter of choice. I willingly walked the path she set for me from my earliest years, never doubting even for a moment that it was the right path."

Sadly, tragedy would strike Duane early in life. He had strong recollections of his grandfather, his wonderful Papere, "holding me by the hands as he jiggled me up and down on his foot while singing ribald French Canadian songs of women and college days in his past. At other times, he would just hug me and dance around the living room to imaginary music. Although it was Mamere who provided the guidance, it was Papere who gave me love and the most heartwarming memories. He was a great bear of a man with enough affection to go around for everyone." Duane was only six years old when he witnessed a kerosene heater in his grandparent's house explode into flames, killing his adored Papere. The horror of that day remained a brutally vivid memory, and the thought of death by fire always haunted him.

Life continued after the accident, and he was thankful to his grade school teacher, Iris Wheeler, for developing and nurturing his interest in science. In one such instance she was able to spike her young student's curiosity by "the simple act of placing a jar of frog eggs on my desk so that I could more intimately watch the almost hourly change from egg to tadpole, and this probably more than any other thing pointed me along the path of scientific inquiry."

His many interests also extended to the sporting field; at one time, he was captain of the football team at Newport High. As he grew up, other teachers influenced his career path. His high school science teacher Arlene Cushing was one who "got my undivided attention with a demonstration of the explosive qualities of a beaker of hydrogen gas," while another teacher, Lyman Rowell, later astounded the young college biology student with his "chalkboard dexterity using two hands simultaneously as he sketched the process of gastrulation. It still impresses me."

The University of Vermont in Burlington had long held a strong appeal for Graveline and seemed a logical college choice after Newport High. It was also not too far from where he lived. He recalled, "Getting home easily seemed to have been a high priority in those early days, when the apron strings were still tight and your mother looked forward to doing your laundry."

It was 1948, and the college was packed with older war veterans recently out of the military, all taking full advantage of the government's free college education program. As well, it had a compulsory ROTC program, and Graveline soon grew to love the disciplines involved. In fact, he became so accomplished in close order drill that he was made squad leader. "They later offered me the officers' training program, which I would have accepted, but it was designed for a four-year college curriculum. And I knew that when my third year of college ended, I would have all my graduation credits and would be starting medical school. So I could not accept the program. However, my introduction to the military was pleasant and had a very important role in my future career decisions."

As he was trying to cram four years of studies into three, Duane had little time for extracurricular activities, although he did play second trumpet in the university band in his first year. In order to raise a little extra spending money, he also took on a part-time job as an assistant instructor in biology, conducting classwork and special tutoring for freshmen students.

At the beginning of his junior year in undergraduate school, he made the unprecedented move of applying for medical school. The school's initial response was that his application was invalid because he was not yet a senior, but when they checked the records, it was clear he had met, or would soon meet, all the preliminary requirements. As he would have sufficient credits in a few months for graduation with a bachelor's degree in science, his application was finally accepted and approved.

Then, just before he started medical school, Graveline's high school sweetheart Carole Jane Tollerton informed him that she was pregnant. They eloped and were married in Newport, Vermont. He was only nineteen years old, but as he said later, "By my standards, that was the only thing to do." Edgar Graveline was furious and remonstrated with his son, telling him he had just ruined his career.

Despite this, Graveline began medical school in 1951 as a member of the university's June class. Twelve months later he received his bachelor of science degree, and in 1955 he was further awarded a doctor of medicine degree from the university's medical school.

By now, he was keen to join the air force as a flight surgeon, no doubt influenced in this ambition by his father, who had been a pilot in the Civil Air Patrol. Graveline could never understand his younger brother, Norman, not sharing this sublime passion. Following a two-month assignment as an assistant to a family doctor in Vermont, he drove down to Washington DC to take up a USAF Medical Service internship at the Walter Reed Medical Center.

In June 1956 Graveline attended the primary course in Aviation Medicine, class 566, at Randolph Air Force Base (AFB) in Texas. He was subsequently assigned to Kelly AFB, also in Texas, as chief of the Aviation Medicine Service. His job as flight surgeon required him to become familiar with the flight environment, and he loved every minute of this training, during which, "I flew in everything they had with more than one seat."

Reasoning that a pilot might become incapacitated during flight, requiring an accompanying flight surgeon to assume control, the air force trained its flight surgeons to a ready-to-solo level of experience. In this way, he got to fly such aircraft as the C-45, KC-97, C-124, XC-99, and C-119, while he racked up thirty hours of instruction time, "the unforgettable frosting on that delicious flying cake" (as he called it) in the sleek T-bird jet trainers, particularly the Lockheed T-33 Shooting Star. He admitted, "I actually used to feel somewhat guilty when I picked up my paycheck with its extra cash for flight pay. Where else but the air force was this kind of thing readily available to you, and they paid you for it?"

When asked, his favorite recollection of that time was of the many hours he spent flying as second pilot aboard the nimble, two-seater T-33: "During my instruction in this bird, I still remember the thrill of rolling her over into a split S and holding her on 'burble' during pullout. I loved it."

In October 1957 Graveline began attending Johns Hopkins University as part of his Aerospace Medical Association residency, studying the effects of prolonged weightlessness on the human body. It was there, on Friday, 4 October, that he learned the Soviet Union had launched the world's first artificial satellite named Sputnik into Earth orbit, which he described as the defining moment in his life. "All things are supposed to have a beginning," he recalled, "and I guess Sputnik started it for me. From that moment on I did my best to guide my path towards space." His excitement at this event was only compounded the following month when canine passenger Laika was sent aloft on a one-way orbital journey aboard Sputnik 2.

"Little did I know then that only a few years later at Wright-Patterson AFB I would be studying Laika's bioreadouts in the top-secret labyrinth of FTD, our Foreign Technology Division," he revealed. "Through Foreign Technology I learned the true scope of the Soviet bioastronautics program, and it was impressive. By the time we launched John Glenn, the Soviets had given us a tremendous amount of information about spaceflight."

His time at Johns Hopkins ended in 1958 when he departed with a master's degree in public health. Next, he attended the Aerospace Medical Association residency at the Air Force School of Aerospace Medicine, completing his residency training at Brooks AFB, San Antonio, in July 1960.

One of Captain Graveline's major interests at this time was the study of deconditioning future astronauts in a one-g environment after a lengthy period of weightlessness, which he knew would be quite taxing on the human circulatory system. While working at the Randolph AFB hospital, he recruited five young airmen to assist him in an experiment concerning bed rest for future astronauts returning from orbital missions. The selected men were told that they would be spending two weeks doing nothing but lying in bed, during which time Graveline would conduct some baseline and stress tests and take measurements of their muscle function and blood volume. Three of the men conducted sit-ups and other exercises in their beds, while the other two—as required—did very little, but at the end of the two weeks, the results showed almost no difference between the active and nonactive participants.

Convinced that there was a better way to do things, Graveline then decided to begin water immersion experiments in the Aeromedical Research Laboratory at Wright-Patterson AFB. By this time, however, he and his wife were having marital problems. They had four children—all girls. And his burgeoning career, while fascinating to him, was having a negative impact on their family life. He later noted in his memoir,

> My married life was not all fun and games. My wife had decided not to accompany me to the Aeromedical Research Lab in Dayton, Ohio. She and the kids had gone back home. She was fed up with raising the kids herself. She thought she was marrying someone destined to be a regular family doctor but instead I had become infatuated with space medicine and our relationship was deteriorating. With my almost constant travel and

focus on research and training, the sore spot in our relationship became an abscess that gradually worsened. Instead of providing support and recreation, the officers' wives group was a threat to her. She had no one to lean on. I was advancing, so to speak, while she was still a hometown girl, tied to her folks. I was smart enough to know that without family support I was vulnerable, not necessarily to other women, but to the customs and tradition of military officers. Without a wife you are incomplete and I knew it.

Nevertheless, he pressed on with his plans to begin a program of water immersion tests at the Dayton laboratory. This involved four subjects wearing specially designed scuba suits and a modified pressure helmet while individually immersed for six-hour periods in a nine-foot-cubed room filled with body-temperature water, and it later increased to twelve and then to twenty-four hours. The room was equipped with viewing ports to allow Graveline and others constant monitoring of the subjects.

Once again, he felt there had to be a better option. In order to better determine the effects of postflight recovery, he volunteered to become the subject of a different seven-day immersion experiment, once again simulating weightlessness through flotation. In this experiment, he would remain almost fully immersed in a tank measuring three feet by seven feet, filled with water heated to 33.5°C (92.3°F). He would conduct the test while clad in a conventional scuba dive suit and seated semirecumbent on a Mercury spacecraft-type of seat, with his head supported above water by a padded headrest and with his ankles secured. The size of the tank precluded almost all free body movements, which were restricted to motions of the forearms through limited arcs to operate levers and carry out problems on an electronic panel. To alleviate the boredom somewhat, he also had a small TV set mounted in front of him, but even then, "having nothing to do but watch daytime TV was the hardest part of my experiment."

It was a very exhausting seven days in which his muscles shrank and became weaker, and in all that time, he would only manage to get a total of seven hours of sleep, recorded as just three to five minutes at a time.

Once he was removed from the tank, Graveline recalled, "My limbs felt like lead. . . . Predictably the results showed substantial deconditioning with the most critical period being the first few days. . . . There was no real doubt that special measures would have to be taken to protect the astronaut for mission durations beyond this length." Applying the knowledge gained from this experiment, he conceived and developed a lower-body pressure device prototype, later flown on the *Skylab* and *Mir* space stations and on space shuttle missions.

Due to his deep interest and research into the biologic effects of weightlessness, Captain Graveline (now known to one and all as Doc) became a medical flight controller for NASA's Mercury program. In this capacity, he was involved in events leading up to the orbital mission of astronaut John Glenn, especially biomedical studies surrounding the precursory spaceflight of chimpanzee Enos. At this time, he was temporarily based on Canton Island in the South Pacific. He then continued working for NASA as a flight controller in the early phases of the Gemini program. During this period of his life, he was also still working with the FTD as a medical analyst, attempting to deduce what the Soviets were doing in their bioastronautics program.

Eventually, he carried out two tours at Canton Island and two tours aboard the tracking ship *Rose Knot Victor*. While conducting his studies on one of these seaborne tours in March 1965, he was engaged in some particularly rewarding work during the flight of cosmonauts Alexei Leonov and Pavel Belyayev aboard their *Voskhod 2* spacecraft.

"I was able to direct our entire worldwide tracking network to monitor the biodata emanating from a Voskhod mulitmanned spacecraft, coincidentally launched by the Soviets during our deployment," he said of his duties. "All we needed were our high-frequency receivers and simple antennas— standard items at every tracking station. The frequencies and orbital parameters were carried in my head."

There was also something brewing at that time in the life of Doc Graveline. In October 1964 NASA had announced that it was looking for a number of scientists to join the space agency's astronaut corps. By January the following year, 1,492 letters expressing interest had been received—including one from Graveline. Of these, 422 met the preliminary qualifications, and their files were forwarded to the National Academy of Sciences (NAS) for further perusal. Eventually the number of candidates was winnowed down to just sixteen. To his delight, he found he was still in the running.

It proved to be a long and anxious wait of nearly a year for the applicants, as their numbers were slowly culled through a process of elimination. The NAS review board eventually recommended that Graveline be one of a group brought to the School of Aerospace Medicine at Brooks AFB for evaluative testing.

"The screening process took several weeks," Graveline reflected, "and included the usual assortment of medical tests, prodding and probing into every nook and cranny, personality and emotional evaluation with all the usual inkblot, Rorschach, and MMPI [Minnesota Multiphasic Personality Inventory] tests, and even intelligence testing with all the latest methods."

When asked about the rigorous testing to which he was subjected in the latter stages of the selection process, he recalled his experience pulling 10 g's on the centrifuge as the most difficult: "At that time, I was thirty-four, but even then, transverse g's at those levels were very uncomfortable. Perhaps, as a doctor, I was aware that the discomfort was coming from the stretching of tissues in my body not designed for this kind of thing."

NASA flight surgeon and navy pilot Dr. Fred Kelly (himself an unsuccessful applicant for the same group) had previously worked with Doc Graveline and was watching his application with interest, as he later wrote in his book *America's Astronauts and Their Indestructible Spirit.*

> *Duane Graveline—now there was a fierce competitor. He was real competition. He was firmly established as one of the leading researchers in aerospace medicine, had performed most of the basic research into the physiology of weightlessness, and was the first to use underwater simulation of weightlessness. He was now assigned by the U.S. Air Force to monitor the biological data from every spaceflight the Russians had put up. He probably knew more about the Russian space program than the Russians. In addition to all of his professional qualifications, he was young, articulate, ran three miles every day, and certainly had the motivation. I would be disappointed in the system if Duane were not selected. Duane was definitely my first choice—after me.*

Then came the news Graveline had waited and hoped for; he had been selected as one of six group 4 scientist-astronauts. It all happened on Saturday, 26 June 1965, when NASA disclosed the selection of six scientists who would undergo training as astronauts for flights to the moon in the following decade. Their selection was not supposed to be formally announced until the twenty-ninth; however a local newspaper, the *Houston Chronicle,* printed a story in its Sunday edition, naming the six men. Officials at the

5. The six scientist-astronauts selected in June 1965. *Front row, from left*: Owen Garriott, Harrison (Jack) Schmitt, and Edward Gibson. *Back row*: Curtis Michel, Duane Graveline, and Joe Kerwin. Courtesy NASA.

Manned Spacecraft Center were then forced to confirm the report. According to the newspaper, NASA officials had hoped to get ten to twenty scientists, but the space agency's qualification standard had proved too high. As reported by the *Chronicle*, the six scientists chosen were F. Curtis Michel, a thirty-one-year-old physicist; Owen Garriott, a thirty-four-year-old electronics engineer; Edward Gibson, a twenty-eight-year-old physicist at the Applied Research Laboratories in California; Duane Graveline, a thirty-four-year-year-old NASA doctor; Harrison Schmitt, a twenty-nine-year-old geologist; and Joseph Kerwin, a thirty-three-year-old naval flight surgeon.

Now there was another difficult decision for Graveline to ponder: "After my acceptance as a NASA scientist-astronaut was announced, I made my decision to leave the air force. I was a major at that time. My reasoning was that I wanted to be permanently with NASA in a civilian capacity, not as an air force 'loaner.' I thought my career in NASA would be better if they 'owned' me." It was a decision that would soon have an enormous impact on his future life.

Graveline took to his new vocation with undisguised enthusiasm. Due to his previous air force experience, he was not at all fazed by the upcoming supersonic flight school training the six men would undertake at Williams AFB, Arizona, prior to commencing their initial astronaut training. Soon after leaving the air force, however, things rapidly began to unravel for the talented young flight surgeon.

Carole Graveline was a quiet, unassuming country girl from Vermont and felt ill at ease in the increasingly powerful circles in which her husband was moving as his career rapidly advanced. On 20 July 1965, just three weeks after her husband's name had been announced as a NASA scientist-astronaut, she was granted a temporary court order forbidding her husband from visiting or disturbing her.

The news hit a stunned Graveline on the same day he and the other five scientist-astronauts were having their official NASA portrait photos taken. In a case of bad timing, his photograph session took place only an hour after his wife's lawyer had phoned to say, "Don't come home. She won't be there. She has filed for divorce. I have advised her to go somewhere for the next few weeks. I don't know where, and no one does. Don't be too surprised at what you see in the newspapers. That's how we have to do things here in Texas." The abject misery he experienced that day is clearly reflected in his official NASA photograph, with disbelief and confusion evident in his solemn expression.

The following day, Carole Graveline's lawyer filed a divorce suit against him in San Antonio's Forty-Fifth District Court, seeking an end to their fourteen-year marriage. Her lawyer was right about what might appear in the newspapers over the next few days, with sensational claims—obviously at the instigation of his office—of mental cruelty and emotional instability. Duane Graveline was understandably devastated. "There was no way I could fight this," he reflected. "There was no need to fight this. The damage already had been done. . . . There did not seem to be anything else for me to do, except to start the T-38 program and see what happened, but intuition told me I was dead." While understandably upsetting news for him, it created a massive media headache for NASA, which at that time was desperate to maintain the pristine, all-American image of its astronauts.

Surprising as it may now seem, reporters, editors, and other media people had cooperated with NASA, up to that time, meekly complying with the space agency's carefully crafted image of the squeaky-clean, untarnished hero, and chose not to report on many of the wilder activities and affairs readily ascribed to many of the early astronauts. Now, fueled by adverse publicity, reports of a potentially nasty astronaut divorce caused immediate concern for NASA.

Amid the mounting confusion, the newly selected scientist-astronauts continued as normal with their preparations to go to supersonic flight school in August. Following this, they would undertake their initial astronaut training in the summer of 1966.

An uproar over the divorce issue quickly descended like a black cloud on the Astronaut Office, and chief astronaut Deke Slayton was far from impressed. "The program didn't need a scandal," he told interviewer Michael Cassutt, his coauthor on the autobiographical *Deke!* "A messy divorce meant a quick ticket back to wherever you came from—not because we were trying to enforce morality, which was impossible, anyway, but because it would detract from the job."

The space agency could no longer keep a lid on the situation. Faced with this dilemma, NASA director Dr. Robert Gilruth had to make a quick decision, and his verdict was soon dispatched to the Astronaut Office for prosecution. The news hit a bewildered Graveline like a blow; he was out—end of story. As Deke Slayton later stated, "Graveline was the first to get it. He was back in the Life Sciences Division so fast he never even made it to the group photo."

It was also a salutary lesson for the other astronauts, as evinced by Walt Cunningham from the previous group, selected in October 1963: "That was as dramatic an example to the rest of us as a neck attached to a swinging rope was to horse thieves in the Old West."

The fact that Carole Graveline later withdrew the damaging charges filed by her lawyer seems to have had little or no effect on NASA's decision. The damage had been done, especially after newspapers across America carried prominent articles repeating the charges against one of NASA's newest astronauts.

The whole sordid business outraged Graveline's friend and fellow NASA flight surgeon Fred Kelly, and he later wrote of his disgust at the way the whole affair had been handled. Like other insiders at the space agency, he knew that many of the astronauts were far from innocents themselves and were living perilously close to the marital edge. It was well known that two of the Mercury astronauts, for instance, had only maintained their failed marriages for the sake of keeping up appearances and to remain part of the space program. As Kelly stated, "Astronauts were supposed to be immune from social and marital ills. They were all fair-haired boys living in vine-covered cottages in perfect harmony. Duane's wife called a press conference to deliver an indictment so devastating that NASA had asked for his resignation. It was more than a request; he was out! Here was a man I considered head and shoulders above all the other scientist astronaut selectees. He was wasted because his wife had filed for divorce. If this was going to set a precedent, they would have to select more astronauts."

Looking back, Doc Graveline could afford to be philosophical and forgiving to an extent and said he could not help but "deeply envy" those of his colleagues who realized their dreams of living and working in space. Choosing his words carefully, he mused,

> *I had no problem with NASA's reaction. This was their first publicized divorce of one of their shining knights. Their reaction was entirely reasonable and even predictable. What else could they do?*
>
> *With respect to Dr. Gilruth, it was his decision that day, in his office at NASA. I bear him no grudge. My divorce publicity was anything but appropriate for a newly appointed astronaut. He did what he had to do at that time. I have to admit that when the publicity came out, I felt like someone who had just received a lethal dose of radiation—I knew I was dead but was just not sure of when it would happen. Five months after the ruinous publicity, and well into the flight-training program, I resigned from NASA officially "for personal reasons" . . . the hardest decision of my life.*

Following her husband's resignation from NASA, Carole Graveline chose to withdraw her divorce suit, but it was all too late. The couple reconciled soon after, and Doc Graveline moved back into the family home.

"It was a reconciliation doomed for failure," he said, "for every time an Apollo mission occurred, I was pulled more deeply into self-doubt and troubled thoughts. A year passed, and finally, like Thoreau, I moved alone into my little cabin in the woods of northern Vermont and gradually regained my footing."

The divorce finally went ahead, but it was a muted affair after the early, scandalous publicity that had ruined his career as a scientist-astronaut. He would never speak publicly of Carole's motivation, except to add that she later admitted her timing could have been better. "I consider that a masterpiece of understatement," he commented with obvious feeling. "She was young and confused. If she had planned to hurt my prospects within NASA, she could not have done a better job."

With a return to civilian life, Duane Graveline once again began to practice medicine as a family doctor in Burlington, Vermont. During this time, he also served as a flight surgeon for the Vermont Army National Guard.

Prior to the first space shuttle flight in 1981, Dr. Kelly invited his friend to make a temporary return to NASA as the director of medical operations. Happy to be involved, he took a six-month leave of absence from his family practice to assist Kelly on the first four shuttle missions. "Otherwise," he explained, "my only NASA contact has been as a regular participant in the Longitudinal Study of Astronaut Health, getting my annual physical checkup at Johnson Space Center."

In 1999 Doc Graveline's life would suddenly take an unexpected and dramatic change for the worse. Following one of his annual NASA checkups, he was informed his cholesterol level had hit 280, and he was given a prescription for ten-milligram doses of the statin drug Lipitor.

"I went along with it because I had no reason to be particularly worried about statin drugs," he said. "I had used it a year or so before my retirement, but I wasn't a big user." Then everything went seriously wrong: "Six weeks later I experienced my first episode of what was later diagnosed as transient global amnesia. This is an unusual form of amnesia wherein you immediately, without the slightest warning, are unable to formulate new memory, and you can no longer communicate. Not because you cannot talk, but you can't remember the last syllable that was spoken to you. So nothing you say is relevant anymore. In addition, you have a retrograde loss of memory, sometimes decades into the past."

Immediately, he stopped taking the drug, but his doctors reassured him that the drug was not to blame and that it was merely a coincidence. Later that year, with no further relapses, his cholesterol was still hovering around 280, so he went back on the statin drug. But this time he was limited to just half the earlier dose. "Eight weeks later," he recalled, "I had my second and my worst episode. . . . For twelve hours, I was a thirteen-year-old high school student who knew my subjects, teachers, and every kid in my class (according to my worried wife) but with no memory of my entire adult life. I laughed when they told me I was married with children and a doctor. I could not have doctored a mouse and certainly had no children. I was thirteen! Fifty-six years of rich and fulfilled adult life had vanished from my mind as if it had never occurred."

This frightening, drug-induced fantasy finally convinced him there was something wrong with statin drugs: "This took me out of retirement, and I've been actively involved in researching statin drugs ever since."

Over the next few years, Doc Graveline conducted deep and extensive research into the effects of statin drugs and began waging a well-publicized campaign, particularly against the use of high doses of the supposedly safe cholesterol drugs. His ongoing fight with the powerful drug companies and disbelieving doctors led to several books, talks, and media appearances on the subject. For Doc it was a worthwhile and well-informed crusade. He toured the United States and gave talks as far away as Sydney, Australia, always finding people who had suffered similar episodes and physical ailments they related to their use of large prescribed doses of statin drugs. They were astonished at Doc's findings and outraged that the medical profession was so ill informed on the subject. His four revealing books on the subject—*Lipitor: Thief of Memory*, *Statin Drugs Side Effects*, *Statin Damage Crisis*, and *The Dark Side of Statins*— became medical best sellers. Away from that subject, he also became a prolific author of science fiction thrillers, with nine published novels to his credit.

Doc Graveline was now living a far quieter but still productive life, with his supportive wife at his side. Suzanne Gamache had lived in California, Hawaii, and Florida before they met. "Both her parents were born in Canada," he told me, "making this French Canadian beauty the perfect match for me. We were married in Newport, Vermont."

When asked if he would change any facet of his life, the smile and answer came quickly and easily: "I would want to turn back the clock to 1955 and meet my present wife Suzanne just as I started my USAF internship at Walter Reed Army Hospital. We are a perfect pair—we just found each other thirty years too late. I would love to restart my life with her and travel my same path to astronaut selection."

In his later years, Doc and Suzanne lived in quiet contentment on Merritt Island, Florida. It must have been a very wistful experience for him at times, living within hailing distance of Cape Canaveral and the Kennedy Space Center, watching with interest from their front lawn as a succession of mighty launch vehicles ripped a path into the Florida skies, often with crews on board. For him, however, there must always have been a certain sense of achievement in having been able to ascend from a one-room-schoolhouse education to the renowned position of a U.S. Air Force flight surgeon and research scientist, a respected authority in his ongoing campaign against the unnecessary overprescription of statin drugs, and a published author. And albeit briefly, he was one of his nation's very finest—a NASA astronaut.

To the end of his days, Doc Graveline was still writing papers on and conducting space medical research. He remained affiliated with the space program as a consultant on one of his greatest concerns for the future of space travel—the life-threatening hazards of galactic cosmic radiation that astronauts will encounter on lengthy lunar habitation or protracted expeditions to other planetary bodies. He called it "our biggest challenge for deep space travel."

As he explained, the effective shielding of our human-tended spacecraft or lunar dwellings is "an ongoing and unfinished task that requires the interaction of physicists, engineers, and biologists. Furthermore, independently of spacecraft-shielding configurations, astronauts will always face the risk of these novel types of radiation and require specific countermeasures. We must do what we can and improvise where possible to seek out other means such as the use of biochemical agents and gene modification to modulate the harmful effects of galactic cosmic radiation on man. Such studies are just beginning. Any long-term return to the moon or manned Mars exploration is simply not possible with existing technology."

Effective shielding from cosmic radiation, he believed, is still many decades away, and the need to study ways to protect the crewmembers is, in his words, a subject "of paramount importance."

Duane Edgar Graveline, MD, a longtime friend of the author, passed away in a hospital on 5 September 2016, and his ashes were respectfully interred at Arlington National Cemetery during a well-attended ceremony on Wednesday, 3 May 2017.

For Suzanne it was a very emotional and moving service, which she likened to "being at the funeral of a head of state. Close to a hundred uniformed military personnel attended, along with a horse-drawn gun carriage." Doc would have been honored and certainly humbled by the number of people who had gathered at Arlington that day to pay their last respects and celebrate his extraordinary life.

As Suzanne later reflected on her late husband's life and proud legacy,

It is a regrettable situation that Doc's enforced resignation from the astronaut corps more than fifty years ago completely overshadows a truly stellar medical career—during which he helped and treated countless thousands of people. He also served with pride and distinction in the military and with the National Guard, including some twenty-three years as a flight surgeon. Then, later, there were literally hundreds of thousands more he assisted and guided with his writings and lectures on the often-pernicious side effects of statin drugs.

These and other achievements are what Doc should rightfully be remembered for, and not just a few months of his life as an active astronaut with NASA.

It has to be said that by unreasonably overreacting to news of his pending divorce back in 1965, NASA missed out on flying one of the most experienced and potentially valuable flight surgeons and space scientists, in Duane Graveline. His insights into spaceflight and human physiological conditions would have been incomparable. He had been involved in some particularly relevant studies, at times the voluntary subject of his own experiments and tests regarding the human condition as it applied to space travel. In doing so, he had also worked alongside some of the doyens of space medicine and aerospace physics.

There is little doubt that had he remained an astronaut with NASA, Doc would have proven to be one of the best and most resourceful persons ever selected to fly into space. Sadly, he fell victim to prevailing taboos within a publicity-timid space agency and the very different times in which he lived.

Despite this, to the end of his days, Doc Graveline remained humbly grateful for the many alternate opportunities NASA gave him. "My entire career has been devoted to the space program," he once told the author. "The cape seems to fit me."

3. Born beneath the Southern Cross

NASA's Group 6 Astronaut Philip K. Chapman

> Bad times have a scientific value.
> These are occasions a good learner would not miss.
>
> —Ralph Waldo Emerson

It was Friday, 21 July 1967, and Phil Chapman was sitting alone in his office at the Massachusetts Institute of Technology (MIT), in Cambridge, Massachusetts, when the telephone began to ring. It was a call he was expecting, and a long, nervous wait was almost at an end. He hesitated briefly before lifting the receiver, knowing that in the next few moments, he would receive either the best news of his professional life or the most disappointing. One way or the other, it was probably the most important phone call he would ever receive.

As he had presumed, it was Alan Shepard calling from the Manned Spacecraft Center in Houston. Shepard, the first American to fly into space, was now the head of the Astronaut Office and the man in charge of his nation's astronaut team. Chapman had applied to NASA with hopes of selection as a scientist in the space agency's latest astronaut group. He had been through all the rigorous interviews and tests and knew that he stood a reasonably good chance of being selected. Today he would know that decision.

Shepard's call was very brief and to the point. Did the young scientist still wish to be an astronaut? Chapman could hardly believe his ears. He was being offered the job of his dreams, which he quickly accepted. Shepard congratulated him and added that he would call him later at his Massachusetts home with more details.

After Shepard hung up, Chapman laughed with excitement. He had made it. At thirty-two years of age, the Australian-born scientist was going to train as an astronaut and perhaps one day fly into space—maybe even to the moon, although he realized the chances of that happening were quite remote. Nevertheless, it was an exciting prospect, and one he could scarcely believe was now within his grasp.

Philip Kenyon Chapman was born in Melbourne, Australia, on 5 March 1935, the son of Phyllis (née Kenyon) and Colin Robison Chapman, a journalist. When he was four years old, his father took on a job with the *Sydney Daily Telegraph* newspaper, and the family moved north to New South Wales. His parents purchased a house in peaceful Mosman, a northern suburb with glorious, sweeping views of Sydney Harbour. Young Philip could not have imagined a better place in which to live. He learned to swim with other children in nearby seawater pools and enjoyed exploring the rocky cliffs rising up from local beaches.

He cannot recall how it happened, but when he was eight years old, he met and became friends with Ethel Turner, the renowned author of *Seven Little Australians*, regarded by many as the most successful Australian children's novel of all time. Turner, then in her seventies, owned a house with a wonderful, mysterious garden overlooking Balmoral Beach.

"I often went there after school," Chapman recalled, "and spent a lot of time reading on her verandah. I also remember using her telescope to inspect departing ships, wondering what lay out there across the ocean, beyond the Sydney Heads."

Chapman had learned to read when he was three, and Ethel Turner had a library filled with books. As their friendship grew, she introduced him to the works of John Buchan, H. G. Wells, Jules Verne, and a favorite author—Edgar Rice Burroughs. "I think it was John Carter's adventures under the hurtling moons of Barsoom that first made me a space buff," he reflected.

Having taken his early education at a Mosman primary school, he advanced to Fort Street Opportunity School when he was nine. Teachers and friends at those schools, and later at Parramatta High School, often teased him about his fascination with rocket ships and space travel. In 1951 he won a book prize of his choice at school and requested Arthur C. Clarke's *Interplanetary Flight*. Chapman recalled, "At the presentation, the headmaster joked about wasting my time on fantasies. Many years later Arthur Clarke and I became friends, and he autographed my tattered copy. While I was an astronaut, I returned to Parramatta High for a tree-planting ceremony, bringing the book with me. My old headmaster had retired but he was there, and I was glad to make him eat his words."

His interest in space travel even led Chapman to write a letter to the Australian prime minister, Robert Menzies, in which he stated that the proposed rocket launch facility at Woomera in South Australia would be pointed in the wrong direction for launching satellites. "Oh, yes, Menzies wrote back," he recalled with a smile. "He thanked me for my interest but told me I should not worry, since his experts assured him that launching a satellite would always be impossible!"

Nevertheless, Chapman remained convinced that people would fly in space during his lifetime, and when he was fourteen years old, he set about maximizing his chances of being one of them. An obvious step was learning to fly, but it was a costly proposition. He knew that when he turned eighteen, he had to spend a compulsory six months doing national service military training and that a very small number of trainees—thirty from each intake, nationwide—were given flying lessons by the Royal Australian Air Force (RAAF). That was still four years away, so in order to make himself a better candidate, he joined the high school army cadets, rising to become the senior cadet officer by his final year at Parramatta High.

After passing his high school leaving certificate (with the highest grade in the school), he enrolled in a degree course in physics and mathematics at Sydney University. Then, by joining the university's RAAF Reserve Squadron, he ensured he would do his national service in the air force rather than the army.

His plan worked; he spent two summer vacations as an aircraftman (recruit-minor) at Bankstown Airfield, learning to fly Tiger Moths. He was rewarded with his private pilot's license and many happy memories of flying a biplane with his head stuck out in the slipstream.

Having graduated from Sydney University with his bachelor of science degree in May 1956, Chapman became an electronics engineer with Philips Electrical Industries. The following year, he applied for a job as a physicist with the Australian National Antarctic Research Expeditions (ANARE), administered by the Antarctic Division of the External Affairs Department. Unfortunately, he was too late responding to the advertisement and, to his disappointment, was told that the expedition teams had already been chosen, although he was asked to apply again the following year.

In early December, Chapman was working in his laboratory at Philips when a member of ANARE called to say that a physicist who was scheduled to spend the next year at Mawson Station in Antarctica had just broken his leg. Could Chapman join the expedition in his place? "Of course" was his immediate response. The ship was nearly ready to sail; could he make his way to Melbourne immediately—like, today? Chapman went to see his supervisor and gave him ten minutes' notice that he was leaving his job. Fortunately, the man was very understanding, and Chapman was on a plane to Melbourne that evening. A week later he found himself aboard the MV *Thala Dan*, plowing a rocky path through seventy-foot waves in the Southern Ocean.

The year 1958 had been designated as the International Geophysical Year by the worldwide scientific community, intended as a period of intense study of our planet. Chapman's principal job was to observe the *Aurora Australis*, the delicate, luminous curtains that light up the night sky in Antarctica. One of his objectives was to take simultaneous photos of the aurora, using a camera mounted on a theodolite at Mawson and another one at a camp beside an emperor penguin rookery at Taylor Glacier, some fifty miles west of the base. The display typically takes place at an altitude of around fifty to sixty miles, and the two photos would form a stereo pair, allowing the plotting of its position in space. These studies required Chapman to spend most of the Antarctic winter at Taylor Glacier, although for safety reasons there was always one other man with him.

Now twenty-three, Chapman found life at Taylor an exercise in self-reliance and a truly formative experience. If an emergency arose when the weather was fine, a de Havilland Beaver aircraft from Mawson could be there in less than an hour, although for several weeks around midwinter there was too little daylight for flying. As well, the weather was appalling much of the time, especially in the depth of winter, with temperatures often dropping below –40°C, with winds blasting at over one hundred knots, and with the visibility zero in snow so cold and dry that it would sandblast any exposed skin in seconds.

The first hut intended for Taylor Glacier had been blown away in a blizzard, so the two men lived in another, manufactured from a packing crate measuring eight feet square and six feet high. Their toilet was a tide crack where the sea ice met the land, and the ferocious weather soon taught them to be quick about it. Most of their food came in cans, which they stored in a stack of wooden crates that blew away one night. The crates all broke open, but the two men managed to recover many of the cans, which were spread for miles across the sea ice. All the labels had come off, so dinner thereafter was generally a surprise.

The world's first satellite, Sputnik, was launched on 4 October 1957, shortly before Chapman traveled to Antarctica. While he was there, the American satellite Explorer 1 was launched and discovered the Van Allen radiation belts, proving that the aurora is caused by high-energy particles from the solar wind trapped in Earth's magnetic field. By early 1959, when the *Thala Dan* relieved the expedition, the aurora was better understood by physicists everywhere, except for those who had been out of touch because they were busy studying it in Antarctica.

The space age was now well under way, and Chapman knew it was the right time for him to move to the United States. Engineers and scientists were in great demand, and he had no trouble receiving a job offer from the Massachusetts Institute of Technology. This put him on the first-preference list for a U.S. immigrant visa, but getting one would still take time, as the Australian quota was then only fifty per year.

In December 1959 he married Pamela Gatenby from Herberton, Queensland. They left the next day on a sea journey that eventually took them to Montreal, Canada, where Chapman found a temporary job as an engineer working in flight simulators for Canadian Aviation Electronics. The main attraction of Montreal was that he could drive down to MIT every few months, to ensure he would still have a job there when his immigrant visa finally came through.

Finally, in April 1961 the visa was granted. The young couple moved to Boston with their first child, Peter Hume, born the year before. At MIT Chapman became a staff physicist in the Experimental Astronomy Laboratory of the Department of Aeronautics and Astronautics.

This was a momentous period in the history of human space exploration. On 12 April a young Soviet air force lieutenant named Yuri Gagarin made a single orbit of Earth in 108 minutes aboard his Vostok capsule. Doubly promoted to the rank of major while in orbit, he will forever be remembered as the first person to fly into space.

Just three weeks later Alan Shepard also made the journey into space, this time on a short, suborbital ballistic mission lasting fifteen minutes, thus becoming America's first spaceman. President John Kennedy responded with a stirring speech in which he committed his nation to the goal of landing a man on the moon and returning him safely to Earth, before the decade was out. It was an incredible undertaking, and MIT was heavily involved.

The Experimental Astronomy Laboratory was an offshoot of the MIT Instrumentation Laboratory and was responsible for building the inertial guidance system that would one day take Apollo spacecraft to the moon. It was one of the best possible places to begin a career in the relatively new field of astronautics. Chapman's office mate was Russell (Rusty) Schweickart, who later became one of NASA's third intake of astronauts and flew in Earth orbit on *Apollo 9*. Buzz Aldrin, the second man to walk on the moon, and Dave Scott, of Gemini and Apollo fame, both had degrees earned through that laboratory.

In 1963 the Chapmans traveled to Washington DC, where the Australian ambassador invested Phil with the British Polar Medal, for his services in Antarctica. His job also allowed him to take courses at MIT, which in 1964 led to a master of science degree in aeronautics and astronautics and in 1967 to a doctorate under the joint auspices of the Departments of Physics and of Aeronautics and Astronautics. His doctoral dissertation was titled "Theoretical Foundations of Gravitational Experiments in Space."

By this time, the so-called space race between the United States and Russia was heating up. Russia had sent not only the first man into space but also the first woman and the first three-man crew. In 1965 cosmonaut Alexei Leonov became the first person to "walk" in space, outside the two-man *Voskhod 2* spacecraft.

The year 1967 was also when space exploration was marked by profound tragedy. On 27 January NASA astronauts Gus Grissom, Ed White, and Roger Chaffee died when the interior of their Apollo capsule was consumed by fire during a training exercise on launch complex 34. In April, Russia's experimental *Soyuz 1* spacecraft crash-landed following in-flight problems and a catastrophic parachute failure. The sole cosmonaut on board, Col. Vladimir Komarov, was killed when his capsule slammed into the ground at high speed and exploded into flames.

Soon after receiving his doctorate, Phil Chapman applied for American citizenship, which he knew was mandatory for any astronaut applicant. He completed the necessary paperwork and, on 8 May 1967, became a citizen of the United States.

By this time, as he had hoped, NASA had announced that it was looking for a second group of scientists to train as astronauts, and Chapman mailed in his application. He recalled, "I was fortunate to know several astronauts, who had told me a lot about the program. There is also no doubt that my year in Antarctica was a great advantage, because it suggested that I could survive in isolation and under stress. I met all the requirements, all right, but I also knew there were 1,100 applicants." NASA wanted only the best, and only one in a hundred applicants would eventually make the grade.

The selection process initially sorted out any suitable applicants from those who lacked the necessary qualifications. The selection panel then questioned the candidates endlessly about their experience and background and established their motive for wanting to become an astronaut. As they were not pilots, or had limited flying experience, the applicants were subjected to dizzying flights aboard jet trainers to test their reaction to heavy g-loads and unusual attitudes. They were informed that as a NASA astronaut, they would be learning to fly those same jets themselves.

While pressing ahead with its space program, NASA was also undergoing a profound reexamination of its policies and procedures to ensure that preventable accidents like the *Apollo 1* fire would never happen again. Chapman was well aware of the risks inherent in human space exploration, but he remained quietly confident that the country's best scientific and engineering brains were working on solutions. Any scientific exploration demanded that people resolve to press ahead, despite any losses that might occur along the way. It was something he accepted and then set aside.

Much to his elation, Chapman made it through. On 4 August 1967 he was officially announced as one of eleven scientists selected in the space agency's sixth group of astronauts. Immediately, he found himself under the media spotlight, as he and fellow candidate Tony Llewellyn, from Wales, were the first NASA astronauts to have been born outside the United States— something of a novelty back then. The other nine scientist appointees were Joe Allen, Karl Henize, Tony England, Don Holmquest, Story Musgrave, Bill Lenoir, Brian O'Leary, Bob Parker, and Bill Thornton.

One exciting event for the new astronauts took place on the morning of 22 January 1968, when they were at Cape Kennedy to witness the lift-off of the unmanned *Apollo 5* test mission. The Saturn 1B rocket used for the launch was some five times less powerful than the mighty Saturn V, which was still under development, but the Saturn 1B would carry a prototype lunar module on its maiden test flight. The new astronauts could hardly believe the noise and power of the launch and urged the huge rocket on as it cleared the gantry and thundered off into space. Chapman hoped he might one day be strapped into an Apollo spacecraft on top of a similar rocket, soaring out over the Atlantic Ocean on his way into orbit or beyond. Nevertheless, he was a realist and knew that any seats on upcoming flights were taken or coveted by pilot astronauts from earlier groups. Little wonder that the "new guys" began calling themselves the xs-11 (Excess Eleven).

The next phase of their training, which began in March 1968, was learning to fly. Apart from Chapman, only Story Musgrave had ever piloted an aircraft before, and none had flown a jet aircraft. With the exception of Don Holmquest, who would join the group later in their training, they were sent to flight schools at several U.S. Air Force bases, where they would train alongside air force hopefuls. Chapman's assignment was to Randolph AFB in San Antonio, Texas, the headquarters of USAF Training Command. As the base was only two hundred miles from Houston, it made it easy for him to keep in touch with the work on Apollo at the Manned Spacecraft Center.

Their fifty-three-week flight training began with six weeks in a modified version of the Cessna 150, a single-engine high-wing aircraft commonly used in civilian flight schools. The main purpose in this phase of their training was to identify, at minimum cost and risk, any students who had little chance of completing the course. Chapman was quite comfortable, as the Cessna was similar to aircraft he had flown before. The students then moved on to the subsonic T-37 jet trainer, affectionately known as the Tweety Bird due to its whistling engines, and finally to the supersonic T-38 Talon, a two-seat training version of the F-5 fighter jet. NASA owned a fleet of T-38s, which were in constant use by the existing astronauts.

The nonastronaut students taking part in the pilot training were fresh out of university, so at thirty-three, Chapman was the "old man" in his class. He was also the only civilian. As he told the author,

6. Dr. Philip K. Chapman, NASA scientist-astronaut designee. Courtesy NASA.

I normally wore a flight suit around Randolph, but I had no rank insignia. Even worse, I had no hat, which was a serious infraction for the military students. Occasionally some colonel I passed in the street would tear a strip off me for being out of uniform, but of course he always apologized when I explained that I was a NASA civilian. I soon learned that if I made firm eye contact with an approaching officer, he would usually leave me alone. Sometimes, confused by seeing this rankless, hatless person in flying clothes, he would play it safe by actually saluting me. My best effort in this game was a salute from a two-star general.

Chapman was enjoying this phase of his astronaut training.

I really loved flying jets, especially the T-38. It is an extraordinarily agile machine, and it needs a very light touch on the controls. If you push the stick hard over, it will complete an aileron roll in less than two seconds. My first few solos were quite scary, but it became very easy to fly once I was used to it. Then we moved on to formation flying, which was scary all over again. It is quite intimidating to see your wingtip only a meter away from the lead's wingtip when you are moving at five hundred knots— but it is easier than it looks. The slipstream from the lead aircraft pushes you away, so colliding is unlikely.

At the end of pilot training, Chapman graduated second in his class. This was at the height of the conflict in Vietnam, so he was not surprised that the best students all wanted to be fighter pilots. "I admired their spirit," he said, "but dodging SAMs over Hanoi didn't seem like the best possible career move. I would have selected something a little less lethal. Test pilot school, perhaps."

Some of his fellow astronaut trainees, however, had found the flight training hard going. A month after it began, Brian O'Leary came to the difficult conclusion that he could not handle the flying part of being an astronaut. He also foresaw very little opportunity for scientists to be on spaceflights for several years and reluctantly decided to resign from the astronaut corps.

O'Leary had made a valid point about a lack of mission opportunities for the scientist-astronauts, but Chapman was far more committed and decided to ride it out, just to see what NASA had in store for him. He knew that the national objective was to get men to the moon and back, and only the best, most experienced pilots would be among those assigned to the first missions. Once NASA had demonstrated that its astronauts could land on the moon and return safely to Earth, he felt there would be a need for scientists to follow in their path.

Then, on 23 August 1968, another member of the XS-11 tendered his resignation. The loss of Wales-born Tony Llewellyn, who also decided that he simply did not have the aptitude for learning to fly fast jets, brought their number down to nine and the total number of NASA astronauts to fifty-two.

A baby girl christened Kristen de Querilleau rounded out the Chapman family in October 1968. Two months later Frank Borman, Jim Lovell, and Bill Anders flew their *Apollo 8* spacecraft around the moon, the first humans to do so. America, through NASA, was now poised to send astronauts to land on the lunar surface.

When the family returned to Houston in early 1969, Chapman had qualified as a jet pilot. NASA wanted all its astronauts to maintain their proficiency by flying thirty or forty hours each month, but it was not easy to find the time, as work on the Apollo program was intensifying. He was now flying all over the United States, attending technical meetings and giving public lectures about the space program, but like his fellow astronauts he spent most of his time helping with the development of equipment for the lunar landing. As an example, the Apollo command module had been designed to enter Earth's atmosphere under automatic control. If the guidance system failed, the pilot could reenter by flying manually, using a display that showed the deceleration as a function of time. If the deceleration was too great, the descent path would become too steep and the capsule would burn up. If it were too little, the capsule would bounce out of the atmosphere. It was not clear that a pilot could handle the controls under the stress of atmospheric entry, so Chapman flew several simulated manual trajectories, pulling 7 or 8 g's in a command module mock-up mounted on a centrifuge. The conclusion was that manual reentry was feasible, but only if the pilot had practiced it beforehand.

On the *Apollo 9* mission, three astronauts orbited Earth during a ten-day mission to check out rendezvous techniques between the command and lunar modules. Then, in May, the crew of *Apollo 10* flew their lunar module to within nine miles of the moon's surface before rendezvousing once again with the orbiting command module.

Everybody understood that Project Apollo was President Kennedy's response to the Soviet Union's early supremacy in space. Now it seemed quite probable that the first people on the moon would be Americans, not Russians. The problem now facing NASA was that beating the Russians too decisively might lead Congress to cut back future funding for human spaceflight. Chapman said,

> *Soviet cosmonauts visited Houston several times while I was there, and we usually put on a party for them at the home of one of the astronauts. They claimed to speak little English and were always accompanied by*

7. Chapman sits inside the Lunar Module Mission Simulator in Building 5 during familiarization training at the Manned Spacecraft Center. Courtesy NASA.

"translators," who were actually zampolits *(political officers). Our standard procedure was to have some pretty girls on hand, in miniskirts, who would distract the* zampolits *while we fed alcohol to the cosmonauts. Their English improved remarkably after a few scotches. I remember one of them urging us to do something spectacular in space, and soon, because otherwise the Politburo would cut their funding. The space programs of both countries depended on the Cold War.*

A few months before Apollo 11, I was sitting in a bar with a few other astronauts, when the conversation turned to what we could do if the USSR quit the space race. Somebody suggested that we should create a fake alien artifact and give it to Neil [Armstrong] to "find" on the moon. Evidence that an alien civilization had visited the moon in the past would surely stimulate a major effort to find out more. To be convincing, the artifact had to be something subtle. Our solution depended on the fact that sugar molecules exist in two forms, called isomers, that are mirror images of each other. Sugar produced chemically contains an equal mix of both isomers, but biological sugars contain only one, and it is the same one for all life on Earth. Our plan was to obtain some goat urine, remove the sugar, and replace it with the other isomer. Neil would contaminate a soil sample, let it bake in vacuum until he was ready to leave, and bring it home. Then the chemists would discover that somebody or something not of this earth had taken a leak on the moon. Of course this was a joke (almost), and we never did anything about it. I rather wish we had; we might now be much farther ahead in space.

On 20 July 1969 Chapman was present in mission control when lunar module *Eagle* touched down on the Sea of Tranquility and Neil Armstrong became the first person ever to set foot on another world. For the rest of his life, the Australian scientist would never forget the profound awe and elation he felt in being present at—and part of—that remarkable occasion. He thought it might prove to be the most significant event in the history of life since the first gasping fish crawled ashore and started the evolution of animals on land during the Devonian era, 400 million years ago.

The crew of *Apollo 11* returned to a hero's welcome, and their flight was successfully repeated four months later when Pete Conrad's crew journeyed to the moon on *Apollo 12*. By this time, following several mishaps, Russia had abandoned its plans for landing cosmonauts on the moon and was instead developing crew-tended laboratories that would be placed into Earth orbit.

Tragedy nearly struck the Apollo program again on the following flight when Jim Lovell, Fred Haise, and Jack Swigert suffered an explosion in their service module. However, the cold and exhausted crew of *Apollo 13* finally made it back safely after a perilous loop around the moon.

Prior to this flight, Chapman had been handed a choice assignment as mission scientist for *Apollo 14*. He was not on the prime or backup crew, but he became an essential part of the team, helping to organize the scientific training of the crew, coordinate lunar experiments, and provide the interface between the scientific team and the crew on the moon. After the mission returned, he served as chairman of the editorial board for the *Apollo 14* preliminary science report.

In January 1971 Alan Shepard and his crew successfully made it to a lunar landing, and in one of the lighter moments, he even managed to whack a couple of golf balls a considerable distance in the airless moon's low gravity, using a specially built club.

While Chapman was glad to have taken an active role in a lunar mission, his work on *Apollo 14* strengthened his growing concern about prevailing attitudes in NASA management. In particular, he disagreed strongly with Deke Slayton, one of the first Mercury astronauts, who was head of the Manned Spacecraft Center Crew Systems Division, which included the Astronaut Office. Slayton's position included a responsibility for selecting crews for each mission. Chapman mused,

> *Problems with Deke became apparent soon after I joined the program in 1967, when John Glenn sent a memo to all of us, complaining that Deke had revoked his access to mission control. Glenn had left NASA, but he was of course still in great demand by the media. Cutting him out of the picture, instead of using him as a spokesman, was an act of breathtaking stupidity. It was hard to believe, but it really seemed that Deke was motivated by nothing more than envy because Glenn was a hero enjoying the limelight, while he had been grounded by a heart murmur.*
>
> *Removal from flight status was of course a great disappointment for Deke, so nobody minded much that he was usually irascible. Everybody knew he had been given his senior desk job as a consolation prize—but I didn't think a heart murmur was an adequate qualification for such a responsible position. To put it plainly, it seemed to me that Deke had no understanding that leadership is a two-way street and no vision of spaceflight beyond keeping it as his own little fiefdom. Furthermore, he apparently thought that the only legitimate purpose of a space mission was flight-testing a vehicle, that science in space was a worthless distraction, and that scientists were inherently unacceptable as astronauts, regardless of their flying skills.*
>
> *I believed then, and still do, that pilot training is very useful. Like spaceflight, flying is an activity that is not normally dangerous, but it is intolerant of mistakes. If you do the wrong thing, you die. Flying thus teaches you to be calm under time-critical stress—or, rather, to postpone the panic attack until you are safely on the ground. I had nothing but admiration and respect for the coolness shown by pilots such as Neil Armstrong and by the entire crew of Apollo 13. While I was not sure that I could have matched it, I did not believe that we scientists would endanger any mission. We had all been tested under stress and would not have been there if we were unstable.*

Deke made his attitude very clear while I was working on Apollo 14. As in all lunar landings, the command module pilot, Stu Roosa, would wait in orbit while the other two crew went down to the surface. Stu would have very little to do, and he asked me if I could suggest useful activities or observations he might undertake. I talked to various friends in the space sciences, and we came up with an interesting list. None of our suggestions involved any special equipment or had any impact on other mission tasks. For example, a Polish astronomer named Kordelewski, using an earthbound telescope, had reported seeing very faint clouds at places in the plane of the moon's orbit called L4 and L5, which are located so as to make equilateral triangles with the Earth and moon. These are points of stable gravitational equilibrium, and it was possible that dust or larger meteors had collected there. This was of great scientific interest, since it offered the possibility of obtaining meteoritic material that had not been altered by passage through the earth's atmosphere. There were times in lunar orbit, on the nightside of the moon, when the Kordelewski clouds (if they existed) would be within the line of sight and illuminated by the sun. All Stu had to do was to point a camera in the right direction at the right time, and he might make a major scientific discovery.

Unfortunately, Deke heard about this list, and he carpeted Stu and me. He pointed out that scientists whose proposals had been rejected would be angry if we undertook experiments that had not been through the formal selection process. I agreed but said that formal experiments were only accepted if there was a good chance of completing them. This conservative approach meant that there would always be some spare time, and we should not waste it just to avoid upsetting a few individuals.

Deke refused to listen and told Stu that he would be removed from the flight crew if he did not get rid of the list and that he would never fly in space again if he made any observations that were not specifically shown in the official flight plan. As a result, we still do not know if the Kordelewski clouds are real.

Later, Deke sent a memo to all the astronauts, saying that TV commentators always judge the success of a mission by the percentage of the mission objectives that have been achieved. The obvious way to maximize that number, he said, was to reduce the number of mission objectives. In future, therefore, the Astronaut Office was to do everything it

*possibly could to eliminate scientific experiments on every mission. I was
dumbfounded by the idea that the way to increase interest in spaceflight
was to minimize the useful results, and insubordinate Australian that I
am, I told Deke what I thought of his new policy.*

The final straw came when Slayton announced that he would never
assign any scientist-astronaut to a lunar mission (nor to any other mission, if he could help it). Chapman had no real expectation of going to
the moon himself, but geologists Jack Schmitt and Tony England were
clearly the astronauts best qualified to investigate lunar geology. They were
both very competent pilots, and Chapman thought that excluding them
for no better reason than blind prejudice was tantamount to sabotaging
the space program.

"I had always tried to be a team player, disagreeing with Deke only in
private, but this was much too much," Chapman recalled. "After some soul-
searching, I discussed the issue of scientists on the moon directly with Jim
Fletcher, the NASA administrator. I don't know whether what I said influenced his decision, but in any case, Deke was overruled, and Jack Schmitt
went to the moon on *Apollo 17*, the last Apollo mission."

Shortly after *Apollo 14*, Chapman gave a talk about spaceflight at a meeting of the Ninety-Nines, the international association of women pilots. He
shared the podium with Sheila Scott, a well-known British aviatrix who
had just arrived from Fiji in her single-engine Piper Comanche. She told
him that she was getting ready for a flight from equator to equator, over
the North Pole.

"I knew that NASA had developed a transponder that gave a position
report to the Nimbus weather satellite," Chapman said. "It was intended
to hang around the neck of a caribou (a North American reindeer), so as to
track their migratory patterns. I persuaded NASA to lend one to Sheila. This
meant that the Goddard Spaceflight Center in Washington would get a fix
on her every ninety-six minutes, when Nimbus passed over the pole. If she
came down anywhere in the Arctic, we could tell rescuers where to find her."

Chapman was at Goddard with Dick Hoagland, another friend of Sheila's, when she left Norway in a twin-engine Piper Aztec, heading for Point
Barrow in Alaska. It was a strenuous flight, which Sheila later described in
her book *On Top of the World* (to which Chapman contributed a foreword).

At Goddard, in between Nimbus fixes, Chapman and Hoagland were discussing a request by Dave Scott, commander of the upcoming *Apollo 15*. He wanted something interesting that he could do before leaving the moon, just to be one up on Alan Shepard's demonstration of lunar golf. The suggestion that they came up with turned out to be one of the most memorable but simple exhibitions of pure science carried out in the Apollo program.

Toward the end of his lunar visit, Dave Scott told a live television audience back on Earth that he was hoping to demonstrate that Galileo Galilei had been right. Galileo, the Italian physicist and inventor, stated that objects of different weight would always fall with the same acceleration under gravity. Scott therefore produced a hammer and a falcon's feather (taken from the mascot of the U.S. Air Force Academy), held them out, and dropped them at the same instant. On Earth the ultralight feather would have floated down, but on the airless moon, both objects fell together. Because lunar gravity is only one-sixth that on Earth, they fell quite slowly, but they hit the lunar soil simultaneously. The video of this simple experiment is still widely used in schools to demonstrate the nature of gravitation.

By the time *Apollo 15* flew, Americans were rapidly losing interest in the space program. President Richard Nixon did nothing to stem this decline or to help NASA find the best direction for the future. Despite the staged enthusiasm he displayed during his phone call to Neil Armstrong and Buzz Aldrin while they were on the moon, Nixon had no real interest in spaceflight and was already sinking into a paranoid preoccupation with his political enemies that would lead to the Watergate break-in and his eventual resignation. Lacking strong support from the White House, the NASA budget was diminishing each year. Conversely, the enthusiasm that was evident when *Apollo 11* landed had been replaced by a growing uncertainty about the future.

Budget cuts eventually led to the cancellation of Apollo missions 18, 19, and 20 and led to a debate within NASA about its future programs. *Skylab A*, as it was known, was being developed as America's first space station and was scheduled for a launch in 1973. It was planned that three crews would spend months aboard that workshop, but after that, it would be abandoned. Each of the three crews would include a scientist-astronaut, but none came from Chapman's group.

A second workshop, *Skylab B*, was under planning for 1975. Chapman was a member of a committee, headed by Frank Borman, that advocated simple changes that would permit repeated resupply and refurbishment, in order to give the station an indefinitely long life on orbit.

There was, however, another influential faction in NASA, which urged the development of what became the space shuttle. They claimed that a space station was unnecessary, as the shuttle would prove so inexpensive to operate that astronauts could sleep at home and commute to orbit each day. Chapman had no faith at all in these claims. In his judgement, the estimates used to support them were simply fraudulent, and radically new technologies required by the shuttle precluded any meaningful prediction of costs. He firmly believed that NASA should work on such advanced technologies as relatively low-cost research projects and not commit to using them in an operational vehicle until they had been proven. While the necessary research was underway, NASA could use *Skylab* to establish a low-cost, permanent space station.

Chapman suspected that the real problem with a space station, as perceived by Deke Slayton and his ilk, was that it just sat there in orbit. No "real" flying would be carried out, and the role of the pilot would essentially be reduced to monitoring the automatic guidance systems that controlled launch, docking with the station, atmospheric reentry, and descent under parachutes. The shuttle was more appealing, because it had wings and could actually be flown manually, at least during the final descent to a landing.

The space station was a step toward a future in which different people could live and work in space—engineers, scientists, steel workers, doctors and nurses, even farmers and cooks. That prospect, according to Chapman, was very threatening to those who were more interested in retaining control of the program than in a growing human enterprise in space.

Faced with a declining budget and rising costs, NASA made cutbacks in several areas. The Borman committee recommendations about making *Skylab B* permanent were rejected, and the entire second Skylab project was canceled. This was a major blow for Chapman, as he had hoped to fly in that workshop and was developing two experiments he could undertake there. "The *Skylab* in which I hoped to live is now a tourist attraction in the Smithsonian Air and Space Museum," he laments. "I sometimes visit it when I am in Washington, but it is very sad to see it wasted."

It was now abundantly clear that none of the XS-11 would make it into space for at least another decade. In July 1972 Chapman reluctantly decided that he had to find a better way to contribute to spaceflight than simply hanging around in Houston, working in a program in which he had lost confidence. He handed in his resignation and spent the next five years working at the Avco Everett Research Laboratory in Massachusetts, helping to develop laser propulsion. The lab had built the most powerful lasers in the world, mostly for military purposes, and had conceived the idea of developing a rocket engine that would derive its energy from a laser beam rather than from combustion. A launch vehicle using such an engine would climb up the beam into the sky, which would make achieving orbit extremely cheap and easy. The cost per pound in a conventional launch to orbit is in excess of $400,000. In principle, laser propulsion could reduce that to less than $4 per pound, making spaceflight cheaper than airline travel.

Meanwhile, back at NASA, another scientist from the group, Donald Holmquest, handed in his resignation in September 1973. Any spaceflight was still several years away, and he wanted to resume his own life's work and studies.

Altogether, Chapman spent five years at Avco, helping to build several test engines. The results were promising, but it became clear that an extremely large laser, with a power output of at least a gigawatt (a thousand million watts), would be required for a practical space launch facility. Such a laser could be built, but it would be massively expensive.

In 1977 he went to work for Peter Glaser, of Arthur D. Little, Inc. (ADL), in nearby Cambridge, Massachusetts. He spent the next four years there, working on the solar power system (SPS), with funding supplied by the Department of Energy. This entailed placing solar arrays in geosynchronous orbit to produce five to ten times more energy per square yard than terrestrial solar arrays. Next, he was appointed president of Echelon Development, a computer software company, also based in Cambridge.

Although he was working on important technologies that offered great promise for spaceflight, it was not easy for Chapman to give up his lifelong goal of becoming an astronaut. He had come very close but was finally let down by what he thought were idiotic decisions by NASA management. These stresses ultimately cost him his marriage to Pamela, and they were divorced in 1976.

The following year he was elected president of the L5 Society, a space advocacy group that later merged with the National Space Institute, becoming the current-day National Space Society. Four years later the space shuttle finally became operational, and in 1982 Bill Lenoir and Joe Allen from Chapman's astronaut group finally made it into space, having waited fifteen years for the opportunity. The other five group 6 scientist-astronauts, who had resolutely stayed on with NASA, would eventually fly on science missions aboard NASA's shuttle fleet.

Phil Chapman spent most of the 1980s working for himself as a consultant to industry and government. In 1984 he married Maria Tseng, daughter of an ancient and respected Chinese family, who can trace her lineage back for 2,500 years. She was born in Hong Kong but grew up in Manhattan, holds a master's degree in business administration, and works in the computer industry.

In January 1989 he returned to Antarctica, leading a privately funded expedition aimed at investigating mineral resources in the vicinity of Enderby Land. The team chartered an ice-strengthened ocean-going tug in Cape Town, which gave them an interesting passage through the monstrous seas of the Southern Ocean. Pack ice blocked the way when they were forty-two miles from their objective, but they went ashore by helicopter.

"There was talk about banning all mineral activities on the ice," he revealed, "and we wanted to see what was there while we still could. We didn't find much of real commercial potential. But it was a great adventure, and we had a wonderful time. I was especially pleased that Maria was with us and had a chance to see that magnificent place and to understand why it has been such an influence in my life. What we were doing was entirely legal at the time, but in 1998, prospecting was prohibited by U.S. and international law."

In the mid-1990s Chapman served as chief scientist for Rotary Rocket Company, a start-up group keen to develop a single-stage manned launch vehicle called the Roton. The design and construction of the Roton went ahead without major technical problems, and the rocket underwent initial flight tests at the company's facilities in California's Mojave Desert. Unfortunately, funding for the innovative project dried up in the stock market collapse late in the decade.

In summing up, Chapman said, "I have enjoyed an adventurous, rewarding life. I am of course sorry that I didn't get into space, but that experience would have been just one more trinket on my string of memories. What is deeply frustrating is that NASA has betrayed the dream, and that means that I shall not live to see our society liberated from the constraints of this fragile little planet."

Today he and Maria live in Sunnyvale at the southern end of San Francisco Bay, where he devotes some of his free time to writing. He also currently serves as chairman of the Solar High Study Group, a team of experienced senior managers and technologists who believe that space-based solar power can solve the problem of bringing clean, affordable energy to people anywhere on Earth or in space.

Dr. Philip Chapman's assured place in spaceflight history is that of the first person born in Australia to be selected and trained as a NASA astronaut. In October 1984 another scientist, Sydney-born oceanographer Dr. Paul Scully-Power, was launched into orbit aboard the shuttle *Challenger*, although he flew as a non-NASA payload specialist.

It would be just on twenty years after Philip Chapman's resignation from the space agency that the next person from his country of birth, Andy Thomas, would follow his example and join NASA's elite astronaut corps. Thomas would fly into space five times and spend nearly five months living and working aboard Russia's *Mir* space station.

4. Svetlana's Story

Russia's Journalist-in-Space Program and Cosmonaut-Journalist Svetlana Omelchenko

I would not say that female cosmonauts are not welcomed in the
Russian space program. I must say, however, that all spaceflight
hardware, including space suits and spacecraft comfort assuring
systems, were designed mostly by men and for men.

—Valentina Tereshkova

It was once planned as part of the Soviet-CIS space program to send a professional journalist into space. One of the six aspiring cosmonaut-journalists who completed her training in February 1992 was a reflective but fun-loving woman named Svetlana Omelchenko. Although she would never fulfill her cherished dream of writing about life in space or our blue planet as seen from orbit, Svetlana agreed to share her story through a lengthy Q&A mail correspondence with the author.

On 11 May 1990 the Soviet Joint State Commission approved a new group of fourteen cosmonaut trainees. Included in this number were six journalists from the Union of Writers who had been selected as cosmonaut candidates four months earlier. All were keen (and competitive) to assume the title of first journalist in space. The only female in this group was Moscow-based Svetlana Oktyabrevna Omelchenko.

As a young girl, Svetlana (known to her family as Sveta) first became entranced with spaceflight through her father Oktyabr (October) Yeremeyeva, who loved nothing more than sitting in their back garden of an evening with his two young daughters, Svetlana and Lyudmila, patiently describing to them the wonders of the cosmos. A pipe smoker, he was banished from the house by his teacher wife Anna Nikitichna (née Doroshenko), who did not want her curtains fouled by tobacco fumes.

Their modest home was situated in the Stavropol district of southern Kavkas, an area later devastated by fighting during the fall of the Soviet regime. Svetlana and her little sister Lyudmila would often nestle up to their father as he explained some of the mysteries of the vast heavens to them and discussed the possibility of other civilizations inhabiting the infinity of space. A journalist by trade, and named after the October Revolution by his patriotic mother, Yeremeyeva talked to his daughters easily, pointing out stars and planets to them in the night sky with his pipe, telling them that one day humans would venture out into space. He was looking forward to that day. "He was a marvelous father," Svetlana recalled with affection, "and gave a lot of himself to us children."

On 4 October 1957, soon after Svetlana's sixth birthday, the first Sputnik satellite was launched into orbit. Her father was so excited and proud; Svetlana said it was almost as if he had helped launch the satellite himself. One day soon, he promised his daughters, a man would ride a similar rocket into space.

Sadly, Oktyabr Yeremeyeva would not live to tell his daughters about a man named Yuri Gagarin. On 16 July 1958, just three years before the first human spacefarer ventured into the relatively unknown mysteries and dangers of the cosmos, a fatal motorcycle crash took the thirty-three-year-old Yeremeyeva prematurely from their lives. But his fascination with the heavens had left an indelible impression on his older daughter.

Svetlana Oktyabrevna Yeremeyeva was born soon after midnight on Monday, 20 August 1951 in Sleptsovsk, Chechen-Ingush ASSP. It was a significant date in Russian history. On that day in 1882, Tchaikovsky's rousing *1812 Overture* had made its debut in Moscow, while in Mexico City in 1940, the exiled Russian revolutionary Leon Trotsky was fatally wounded with an ice ax wielded by Ramón Mercader, a Spanish communist. Mercader was sentenced to twenty years in prison but was presented in absentia with the Order of Lenin by a delighted Joseph Stalin (who historians believe had actually recruited the killer). Such was Russian politics in those desperate days.

The area surrounding Svetlana's birthplace had been the scene of bloody fighting and bombardment over the decades, but it began in earnest in

March 1992 when Chechen leaders refused to sign the federation treaty. By early winter in 1994, Boris Yeltsin had sent troops into Chechen-Ingush to put down the revolt and prevent the republic from seceding.

"I saw on television these tragic happenings and the helplessness of the Russian government to do anything about it," Svetlana mused. "When I watched it, I wept and was grateful for the true journalists who produced this show." Over the next two years, the Chechens fought a demoralized, poorly equipped, and ill-led Russian army to a bloody stalemate. The province became independent in fact, if not in name.

When she was just two years old, Svetlana's family made the move to southern Kavkaz. The Stavropol area was very primitive, with no electricity or water. Typically, Oktyabr Yeremeyeva was the first in line to organize and install electric power, which meant the family could finally do away with kerosene lamps. They were poor, but their house was in an impoverished area where everyone lived and fared in the same frugal way.

Despite their circumstances, Svetlana recalled this period of her life as "very joyous." Memorable days were now spent watching soccer matches and attending occasional dances with a wind instrument orchestra providing the music. On 15 July 1955 her sister Lyudmila was born, and six years later a momentous event in the history of the Soviet Union fired Svetlana's youthful imagination.

"I was in third class at school when I first heard of Yuri Gagarin's flight," Svetlana recalled. "People were celebrating in the streets in all the cities when this happened. I remember how even before this, father used to convince mother that I would fly to the moon, and this would eventually become as simple as a trip to a neighboring village."

It would be nearly three decades before Svetlana or anyone would know how perilously close Gagarin had come to a fiery end following his single Earth orbit on 12 April 1961. The frightening story was first revealed when a secret report filed by Gagarin after his flight was printed in the Russian newspaper *Rabochaya Tribuna* in 1991. Then, five years later an auction was held at Sotheby's in New York, during which notes made at the time of the flight by military physician Col. Yevgeny Karpov, first chief of the cosmonaut training center, were auctioned off. His notes confirmed the earlier press reports.

According to Karpov, the retrorocket situated in the Vostok spacecraft's instrument module fired for precisely forty seconds, slowing the craft prior to reentry. As the engine shut down, Gagarin felt a sudden jolt, and the descent module he was occupying began spinning out of control. Ordinarily, the instrument module would have explosively jettisoned from the descent module some ten seconds after the engine shutdown. While separation did occur, the two modules remained tethered together by an umbilical cable that had failed to sever. This caused the linked spacecraft to tumble as they arced back into the atmosphere, creating a real risk that the two components could collide and cause a fatal breach in Gagarin's module.

According to Gagarin's top secret report, and in his own words, details emerged of the hazardous reentry.

> *The craft began to rotate . . . at a very high rate. . . . I was just barely shutting the Sun out, so I could keep the light out of my eyes. I put my feet up to the viewport, but I couldn't close the shutters. I was wondering what was going on. . . . On the instrument panel, the "Spusk 1" [Descent 1] light was still on, and the "Prepare for Ejection" was not on. The separation wasn't taking place. . . . I decided that something was wrong. . . . I figured I'd land one way or other . . . somewhere before the Far East I'd land. . . . I transmitted an EN—everything normal. . . .*
>
> *The spacecraft is beginning to turn slowly, about all three axes. It began to swing ninety degrees to the left and right. . . . I could sense the oscillation of the craft and burning of the coating. . . . I could feel the high temperature. . . . Then the g-loads began to grow smoothly. . . . The g-load felt to be more than 10 g. Things started turning a little grey. I squinted and strained again. That helped, and everything sort of went back in place.*

Gagarin was acutely aware that if the problem persisted, he would be incinerated in the unforgiving heat of reentry, but he remained calm and kept reporting his situation into his tape recorder. Finally, after ten perilous minutes, the linked umbilical sheared and burned through in the intense heat with an audible bang, and the instrument module fell away. The cosmonaut's descent module now assumed the correct orientation and continued to plunge through the atmosphere, its forward section quickly growing white-hot from friction with the atmosphere.

With the reentry phase completed, and approaching the ground, Gagarin ejected as planned from the Vostok craft and landed safely under his own

parachute. It was a very near thing, and the Soviet Union had come perilously close to losing their very first cosmonaut.

Nevertheless, throughout the Soviet Union there was unconcealed joy
and rapturous celebrations among the citizens when they heard the news of
this historic feat, and Svetlana rejoiced in Yuri Gagarin's feat. She wanted
to fly in space as well but confessed to the author that she was never very
healthy or strong in her youth. She would also claim that poor reading
habits had a lasting effect on her life: "As I was growing up, I used to read
a lot, sometimes by torchlight under my blanket after mother switched off
the lights, and this ruined my eyesight."

During her early teen years, Svetlana became interested in flying and
would often visit a nearby aviation club. She quickly noticed that there were
no other girls wandering around the airstrip, just young men. Although very
shy, she plucked up the courage to enquire about joining but was promptly
and dismissively told that girls were not accepted.

In 1968, at the age of sixteen, Svetlana graduated from tenth grade in
her secondary school in Livnon. Knowing by now that she wanted to be a
journalist like her late father, she began directing her efforts toward that
goal and also toward becoming a pilot. "After leaving school," she remembered, "I did a little work at a local newspaper called *Primanycheski Stepi*,
and a year later I went to Moscow to study journalism. I tried once again to
join an aviation club but was refused due to my poor physical condition."

Realizing that she might have to find full-time employment to fuel
her ambitions, Svetlana took on work in the construction industry while
attending vocational school 78 in Moscow, graduating in 1970 with her
electrician-for-propulsion degree.

In the meantime, Svetlana had met Ivan Omelchenko, and the two eventually married. On 11 June 1973 they became proud parents to a little baby
girl they named Xenia Ivanovna.

"I was now also working in building and became an electrician. After
graduating from technical school, I was accepted into a faculty for journalism at Moscow State University and graduated from there in June 1975.
Soon I managed to find employment in a small newspaper called [in English]
Aviation Racing and thus got into aviation, although I only flew as a passenger." She would remain at the newspaper until January 1978.

Then began a busy period in which Svetlana worked as a senior correspondent at the newspapers *Vozdushny Reys* (Air travel), *Vozdushny Transport*, and *Delovoy Mir* (Business world).

In March 1989 it was announced that the Soviet Union's cash-strapped Glavcosmos space agency had reached a financial arrangement—said to be worth an unprecedented ¥1.5 billion (US$10 million)—with the private TV network Tokyo Broadcasting System (TBS) for a show to be called *Nihonjin Hatsu! Uchuu e* (which loosely translates to "The first Japanese in space!"). Under the terms of the agreement, a Japanese journalist from TBS would be launched aboard the *Soyuz TM-11* spacecraft to the orbiting *Mir* space station for a week-long stay, broadcasting live daily radio and television reports from space.

A selection process was begun to find a suitable and medically qualified candidate from hundreds of hopeful applicants. Six months later, on 18 September, TBS named the two finalists as forty-seven-year-old, chain-smoking male journalist Toyohiro Akiyama and twenty-four-year-old television camera operator Ryoko Kikuchi, the only female camerawoman at TBS. They would travel to Moscow for training and lessons in the Russian language—after which, one of them would be named as the prime flight candidate, and the other, as the backup.

It has never been revealed which of the two might have been chosen to make the flight, but sadly for Kikuchi, she developed a case of appendicitis just a week before the launch date, undergoing an emergency operation in a military hospital. This meant that by default Akiyama was launched to the *Mir* space station aboard the *Soyuz TM-11* spacecraft on the morning of 2 December 1990, accompanied by cosmonauts Viktor Afanasayev and Musa Manarov. The day before launch a gallant but disappointed Kikuchi had been permitted to leave her hospital bed in order to attend the preflight press conference alongside Akiyama.

During his time aboard *Mir*, Akiyama gave live television reports to his homeland, documenting life and the daily routine aboard the space station. Then, after nearly eight days, he returned to Earth on 10 December aboard the *Soyuz TM-10* spacecraft, along with crewmembers Gennadi Manakov and Gennadi Strekalov, who had been replaced by Akiyama's crew aboard *Mir*.

The purely commercial agreement to send a Japanese journalist to *Mir* had quietly outraged their Soviet counterparts, who felt one of their own should have had the honor of being the first official journalist sent into space aboard a Soyuz spacecraft, not some foreign interloper. In fact, it was hopefully but unsuccessfully argued that twice-flown cosmonaut Vitaly Sevastyanov, a 1980s television commentator, should have been recognized as the first journalist to enter space.

Back when plans for the Japanese flight were still under way, NPO Energia finally decided to select a number of Soviet trainees with journalistic backgrounds for a flight coinciding with the International Space Year of 1992. The selection process came at precisely the right time for Svetlana.

Just before the Aviation Journal *organized a competition into cosmic flight, my mother died, so I was experiencing a traumatic time in my life. I got divorced, experienced a chronic lack of money to live on, endless queues for food, and so on.*

I was not overconfident in my ability in this competition, but my taking part in it was like entry into another world. First, I had to establish why I wanted to fly. I said that mankind can survive without goods but not without dreams and hope. We have to give our children food not only for the body but also for the soul.

Svetlana had many misgivings even as she fired off her application. Not only did she wear glasses, but she was also afraid of heights. Despite this, she must have made a suitable impression, as she was one of six journalists selected as finalists by the Soviet Writers' Union. Three other female journalists had been candidates: Yelmina Akmedova, Lyudmilla Chernyak, and Olga Sasoreova; but Svetlana was ultimately successful. The other five finalists were male—military journalists Lt. Col. Aleksandr Stepanovich Andryushkov and Lt. Col. Valeri Vasiliyevich Baberdin and civilian journalists Yuri Yuriyevich Krikun, Pavel Petrovich Mukhortov, and Valeri Yuriyevich Sharov.

In October 1990 Svetlana reported to the Yuri Gagarin Cosmonaut Training Center in Star City near Moscow to begin her cosmonaut-researcher training, knowing that the process would be highly competitive. The journalists realized that only one of them would be selected, and that person would spend eight days in space aboard the *Mir* station sometime in 1993, so they knuckled down to their studies and training. Svetlana revealed,

In spite of my lack of physical strength, the hardest part of my training was not the physical part but the theory of flight. The first serious training was the theory of survival in the Arctic. There was an imitation of this at the Cosmodrome, with temperatures at –57°C. We were in this for forty-eight hours on emergency rations. This training was so traumatic that some of the persons required medical attention afterward.

We got to know and learned about many things. We jumped with a parachute, piloted jets, experienced simulated weightlessness, worked on simulation machines, and did scuba diving in the pool.

I will never forget my seventh parachute jump, when I was taken up to a height of three kilometers and we were free-falling for fifty seconds. On my first jump, I had only been concentrating on suppressing my fear! The most-frightening flights were on the [Aero Vodochody L39 Albatros] fighters when we were flying various aerobatics at night.

Also, we trained in the bathyscope (ten thousand meters up, with oxygen masks), worked on the centrifuge with a physical distress up to 8 g's, and on the orthotable. More training took place in the Koriolis correlator accelerator chair, for up to thirty-four minutes, and in the thermocamera at 60°C, for fifty minutes. We had to undergo this test twice.

Our group also took on survival training in the polar tundra and then more in summer desert conditions—to me a lot easier than the Arctic!

During her eighteen-month training course, Svetlana got to meet many of the cosmonauts in the Mir program and was occasionally given permission to use the direct line to speak with Aleksandr Volkov and Sergei Krikalev, who were aboard the *Mir* space station at that time. She found it a curious anomaly that she could communicate quite readily with two cosmonauts in Earth orbit but, due to the poor state of the telephone system, often found it impossible to phone her daughter Xenia just twenty miles away!

On January 27 and 31 [1992] we took our state examinations. Everything was very solemn. There were a few dozen people in the small and beautiful White Hall of the [Office of the Government of Russia in Moscow]: cosmonaut heroes, our teachers, scientists, representatives of the space industry, and guests. They were the examinations board. The walls were crammed with diagrams. We were to take theory of flight, spaceship and station facilitation, and space medicine. That was on the Monday. On

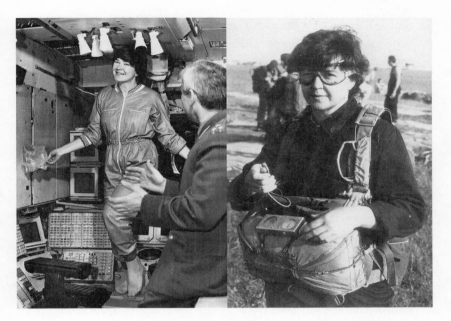

8. *Left*: A lighthearted moment aboard the Mir simulator. With Omelchenko is fellow journalist-cosmonaut Col. Aleksandr Andryushkov. *Right*: Undergoing parachute training.
Courtesy Svetlana Omelchenko.

Friday, station systems and communications, television, electricity, ther-moregulation, motion control, engine plants, antennas and meters, and much more. There was also science and scientific experiments.

At first, I felt uptight because of the solemnity of the situation. Then I looked into the audience and saw a lot of friendly faces. The person who absolutely fascinated me was the chairman of the board—[cosmonaut] Yuri Glazkov. Glazkov is very short, but you forget about it right away because he is so active, lively and "bouncy"—like a ball. He was very strongly for me, especially when someone would ask me a picky question. Anyway, I got As in all disciplines. Only two journalists out of six (me and Valery Baberdin) got all As.

When we were finished with the exams, we wanted to go and buy some wine for dinner to celebrate such a great day. We visited one liquor store after another around Zvezdny Gorodok and finally ran into a big line. Liquor was being sold only to the local people. However, I and Colonel Baberdin talked the manager into selling us a few bottles of wine.

On the way back we ran out of gas, but fortunately we didn't have any problems getting it, since the prices had gone up and the gas station was not crowded. We were on time for dinner and astonished the newly made cosmonauts with our "trophies." Indeed, we were not candidates any-more—we were cosmonaut-researchers!

On 7 February 1992 the certification board officially approved the group's status as cosmonaut-researchers, and forty-year-old Svetlana was awarded a certificate as the 151st graduate. Then followed something of a lighthearted initiation, begun with Yuri Gagarin, in which Neptune, King of the Ocean, takes charge of a graduation ceremony for the novices. They are lined up on the training center's springboard, and then "Neptune" pushes them into the water. After this, the soaked but delighted novices are "officially" accepted as fully fledged cosmonauts. This initiation practice was allowed to lapse for a time but was resurrected sometime in the late 1960s, so Svetlana was accorded a small piece of spaceflight history. "The coach said that I was the first woman to be turned into a cosmonaut through such a procedure," she recalled. "Svetlana Savitskaya [the second female cosmonaut to fly into space] could have done this before me, but it was not in her fashion. Oh, she is an iron lady!"

Unfortunately for Omelchenko's flight chances, it was around this time that the Soviet Union began to break up into independent states. With the country going through extremely hard times, survival became the name of the game. Expertise began to drain from the cash-strapped space program as its trained people, now battling to feed their families, left to find other work. The space program itself suffered massive cutbacks, and Svetlana could see her prospects of flying into space rapidly diminishing with every passing day. Looking at an increasingly uncertain future, she was told that it might be best to return for a while to her former role as an active journalist. Saddened beyond words at these developments, Svetlana moved back into her modest Moscow flat, which she shared with her eighteen-year-old daughter Xenia.

Original plans called for the third seat on Soyuz mission TM-10 to the *Mir* space station to be allocated to either a pilot from the Buran program—possibly Lithuanian Rimantas Stankyavichus—or one of the Russian journalists. The two journalist candidates selected as probable prime and backup crewmembers were Svetlana Omelchenko and Pavel Mukhortov, who wrote for *Soviet Youth* magazine. In the end, only two cosmonauts were launched

9. Wearing a Sokol space suit, Svetlana Omelchenko occupies a seat inside a Soyuz ferry spacecraft. Courtesy Rex Hall.

on the flight, lifting off from the Baikonur pad in Kazakhstan on 1 August 1990 and successfully docking with *Mir* two days later. Cosmonauts Gennadi Manakov and Gennadi Strekalov then entered the space station to take up a four-month tenure as the takeover resident crew. They would return on 10 December aboard the *Soyuz TM-11* craft with—somewhat ironically— the Japanese journalist Toyohiro Akiyama.

These days, with her cherished dream of spaceflight now well behind her, Svetlana Omelchenko is concentrating more than ever on her writing: "I am working for two newspapers, *Air Transport* and *Business World*. I wrote about the problems we encounter with space exploration. Our country cannot now afford the programmers, and, as a result, scientists remain unemployed. Funds are being used for more pressing needs."

Svetlana continued to maintain close ties with the Institute of Medical-Biological Problems and the three doctors who also graduated as cosmonauts— Boris Morukov, Vasili Lukiyanyuk, and Vladimir Karashtin. "They are of great assistance to me in my writings, and we see each other often," she mentioned in our correspondence. "Sadly, the institute does not have enough funds to carry out experiments or even to feed our animals. Our lab assistants go to the fields to collect dandelions to feed our white mice—they are essential to our experiments. Our director receives three thousand rubles per month, which is equivalent to about US$20. For this, one could buy a pair of shoes, but to feed and clothe a family is extremely difficult." In 2015 she would have been upset at the news that Boris Morukov had passed away on 1 January, followed on 2 December by the loss of Vladimir Karashtin.

How tough was life for her after losing her chance to fly into space? "My profession gives me a better-than-average living," she replied. "So my daughter and I are not impoverished." I then asked Svetlana what the future held for her and for space exploration in general.

> I do not know what the future holds. The most important task for the moment? To survive. Of course, the skills I developed when surviving in the polar tundra and in the desert are not likely to be of much help.
>
> Russia pioneered cosmic flight, but now in view of our economic situation we have to come down to earth and consider daily needs against other things like space exploration and research. Only one thing at present is clear: no single country is capable of cosmic flight by itself—we need to pool our resources to achieve this.
>
> I'm sure that despite the difficulties, we shouldn't curb space research. A thousand years will pass by, and it won't be the present difficulties that the people will remember. They will remember the space achievements. They will remember Gagarin and Leonov—everyone who was a pioneer. And of course the American astronauts who were the first on the moon.

Svetlana Omelchenko came tantalizingly close to realizing the dream of a lifetime and is philosophical about the brief time she spent as a cosmonaut-researcher. She can proudly show visitors a framed certificate declaring that she passed examinations to gain cosmonaut certificate number 151. For this, at least, she is grateful.

As the years have gone by, every time Svetlana has read or wrote about cosmonauts who flew to *Mir* or those now working aboard the International Space Station, she reflects on her own cosmonaut training and imagines what might have been for the little girl from Sleptovsk who grew up with stars in her eyes.

5. Unfulfilled Ambitions

Lt. Cdr. Stephen D. Thorne, USN

> And let's get one thing straight. There's a big difference
> between a pilot and an aviator. One is a technician; the
> other is an artist in love with flight.
>
> —Capt. Elrey B. Jeppesen

On 4 June 1985 NASA announced the names of the space agency's latest astronaut cadre, group 11, made up of thirteen candidates selected for future space shuttle missions. They are the only astronaut group to be comprised of thirteen people—pilots and mission specialists—and curiously the only astronaut group never to receive the traditional nickname applied to NASA astronaut newbies. One of the pilot-astronauts selected in that group was a lieutenant commander in the United States Navy named Stephen Thorne. When he received the welcome news of his selection for astronaut training with NASA, Lieutenant Commander Thorne was a thirty-two-year-old squadron aviation safety officer for Strike Fighter Squadron 132 (VFA-132) aboard the aircraft carrier USS *Coral Sea*. He had already accumulated more than 2,500 flying hours in around thirty different aircraft types, including some two hundred carrier landings, and even though he loved the life of a naval aviator, he was looking forward to this exciting new challenge.

Stephen Douglas Thorne was born in a U.S. Army hospital in Frankfurt am Main in the Federal Republic of Germany, on 11 February 1953. His father, James Hilton Thorne, had been born and raised in the small railroad town of Selma in Johnston County, North Carolina. His mother, Eunice Irene (née McCown), came from Anderson, South Carolina, born in a house that had been in the family since around 1890.

James Thorne enlisted in the U.S. Army in Washington DC in October 1936. He wanted to join up so badly he lied about his age, giving his date of birth as 26 March 1918, when he was actually born in March 1920. Later, in his four years of service during World War II, he was involved in battles and campaigns in Rome-Arno, southern France, the Rhineland, the Ardennes, and Central Europe. He was demobilized on 15 December 1944 in the rank of first sergeant, although he would continue his service with the U.S. Army for several more years. Between May 1949 and November 1950 he was assigned as an enlisted ordnance advisor to the South Carolina National Guard, which is likely when he met Eunice McCown in Anderson. They were married in December 1950, and James later moved with his unit to Europe, followed a little later by his new bride.

Although his father did not like to talk about his wartime experiences, Stephen Thorne would always be immensely proud of the man's wartime service to his country. The only thing his father did care to speak about was walking across the captured and strategically important Ludendorrf bridge at Remagen just three days before it suddenly collapsed and fell into the Rhine on 17 March 1945, following months of aerial bombing, artillery hits, and attempts at demolition by the Germans. Unfortunately, when it collapsed, twenty-eight American engineers were killed and sixty-three injured.

The family would eventually leave their temporary home in Wurzburg, west of Frankfurt, and relocate back to the United States. They first set up home in Letterkenny, Pennsylvania, and in 1958 moved to Ft. Benning, Georgia, where Stephen's sister Melanie was born in December the following year. They would finally settle back in Anderson, South Carolina, nicknamed "The Friendliest City in South Carolina," which Steve Thorne would always regard as his hometown. Having continued his military service during (but not fighting in) the Korean War, his father finally retired from the U.S. Army in 1960 with the rank of captain.

While attending T. L. Hanna High School in Anderson, Steve Thorne became a member of the National Honor Society, a commander of the Navy Junior Reserve Officers Training Corps (NJROTC) Unit, an Eagle Scout in Troop 215 (spring 1968), and a letterman in the school's football and track teams. His high school coach Jim Frazier remembered Thorne as "an outstanding young man," who always attended practice and was both punctual and hardworking. As well, Thorne was an active member at his local church, Boulevard Baptist.

His sister, Melanie, recalls a youth who loved reading science fiction books, was a great fan of the *Star Trek* television series, and loved gazing in wonder at the night sky. "He always had an interest in space and science fiction," she said, "and weird things like *The Twilight Zone*. I remember once he got a telescope for Christmas, and for the next six months or so, he would go out every night and look at the stars. It's just like my mother used to say: 'After he got over wanting to be a cowboy, he wanted to be an astronaut.'"

Leaving high school in 1971 as an honor graduate and voted "most likely to succeed," Thorne then headed north to attend the U.S. Naval Academy as a member of the class of 1975. "Going to the Naval Academy is something I'd thought about since I was five or six years old," he once told Anderson reporter Glenna Houston. "I felt it offered a better education than West Point, and there was more flexibility after graduation. You can go into the Marine Corps, submarines, ships, or aviation. I'd always figured I'd go into aviation."

In his lifetime, Thorne would make many close friends, but none more so than Rick Schwarting from Illinois. The two men met as roommates on their first day at the Naval Academy.

That first day began outside the gates of the academy on a typically hot and humid summer day in Annapolis. After jettisoning their civilian suits and sports jackets and arranging to have them sent home, the new midshipmen had their first taste of the academy life that was in store for them over the next four years. "We spent most of the day getting our hair cut and going through long lines to pick up uniforms and toiletry items," Schwarting related. "We did not know any of our classmates that morning, but we started to settle into our assigned rooms by the end of the afternoon." He was assigned to Echo Company, Fourteenth Platoon, which contained around thirty-two plebe midshipmen. The rooms they would occupy in the company area of Bancroft Hall were allocated on an alphabetical basis. "As we went around the room introducing ourselves, I will never forget the southern twang accent of Stephen D. Thorne," Schwarting recalled. "Being a midwesterner from St. Louis and Chicago, Steve's southern accent definitely startled me, but his self-confidence and determination showed through to me on that first evening in Bancroft Hall."

Over the next four years, the two men would become inseparable friends, even though their future goals differed. Postacademy, Rick Schwarting would become a navigator on U.S. Navy destroyers, while Steve Thorne's ambitions were squarely aimed at supersonic aviation.

While studying system engineering at Annapolis, Thorne also earned a highly coveted honor in the first third of his senior year—midshipman commander of the academy's Fourth Battalion. Meanwhile, he had met and hit it off with pretty and talented Sue Graham Lotz, later to become a certified public accountant, from Staunton, Virginia. As Rick Schwarting recalled, he and Thorne had been on the USS *Shreveport* (LPD-12) attending firefighting and shipboard damage control training ahead of departing on their assigned European cruise. On a free weekend, several of them went to the enlisted men's club for a few drinks. "By the end of the evening, none of us were feeling any pain. Steve in particular was very happy."

The next morning, being a Sunday, a few of them decided to leave the ship and head across to Virginia Beach in order to meet and talk with some girls. "I went down the ladder into Steve's berthing compartment to roust him," said Schwarting. "Although he was not feeling very well, he was game to go to the beach." After several hours without managing to strike up any conversations, Schwarting gave up and made his way back to the ship. "Steve and Mike Rabideau decided to stick around. They went to an ice-cream parlor where Steve was fortunate enough to meet Sue."

As she explained, Sue happened to be working at the ice-cream shop following her freshman year in college.

> *My friend and I went there to get some dessert after dinner, so it was around 7:00 p.m. We met Steve and Mike Rabideau, and the four of us hung out in Virginia Beach for the next several hours until they had to leave at about 11:00 to get back to the ship, as it was leaving in the morning. Steve told me before he left that he would write me while he was on cruise and would come back to see me. I was quite skeptical—it sounded like a line to me, so I really didn't expect to ever see him again. But true to his word, he did write me during the six weeks that he was gone and did come back to see me when he returned from the cruise. That was my first inkling that he was much different than the average guy.*

They began dating, and soon the relationship developed and blossomed into love.

There was, however, another love competing for Thorne's affection—a

Pontiac Firebird that he purchased in the fall semester of his senior year at the academy. "He was so proud of that car," Sue recalled, "and I remember that early on we were headed somewhere in it and we stopped for something to eat. Unfortunately, we decided to eat it in the car, and yep, I spilled most of a chocolate milkshake into his gearshift. That I was not left on the side of the road after that is a testament to his self-control!"

On 4 June 1975, Thorne would graduate in the top 10 percent of his class with a bachelor of science degree in systems engineering. He had also received a letter of commendation in his senior year, which is only awarded to around forty graduating midshipmen and is one of the very few things from the academy that transfers to one's military record after graduation. Meanwhile, he and Sue Lotz had dated during the last three years of his academy career, and they both graduated from their respective studies in 1975. "He asked me to marry him on a snowy New Year's Eve in 1975," Sue recalled. Postgraduation, while he was stationed at NAS (Naval Air Station) Meridian in Mississippi, Steve and Sue were married in Staunton on 29 May 1976, with his father acting as best man.

As an ensign, Thorne then entered flight training, eventually receiving his wings as a naval aviator in December 1976. This was followed soon after by an advanced training period in the McDonnell Douglas F-4 Phantom while based at NAS Miramar in San Diego. As Sue recalled, "During the time we were in San Diego while he was going through F-4 training, he was selected from the training squadron to attend the Navy Fighter Weapons School, also known as 'Topgun.'" At the school, naval aviators and flight officers received intensive instruction in fighter and strike tactics and techniques, following which they returned to their operating units as surrogate instructors.

After graduating from Fighter Weapons School, Thorne joined Fighter Squadron Twenty-One (VF-21), known as the "Freelancers," and was deployed to the Seventh Fleet in the western Pacific as part of Carrier Air Wing Two (CVW-2) aboard the USS *Ranger* (CV-61), flying the F-4J variant of the Phantom. Over this time, he accumulated a further 1,100 hours in the F-4 and the A-4 Skyhawk and made around two hundred carrier landings. "A carrier landing has been described as a controlled crash," he once stated. "It's violent, noisy, and uncomfortable, but there's satisfaction in making a good landing on the ship." It was during this time that he picked up the call sign the Fox.

10. Lt. Stephen D. Thorne, USN, in his days as a naval aviator and test pilot. Courtesy Sue and Rick Schwarting.

Much to his delight, in 1981 Thorne was awarded a coveted assignment to the U.S. Naval Test Pilot School at Patuxent River, Maryland, joining the twenty-seven-strong class 80. Also in his class were two future astronauts, James Wetherbee (selected 1984) and Marine Corps aviator Robert Cabana, who would later join NASA along with Thorne in 1985. In addition to academic instruction, they were studying stability and control systems, cockpit assessments, project management, navigation systems, radar evaluations, and carrier suitability. As well, they were kept busy writing detailed reports on aircraft performance. Over the next few months, the students flew and assessed a wide range of navy aircraft types. These included the Schweizer x-26A sailplane; helicopters such as the Boeing CH-46A Sea Knight and the Bell OH-58A Kiowa and AH-1G Cobra; the propjet de Havilland U-6A Beaver; and jet fighters including the North American T-2C Buckeye, the Ling-Temco-Vought A-7C Corsair, and the Grumman OV-1B Mohawk.

The group would also participate in several instructional field trips to the Smithsonian Institution's National Air and Space Museum in Washington DC; the Smithsonian's Paul E. Garber Restoration Facility in Silver

Hill, Maryland; the U.S. Air Force Test Pilot School at Edwards AFB, California; and NASA Ames Research Center in San Jose, California.

"Test pilot school was harder than college," Thorne later admitted. "It demanded a 100 percent effort all the time. One of the reasons I wanted to attend the school was to fly new aircraft and learn more about them. In the eleven months, I flew thirty different airplanes, including multiengine prop planes, helicopters, and jets. Most aviators fly five or six airplanes during their whole careers."

His sister, Melanie, recalls another passion entering into her brother's life—a 1957 Bellanca taildragger airplane: "Flying all those Navy jets gave Steve a desire to have his own airplane. Although it was a 1957 vintage aircraft, Steve treated it as his prize possession. Many times, Steve flew it cross-country. He was a very careful and conscientious pilot. He never took off without going through a checklist to make sure everything was in order, before he would take off into the 'wild blue yonder.'"

After graduating from test pilot school in 1981, Thorne spent the next two years as a project liaison officer and assistant operations officer in the Strike Aircraft Test Directorate, also located at the Naval Air Test Center in Patuxent River. Interviewed at the time by Glenna Houston for the *Anderson Independent-Mail* newspaper, Thorne spoke of his duties and the impact of this work on his life and career. "I troubleshoot aircraft test projects," he stated, "coordinate between project officers and test engineers and track the requirements of the aircraft maintenance commitment when it should be flying." He did admit that his choice of career was tough on his young bride. "She tolerates it," he said. "She knows I wouldn't be happy doing anything else. To me, the toughest thing about the navy is separations. It can be brutal when you're gone for six months on a deployment. I think the navy requires a strong family commitment. That's vital to a career."

As an ordnance test pilot, Thorne carried out flight tests on any new equipment designed for the F-4 Phantom and A-7 Corsair attack aircraft and flew as safety observer during tests on the McDonnell Douglas F/A-18 Hornet supersonic all-weather fighter. "I like the responsibility of supervising fifty people," he said, with pride. "Being a navy manager requires more of a personal commitment, because you get into taking care of your people, both personally and professionally."

He added, "The part of my job that gives me the most gratification is flying. We take small steps, and everything is computer analyzed before we fly. It's not nearly as glamorous as it's thought to be. It's mostly applying engineering and flight experience to plain hard work. I get satisfaction from helping figure out what's best for the future of naval aviation and the pilots in the fleet." He then said, "I was the first navy pilot to drop a Snake-Eye bomb. It has fins that increase drag, slowing it down. That gives the aircraft a chance to get out of the way."

Then, in 1984, he applied to NASA, following the space agency's call for a new group of astronauts, but when the identities of the group 10 astronauts were announced in May 1984, his name was not among them. He subsequently completed F-18 Hornet transition training in October 1984 and joined Strike Fighter Squadron 132 (VFA-132, also known as the Privateers), based at NAS Cecil Field, Florida.

Over the next few months, while serving with the squadron, he impressed everyone with his exuberance, flying skills, and humility. One of those was Dominic (Dom) Gorie, who joined NASA's pilot-astronaut ranks in 1994: "I had the great pleasure of flying with Steve just a short time during our tours in VFA-132. Steve was handpicked to be a department head in this squadron that was starting up from scratch. He was quickly known for his calm professionalism under pressure as well as his being a great guy. Steve was the leader that younger pilots wanted to fly with and the guy his peers and juniors wanted to use as a role model."

Thorne also formed an enduring friendship with Lt. Cdr. Bob Stumpf, who had come to admire what he saw in his fellow aviator. Stumpf told the author,

> In my forty years as a professional pilot, I never knew anyone who loved to fly more than Steve. He loved the aesthetic beauty of flight; the flow of air over the wings that magically lifts his airplane off the ground and keeps it aloft, much like the sailor who hoists his sails and feels the boat surge forward on the breath of the wind alone. Steve loved the beauty of the clouds and sky, the sunsets and sunrises, the majesty of a distant thunderstorm at night, the endless vistas from all directions on a clear day at forty thousand feet, the countless stars on a moonless night far away from any ambient light made by man.

Steve loved, too, the thrill of flight—the breathtaking catapult shot, the violent tug of the arresting cable on his tailhook, the loops and rolls, spins and stalls of precision aerobatics. The low-level raging around at six hundred knots only two hundred feet above the ground, where vision to either side is blurred, objects flying by too fast for the brain to process their images. The dogfight, where every flying skill is combined into an art form, a stage for one pilot to compete man-to-man with another in high-g flight and airspeeds from nothing to supersonic.

But unlike many pilots, Steve also had an intellectual curiosity about how the magic worked. He studied hard to understand lift, thrust, and drag; the flow of air molecules over the wings; the flight controls; the many mechanical systems in a modern jet fighter. He dove into concepts of energy management to maximize the performance of one fighter over another. Steve earned a degree in engineering at the Naval Academy, then went on to attain what many consider the top of the aviation pyramid—test pilot. He drove airplanes to their operational limits, then beyond those limits to document what happens outside the envelope. He was one of the best. That's why NASA selected him to become an astronaut.

Beyond flying, Steve loved the special camaraderie among all pilots, but especially those bonds between pilots in a fighter ready room and their families. In many ways, a fighter squadron is a family, who love and care for one another at home or at sea for months on end. Steve loved our squadron, the Privateers. We were new, we were brash, and we flew the best fighter in the world. Steve flew the iconic Phantom and the venerable Crusader before coming to the Privateers, but confided to me that the Hornet was by far the best. That is why, when NASA gave him the call, he struggled. He wrestled with God over the two forces pulling him apart—loyalty to his squadron mates and the inexorable force calling him to do something extraordinary, something few have ever done.

That Steve had so much trouble making the decision explains the kind of man he was. To most of us, it would have been an easy choice. But then, not many have the strength of character that was Steve. In his farewell address to his squadron mates and their wives, Steve said that he wished he could be two people—one to fly the shuttle in outer space and the other to fly the Hornet with his friends. In the end, maybe Steve decided to move on at the behest of his friends, for we who loved him

*could not, would not deny him the opportunity of a lifetime. We missed
him when he was gone, but we took great pride and joy in his superb
accomplishment and great new adventure.*

*Steve Thorne was one of the very best people I have had the privilege
to know. He was one of the best friends I ever had, the best roommate.*

Thorne continued serving with the Privateers aboard the USS *Coral Sea*
(CVS-43) until 4 June 1985, when NASA announced he had been selected
for astronaut training. Sue Schwarting (then Sue Thorne) agrees with Bob
Stumpf's words on her husband's struggle with leaving his squadron to
join the space agency:

*He felt like he was letting his squadron mates down by heading to NASA.
It tore him apart when they actually began fighting in the Middle East;
he felt so guilty not being there with his guys. I was also torn about moving to Houston, as I would be leaving some very good friends as well. But
you can't deny someone the realization of their dreams. And I remember
thinking, after he accepted the offer from NASA, "Well, at least I won't
have to worry so much about something happening to him" . . . quite
ironic since the squadron had no casualties while on cruise.*

Dom Gorie, a veteran pilot of four shuttle missions, including two as
crew commander, was sorry to lose Thorne from VFA-132, but he was thrilled
that Thorne was on his way to Houston: "NASA recognized Steve's talents
and took him into the astronaut program before we ever deployed with our
new F/A-18s, but my time with Steve significantly affected my desire to follow in his footsteps to NASA. I remember him fondly and am ever grateful for his inspiration."

There were thirteen new astronaut candidates—six pilots and seven mission specialists—who would report to the Johnson Space Center in late
summer to begin a one-year period of training and evaluation. Upon successful completion of the training, they became eligible for assignment to
space shuttle flights. The candidates would join ninety current astronauts,
swelling their numbers to 103 at a time when NASA was preparing for a
launch schedule of two missions per month. Including the new group, NASA
had named 157 astronauts since the beginning of the agency's space program. In making the latest selections, NASA considered thirty-three civil-

ians from the selection rosters developed during the 1984 selection process and 133 nominees from the military services.

Those selected as pilot candidates were Lt. Cdr. Michael Baker (USN), Maj. Robert Cabana (USMC), Capt. Brian Duffy (USAF), Maj. Thomas Henricks (USAF), Stephen Oswald (civilian), and Lt. Cdr. Stephen Thorne (USN). Mission specialist candidates were Jerome Apt (civilian), Capt. Charles Gemar (U.S. Army), Linda Godwin (civilian), Richard Hieb (civilian), Tamara Jernigan (civilian), Capt. Carl Meade (USAF), and Lt. Pierre Thuot (USN).

Two months later the new astronauts began a one-year ASCAN (astronaut candidate) training and evaluation program to qualify them for subsequent assignment as a pilot or mission specialist on future space shuttle flight crews. "I signed up because it is something I want to do, not because I want to be famous," Thorne said following his selection. "I always thought it was kind of neat being an astronaut as I grew up watching the space shots on television. But I never thought there was much chance of me being one. It just happened that the things I did that I thought were fun and interesting were the same things that NASA needed."

Asked about her husband's future as an astronaut and the risks involved, Sue Thorne was circumspect in comparing it to his earlier work flying high-performance aircraft. "I don't think I'll worry about him as much," she admitted. "There are so many people, so much training that goes into making it safe."

Pierre Thuot was one of the new astronauts training alongside Thorne, but they already knew each other from NAS Patuxent River.

I first met Lt. Steve Thorne after I graduated from the U.S. Naval Test Pilot School in June 1983 and reported aboard the Strike Aircraft Test Directorate at Naval Air Station Patuxent River, Maryland. Steve was a Naval Academy graduate, as was I, so we immediately had something in common. Steve graduated from the Naval Academy two years before I did and from the Naval Test Pilot School a year or two before me. Steve was an F-4 Phantom pilot, and I was an F-14 Tomcat Radar Intercept Officer (a backseater, like Goose in Top Gun*).*

My first flight in a navy F-4 was with Steve as the pilot. Coming from an F-14 Tomcat, which at that time was the premier navy fighter, it was a little daunting climbing into the backseat of the F-4, which first became

11. Lt. Cdr. Stephen D. Thorne, USN, NASA astronaut. Courtesy NASA.

operational in 1960 (when Steve was seven and I was five!). It was an old aircraft and a bit finicky. Of course, Steve knew everything about it, all its idiosyncrasies, and he was very supportive and helpful to me as I executed my backseat procedures for the first time. Steve was a fabulous pilot and knew how to get the most out of any aircraft he flew.

In January 1986, as Thorne's astronaut training continued, he received a Navy Commendation Medal. A future that was filled with promise suddenly went catastrophically awry toward the end of that month, when shuttle orbiter *Challenger* and its crew of seven was lost seventy-three seconds after lifting off from the Kennedy Space Center on 28 January. The effect on everyone was profound. Colleagues and friends had died, and the entire shuttle program fell into a dark, soul-searching limbo. Thorne's sister, Melanie, recalls that day as one filled with deep anxiety:

Because Steve would pilot a future mission, he was in the shuttle simulator in Houston going through the same procedures as Mike Smith on the actual shuttle. When the shuttle blew up seventy-three seconds into the flight, all of Steve's cockpit controls went dark. At first, he thought it was a systems failure, but he quickly found out about the tragedy.

I called my brother later in the day. I was upset over the idea, "What if it had been you?" Steve told me that he understood the dangers, but if he allowed that reality to bother him, he would never accomplish anything. The best way to make sure it did not happen was to be as prepared as possible for any emergency. He said the best minds at NASA would be investigating to find out what happened. Steve loved flying and was a very careful pilot.

Three days after the *Challenger* tragedy, President Ronald Reagan spoke quietly but eloquently at a solemn outdoor memorial ceremony held at the Johnson Space Center. In part, he said,

We come together today to mourn the loss of seven brave Americans, to share the grief that we all feel and, perhaps in that sharing, to find the strength to bear our sorrow and the courage to look for the seeds of hope.

Our nation's loss is first a profound personal loss to the family, and the friends and the loved ones of our shuttle astronauts. To those they have left behind—the mothers, the fathers, the husbands and wives, brothers and sisters, and, yes, especially the children—all of America stands beside you in your time of sorrow.

What we say today is only an inadequate expression of what we carry in our hearts. Words pale in the shadow of grief; they seem insufficient even to measure the brave sacrifice of those you loved and we so admired.

Their truest testimony will not be in the words we speak but in the way they lived their lives and in the way they lost their lives—with dedication, honor, and an unquenchable desire to explore this mysterious and beautiful universe.

The best we can do is remember our seven astronauts—our Challenger *Seven—remember them as they lived, bringing life and love and joy to those who knew them and pride to a nation.*

During the memorial ceremony many of the astronauts, including Steve Thorne, solemnly carried out usher duties, seating the dignitaries. It was a profoundly reflective day for all and the beginning of a difficult and searching time, as a deep shadow of blame began to envelope the space agency. Serious questions were subsequently raised about the unrelenting pressure NASA had placed on everyone to maintain an impractical launch schedule. As well, NASA stood accused of ignoring safety concerns raised following a number of missions that had come perilously close to ending in disaster. There must have been a great deal of unease among the astronauts who were in training for future missions, which were suspended while an investigation took place into the *Challenger* disaster and while waiting for the investigating board to resolve and fix whatever problems had caused the catastrophic tragedy that freezing-cold January morning. The board would also be required to issue a series of strict procedural recommendations that had to be implemented before the shuttle program could safely resume.

With seven months of ASCAN training still ahead of him, and an uncertain flight schedule, it would have been an unsettling time for Stephen Thorne and his wife, Sue. Despite the terrible tragedy, however, the allure of flying into space was still there, and a future shuttle mission still beckoned strongly for the young naval aviator.

On Saturday, 24 May 1986, Memorial Day weekend, Stephen Thorne was strapped tightly into the front seat of an Aerotek Pitts Special s-2a skimming through the Texas skies, the pride and joy of its owner, a highly experienced pilot sitting behind him that day.

Taking the small aircraft through its paces was thirty-nine-year-old James Ryan Simons from Montana, a 1969 graduate of the U.S. Air Force Academy. He had attended pilot training at Webb AFB in Big Spring, Texas, and on graduation day in August 1970 received the Commander's Trophy as the top student in his class. He was then assigned to George AFB, in Victorville, California, for upgrade training in the F-4 Phantom II supersonic jet interceptor fighter-bomber. Next, he served as an aircraft commander in the F-4E in Europe before becoming an F-105G Thunderchief aircraft commander in 1973 and joining the Seventeenth "Wild Weasel" Squadron based at Korat Royal Thai AFB, Thailand. While there, he became an instructor pilot.

Simons left Korat in December 1973 and was subsequently stationed at Nellis AFB, Nevada, where he became an instructor in the Fighter Weapons School. In November 1974 he joined the famed USAF Thunderbirds air demonstration squadron, flying solo as number five. Over the next two years, he would fly in more than two hundred aerial demonstrations. While serving at Nellis, he purchased his Pitts S-2A biplane, in which he would often perform aerobatics at local air shows. This freelance stunt flying did not go down well with his superiors, and even though it was not strictly prohibited, he was told he could no longer fly his airplane in public displays. His reaction was to quit the Thunderbirds in protest.

Simons then served an exchange tour of duty with VF-74, an aviation unit of the U.S. Navy, before taking his leave of the U.S. Air Force. Next, he flew briefly with an Air National Guard squadron before joining the ranks of VMFA-112, a reserve unit of the U.S. Marine Corps operating out of Dallas, Texas. In late 1981 he left his flight research work at the Langley Research Center, Virginia, for a position at the Johnson Space Center in Houston. While there, he became a flight control engineer with NASA, serving as a payload officer on night control teams and monitoring space shuttle missions in the Mission Control Center.

Stephen Thorne was essentially a passenger in the Pitts, along for the sheer enjoyment of aerobatic flying. He was unfamiliar with the aircraft type, a single-engine, two-seat biplane, in which Simons had continued to conduct aerial displays at weekend air shows. The two friends had earlier flown out of Houston, and Simons was performing aerobatic maneuvers over northern Galveston County when something suddenly went wrong within the little airplane.

According to Lt. Mike Barry of the Santa Fe, Texas, Police Department, several witnesses said they had been observing the aircraft performing stunts in the air over Runge Park, when they heard what they described as a "pop-ping" noise. As they watched on in horror, they saw the Pitts go into an inverted tailspin, from which it partially recovered before falling straight down and crashing to the ground just south of Highway 6. Both pilots died in the violent impact. The Santa Fe Police Department was notified of the crash at 1:02 p.m., as confirmed by Lieutenant Barry. A wristwatch on one of the pilots, which apparently broke on impact, read 12:58, he added.

According to Sandy Dougherty, a field investigator in the Dallas office of the National Transportation Safety Board (NTSB), the crash happened approximately fifty feet from a house near Runge Park, in Alta Loma, with the wreckage of the airplane situated between two trees and a tree house. Local resident Gary Windham said he was watching television that Satur-day afternoon: "I heard a loud whistling sound, then boom! The ground shook, the windows rattled. I thought a refinery nearby had blown up." He ran outside and found the crumpled remains of a bright-yellow biplane wreckage less than one hundred feet from where he had been sitting. There was no smoke or fire. "My first thought was that there must be people in there," Windham recalled. "I tried to get in and look, but the front was so crunched up."

The NTSB later reached the following conclusions: "A short occurred in the aircraft's electrical system distracting the owner/pilot occupying the back seat of the aircraft. The aircraft was observed, by witnesses, to enter a spin, which went inverted. The front seat pilot [Thorne] may have been able to reach the pedals but had no experience in the aircraft. The spin was stopped at an altitude too low to pull out, and it impacted the ground in a steep inverted attitude."

The crash that day would have yet another devastating effect on the astronaut corps. The pilot, Jim Simons, had recently become engaged to astronaut candidate Linda Godwin, selected along with Stephen Thorne as a member of group 11 in May the previous year. She would later become a veteran of four space missions, marry fellow astronaut Steve Nagel, and have two children before retiring from NASA in August 2010.

Thorne's friend George Holman, who had known Thorne since high school, was devastated when he heard the sad news. He recalled for report-ers that his friend had been a battalion commander at Annapolis, which is among the top posts attained by a midshipman. "Steve was certainly doing what he wanted to do," Holman stated, adding that Thorne, having told Holman in the eighth grade that he intended to be an astronaut, was the only person he knew who fulfilled his childhood dream.

Following a U.S. Navy full-honor memorial service conducted at the Old Post Chapel at Fort Myer, Virginia, Lt. Cdr. Stephen Douglas Thorne was interred at Arlington National Cemetery on Friday, 30 May 1986, not far from the Tomb of the Unknown Soldier and close by the memorial set up for the *Challenger* crew. During the service, navy jets roared overhead, with one breaking off and flying upward, to signify the death of a pilot who has gone to heaven. Two days later, on 1 June, a memorial service was conducted for his family at Anderson's Boulevard Baptist Church. During the service, there was a reading of John Gillespie Magee Jr.'s sonnet to airmen, "High Flight," which President Ronald Reagan had quoted during his eulogy to the *Challenger* astronauts earlier that year.

Capt. George Roper Jr., a former naval officer who was Steve's NJROTC instructor at Hanna, also paid tribute at the Boulevard Church service, saying, "His dedication, motivation, and patriotism made it an honor to assist Steve to go to the Naval Academy. . . . He showed us perseverance and never to stop trying." This quote was printed in the *Anderson Independent* newspaper on 2 June 1986 in an article titled "200 Pay Tribute to Thorne" written by Michael Kersmarki.

At another service held in Houston on 4 June, fellow astronaut Bob Cabana, who had gone through test pilot school in 1981 with Thorne, gave a moving eulogy in which he remembered a friend who was

technically proficient and really good at what he did, or he would not have achieved all that he had done or have been here at NASA. But these are skills many possess. What made Steve stand out was his intense loyalty to his shipmates and friends and his devotion to his bride Sue. Steve was always willing to give of himself. . . . We can seek comfort in the fact that we are a little bit better for having been touched by his life, because in this competitive world where we live, he made us all work a little harder to keep up with him.

Two days later, on 6 June, a private memorial service was held at the Emmanuel Episcopal Church in Sue Thorne's hometown of Staunton, Virginia. During the service, in a quiet voice filled with profound emotion, she read out the following message of love to her late husband, reproduced here at Sue's request:

> *This is probably the hardest thing I have ever had to do. And while it is extremely difficult, it is something I really wanted to do, especially here, not only because this used to be my home but mostly because I knew Steve best and I loved him best. The hardest thing I have ever done was last Friday when I had to say my final earthly farewell to my husband. It was so hard because not only was he my husband but he was also my very best friend.*
>
> *As I thought about what I would like to say, I suddenly realized that I have, in the two weeks since his death, gathered close to me several symbols of some of the things that were so important to Steve. And I felt that if I told you what these symbols were, perhaps you could begin to understand how fine a man he was and just how much he means to me.*
>
> *I have been wearing, both night and day, Steve's Naval Academy ring on my right hand. He was extremely proud to be an academy graduate and intensely loyal to his school and his classmates. This loyalty carried over to his shipmates, his squadron mates, and to his fellow astronauts. He was never ashamed to be bound by the rules of military discipline, even at a time when many of his contemporaries mocked authority. His loyalty and pride in the academy and his friends and classmates never wavered. I dated Steve during his last three years at the academy, and some of my fondest memories are of get-togethers with his company mates. I was so pleased that many of his academy friends were able to be with me in Arlington and another one who was not able to come last Friday has flown in from California and is here today.*
>
> *I have also gathered close to me one of Steve's NASA flight suits and have had it with me every night since his death. To know Steve Thorne was to know his intense love of flying. He was never able to accumulate enough flight time and is one of the few people I know whose vocation and avocation were exactly the same—flying. And if he couldn't actually be flying, the next best thing was to be talking about it or reading about it. I am saddened that he never had the opportunity to fly into space, but it offers me some consolation to know that he died doing the one thing that he so dearly loved.*

At Arlington, I received an American flag that I have kept close to me and will cherish always. His love of this country was evident in his willingness to die for it. He prepared himself to be on the front line of its defense, and he wore the uniform of his navy and his country with pride and dignity. About a month after the Challenger *accident, I asked Steve if he would go up in the next shuttle. His reply was a simple, immediate, and unqualified "Sure!" At that point, I fully realized how far his devotion to his country would go—whatever it asked him to do, he would do it with no hesitation and no reservations.*

I have also worn, either around my neck or on my left hand, Steve's wedding ring. I never once questioned his love for me or for the rest of his family and friends. We often would go many months without seeing our families and sometimes years without seeing some of our friends. But when we finally did reunite, the bond had proved to be only strengthened. I have been able to get through these last two weeks largely through the help of two of his very special friends. They have cried with me, laughed with me, let me take my anger out on them, and totally supported me, and they are with me here today as they have been throughout most of the last two weeks. I will always love them for caring so much about Steve, that they allowed me to lean on them. I know for a fact that only death would pull Steve and me apart from each other. I was confident in his devotion and faithfulness to me and our marriage. I know he made me a better person, and I hope that I made him a better man as well.

I know Steve has returned to his Maker, and I am consoled in knowing that Steve is with his Lord. It is this fact alone that has comforted me the most and will continue to do so in the difficult days ahead. I know that because God gave his only son to die up on a cross, that we are able to have eternal life. Steve has preceded me to our heavenly home and left me here to continue in this earthly struggle. I am comforted by you, my family and friends, and look to all of you for continued support. My ultimate hope and strength is in knowing that someday I will be with Steve again . . . my very best friend.

To honor his memory and achievements, the T. L. Hanna High School in Anderson annually awards the Stephen D. Thorne Memorial Scholarship. The scholarship, $1,000 at its inception, was initiated by Sue and

Rick Schwarting (Thorne's best friend at the U.S. Naval Academy and Sue Thorne's second husband), George Holman, and Bob Stumpf. First presented in 1987 and now valued at $2,000, it is awarded to a graduating student of the senior class whose past performance and potential for future development exemplify the personal and professional qualities of the former student who went on to become a naval aviator and NASA astronaut. As well as achieving academic excellence, all scholarship applicants also must be involved in one or more extracurricular activities; be seeking a degree in engineering, math, or other technical fields; or be interested in pursuing a naval career.

There is also the Stephen D. Thorne Award, presented to the NJROTC student at Hanna who best exemplifies Thorne's can-do attitude in his studies as well as in his work in the program. His sister, Melanie, recalled,

> *Steve was always very dedicated at what he was doing. He was always goal oriented; he saw what he wanted, and he went after it. He was studious, but not to the point that he didn't enjoy life. He was very focused.*
>
> *One thing I remember that was very special to me was the last time we were home together. I had a model of the starship* Enterprise, *from the* Star Trek *show. I asked him to help me with it, and he just about built it, even as busy a person as he was.*
>
> *He was never very talkative about all the things he had accomplished. He was never reckless, but very outgoing and dedicated to what he was doing, whether it was playing football or studying for an exam. Whatever he went after, he achieved.*

Rick Schwarting has many fond memories of his greatest friend.

> *I recall that in the summer of 1979 I had the great privilege of going ashore with Steve and some of his fellow F-4 squadron mates. Both of our ships were in Subic Bay in the Philippines for a period of several days. We had a wonderful time "steaming together" that evening at the Cubi Point Officer's Club. I certainly felt like a fish out of water, hanging out with the "fly boys," since my duty as navigator on a destroyer is not as sexy nor exciting as flying a plane at the speed of sound. I miss my best friend a great deal, and I can only hope my life will measure up to the high standards he lived by.*

Five years after the loss of Steve, Rick Schwarting and Sue Thorne were married, and they now have two grown children: Kathryn Graham and Philip Charles Stephen Schwarting. Philip recently graduated from the U.S. Naval Academy, following hard in the footsteps of his father and Steve Thorne.

George Holman, who helped initiate the Stephen D. Thorne Memorial Scholarship, had known Steve since their days in seventh grade attending the same school. In recalling the death of his longtime friend, Holman said,

Few have had so great an impact on me, and few have I admired or respected more than Steve. He was a very accomplished individual. I was privileged to have considered him my best friend. He made his childhood dream a reality and became an astronaut. His life is worthy of admiration and is an example of determination and accomplishment for all to see. He was an Eagle Scout, was at the top of his class in high school, the very top of his class at Annapolis.

That's the story of his life; he's always been at the top of everything.

6. The Greatest Gesture

Oceanographer Robert E. Stevenson

When one man, for whatever reason, has the opportunity to lead an
extraordinary life, he has no right to keep it to himself.

—Jacques Yves Cousteau

It was a rather incongruous statement delivered by one of the world's most
renowned and respected oceanographers, and even though it seemed right
out of character, he insisted it was true. "I hate ships," Dr. Robert Stevenson once wrote with obvious feeling, "especially when they are floating on
the ocean. They constantly move. Yet, after four years majoring in geology, crawling for days on end through mountain brush and desert sands,
and staring down rattlesnakes, sitting on the deck of a research vessel had
a certain attraction. For fifteen years, I never participated in a research
cruise during which I did not at one time or another curse the ocean, the
ship, and my stupidity for being out at sea."

Bob Stevenson may have hated ships, but he lived a truly exemplary life
filled with research and discovery and rightfully earned for himself the title
of Father of Space Oceanography. And yet when he was offered a dedicated seat on one of America's space shuttles and the unbelievable chance
to view, photograph, and write about oceanic phenomena from the platform of Earth orbit, he had to reluctantly decline. It was the opportunity
of a lifetime, yet this humble man felt he had a far more pressing terrestrial
obligation that made him relinquish that coveted seat to another colleague
and in doing so demonstrated the nobleness and greatness of character that
normally only appears in works of fiction. It truly was the gesture of a very
remarkable and loving person.

Robert Everett Stevenson, known throughout his life as "Bob," was born in the city of Fullerton, in California's then largely undeveloped Orange County, on 15 January 1921. He would be the only child born to George, a builder, and Zella Stevenson, who hailed from New Haven, Connecticut.

He came from a family involved in engineering and stonemasonry back in Manchester, England. In fact, his grandfather Frederick Stevenson, who emigrated to the United States with his family, was a foreman involved in the construction of Yale University in New Haven, built with stone imported from Greece.

"My father, George, married into a Dutch Irish family," Bob once recalled, "and following the Great War they migrated to Southern California. Smart move!"

In his youth, Bob and his father would often gather up their fishing gear and head off on day trips to Newport Bay, situated on the coast some twenty miles south of Fullerton. Here they would spend many happy hours fishing from craggy, exposed sea cliffs full of interesting geological formations that they would often point out to each other and discuss, while also enjoying the sound and rhythm of the sea and tidal surges. On those happy occasions, there was more than enough nature and geology in their surroundings to pique the young boy's curiosity, and it was this intuitive need to explore and question that would forge a challenging path of discovery for him throughout the rest of his life. Later, his PhD dissertation reflected those times, set out under the title "The Marshlands at Newport Bay, California."

From 1935 Stevenson was enrolled at Fullerton Union High School, and following his graduation on 16 June 1939, he spent the next two years attending Fullerton Junior College, where he was awarded his associate of arts degree. In 1942 he began working toward his bachelor's degree in geology at the University of California in Los Angeles (UCLA). Then the war effort finally caught up with him, and he enlisted in the U.S. Army Air Force, as he later explained.

As far back as I can recall . . . I wanted to fly in airplanes. Lindbergh, Doolittle, Roscoe Turner [and] Wiley Post were my heroes. In those days of the 1930s, I read every nickel pulp magazine I could find on the aerial exploits during "The Great War." In June 1940 the government's Civilian

Pilot Training program came to Fullerton. . . . In August I had my civilian pilot's license. For the next fifteen months, I flew whenever I could dig up five dollars [per hour] for the rental of a J-3 Piper Cub.

War came on 7 December 1941 while Robert Finch and I [were flying] over the U.S. fleet in Long Beach Harbor, wondering why the guns on the ships followed us as we crossed back and forth over [their] anchorage. The next day, most of the guys with whom I'd learned to fly enlisted in the Navy Air Arm. "Are you crazy?" [I said]. "Fly off ships over water? Forget it!" About half of them never made it back from the Battle of Midway. I enlisted in the army air force as quickly as possible, not to fight dastardly enemies or to stand firm for any patriotic philosophy, or even home, Mom, and apple pie. I joined to fly!

After graduating from U.S. Army Air Force flight training, Stevenson was assigned the dual rating of aerial navigator and aerial observer with the Eighth Air Force. During his tour of duty as a B-17 navigator, in which he flew nearly thirty bombing mission sorties over Europe out of RAF Thurleigh in Bedfordshire, including two on D-day, he was mentioned in dispatches three times. As well, his division commander personally commended him for observations he had made under conditions when aerial photographic reconnaissance had not been possible. While serving with the 368th Bomber Squadron of the 306th Bomber Group, he also participated in a bombing raid conducted by 377 B-17s on the Peenemünde experimental missile establishment in Germany on 18 July 1944. He would often remark on the irony of taking part in the bombing of these sites, targeting the brutal V-weapons developed by rocket engineer Wernher von Braun during the war, and then working with and assisting him beginning in 1968. In that year, Stevenson had completed the massive task of providing paragraph-long descriptions for most of the 150 photographs—specifically oceanic and coastal areas—for NASA's book *Earth Photographs from Gemini VI through Gemini XII*, which was published soon after. Von Braun was already aware of Stevenson's expertise through Stevenson's oceanography-related papers and continuing work with the astronauts on what to photograph from orbit. He was extremely grateful to Stevenson for providing the lengthy captions for the book, as well as for all the helpful information that he sent—information that von Braun used in the many well-received speeches he gave on the manned space program.

Stepping back in time again, it was during his wartime service in the air with the Eighth Air Force that Stevenson realized he had a better-than-average ability to observe, recognize, and evaluate arenas of action on the ground. Following one particularly hazardous sortie, his expert analysis of the situation resulted in a complete and beneficial change to a tactical plan of attack by the U.S. Army.

During his service with the U.S. Eighth Air Force, Bob Stevenson received the following awards and honors:

Distinguished Flying Cross (1944)

Air Medal with Four Oak Leaf Clusters (1944)

European Theater Medal with Four Battle Stars (1944)

Group Presidential Citation, Eighth Air Force (1944)

Performance Commendation, Ferry Command, Air Transport Command (1945)

On 12 February 1944, while still on active duty, Stevenson married Betty Lou Kurtz, and the union would later produce two sons, Michael George and Robert Kurtz Stevenson. Early in their marriage, Betty Lou worked as a schoolteacher in Compton city schools for four years. On his return to civilian life, Stevenson became a teaching assistant at UCLA until 1946, while studying for his bachelor's and master's degrees in geology in 1946 and 1948, respectively, at the university. From 1947 he also served two years as an instructor at Compton College.

The following year, he began his PhD studies at the University of Southern California (USC), during which time he was also a lecturer at the university. Then in 1951, as a reserve officer in the newly established USAF, he was recalled to active duty following the outbreak of the Korean War. Given his experience as an aerial navigator and observer and his postwar academic education in earth sciences, he was assigned to the Photo Reconnaissance Laboratory at Wright Air Development Center in Dayton, Ohio. Here he was placed in charge of an experimental, classified program, which fell under the jurisdiction of USAF intelligence. The program was established to develop aerial-photographic interpretation techniques. Using these, the terrain, the flora and fauna, and the geology of potential invasion routes could be determined with great precision, enabling the rapid deployment

12. Dr. Robert (Bob) Stevenson in his wartime service with the Eighth U.S. Air Force and during his later years living in Solana Beach, California. Courtesy Robert K. Stevenson.

of U.S. Army and Marine Corps ground forces. The results were so impressive that Stevenson was soon promoted and made head of the Photo-Radar Interpretation Branch of the Photo Reconnaissance Laboratory.

He later stated in a NASA Oral History interview,

So anyway, what helped me when I was at Wright Air Development Center, first of all, were these new techniques. My whole role in being the head of that section was to develop new techniques in photo interpretation, which meant using new, different films. I began to use color film in the field for reconnaissance. They'd never done that because it was so expensive. They had to take the color film and send it back to Eastman-Kodak for processing. Well, we processed it out of the Coleville River that ran by Umiat, Alaska . . . in the summer, with water that ran right into our tanks, and there's no problem. It was just the matter that people hadn't addressed the mechanism or the care that you had to go through in the field to do it. Soon as we set that up, then every reconnaissance unit in Korea began to process color film. Why? You can see a lot more from color film than you can from black and white. So anyway . . . I enjoyed that very much. I would have enjoyed staying in the air force and doing that for the rest of my life, but that didn't happen.

From 1953 to 1961 Dr. Stevenson served as director of inshore research for the Allan Hancock Foundation at USC, during which time he authored numerous scientific papers and was awarded his doctorate in oceanography in 1954. Later, in his capacity as a practicing oceanographer, he spent much of 1959 in England, based in Bridlington, East Yorkshire, while conducting weather and oceanic research of the North Sea under a grant from the U.S. Office of Naval Research.

As Stevenson's younger son (also Bob) told the author,

One of my father's most important scientific papers was on Hurricane Carla, a destructive hurricane that crossed the Gulf of Mexico before slamming into the Texas coast on September 10–11, 1961. Back then (from 1961 to 1963) he was working at the Texas A&M Marine Laboratory in Galveston, first as a research scientist and then as the laboratory's director. One month after Carla's appearance, he ordered the lab's research ship, R/V Hidalgo, to investigate the water temperature of the area in the gulf through which Carla had passed. What he found from bathythermograph data was that the water laying on or close to the path of Carla had decreased by 1.5°C or more. Expressed differently, the amount of heat energy transferred from the water into Carla equaled the amount of heat sufficient to heat for an entire winter 62 million homes located in a climate similar to that of Washington DC. In short, he determined that it was the temperature of the water that gives hurricanes their strength—something scientists and public safety officials had not understood previously. Simply put, the warmer the water the hurricane passed through, the stronger the hurricane would be.

I recall my father telling me the story of his presenting his Carla paper before a roomful of scientists in Europe (probably it was in Germany). At the conclusion of his presentation, all the scientists took off their shoes and started banging the table loudly with them. My father thought, "Oh, oh. I really blew it." Instead, it was just the opposite. The scientists—and it turns out this is a European custom—were bestowing upon my father their highest praise in recognition of his outstanding accomplishment. The scientists were essentially saying, "We take our shoes off for you."

In November 1963 Bob Stevenson's marriage to Betty Lou officially ended in divorce. Later that month, he and Elizabeth Campbell were married. Around then, Stevenson was working as assistant director of the Biological Laboratory of the Bureau of Commercial Fisheries in their fisheries research unit, while at the same time NASA's two-man Gemini space program was sending astronauts into Earth orbit. As a result, a completely new challenge would open for the dedicated oceanographer. He had become quite adept at determining spawning and breeding grounds for shrimp in the Gulf of Mexico, and his findings were proving extremely beneficial to the fishing industry. Then one day he was shown a color photo taken from orbit by astronaut Ed White during the *Gemini 4* mission in June 1965. Dr. Stevenson would later relate,

> *I honestly was flabbergasted. My first thought was that such photos could enormously increase our commercial fishing yield. No, I couldn't actually spot schools of fish in that photo, taken from an altitude of 120 miles. But I could see everything that we were spending months to pinpoint by boat and plane—the shallows, the silt discharges, the upwellings, the estuaries, and the interference currents. And these are the things that determine where fish feed. It really was astonishing; after one look at that photo, I was willing to bet I knew where schools of fish could be found.*
>
> *I also sensed that the biggest breakthrough of the space program might not be the exploration of the moon, but the opportunity to hang a camera out there in space and use it to locate more food from the sea than we'd ever imagined.*

After he had explained the ramifications of this discovery to some fellow scientists and authorities within NASA, he became well known to many of NASA's astronauts, and they began taking specific photographs for him during their spaceflights. In 1966 he was asked to brief the *Gemini 12* astronauts, Buzz Aldrin and James Lovell. Aldrin was the designated photographer on that flight, and his photographs caused a rapturous Stevenson to say, "After I saw the *Gemini 12* pictures, I no longer thought we could locate big schools of fish from space; I knew we could pinpoint them." It was to prove a milestone finding for the fisheries industry.

In 1970 Stevenson began working for the Office of Naval Research at

Scripps Institution of Oceanography in La Jolla, California, initially as scientific liaison officer and then as deputy director of space oceanography.

> *For the next twenty years I monitored, evaluated, suggested new research directions, and brought research results into active fleet practices. My prime area of responsibility was research funded by the navy in oceanography, atmospheric sciences, and the interactions between the ocean and the atmosphere. Mainly for the Pacific Ocean, but I was also involved in the "team" evaluation of similar research programs with navy funds being conducted in the Atlantic, Arctic, and the Southern Ocean around Antarctica. In that, about 90 percent of all the research was cofunded by the U.S. National Science Foundation. I was cognizant, therefore, of just about all the research being conducted in those fields of science by the United States. Furthermore, because nearly every project was "international," I learned, also, the results of the cooperative efforts with scientific centers in Britain, western Europe, Japan, Australia, Canada, New Caledonia, India, South Africa, and South America.*
>
> *In 1975 I became involved in working closely with the officers of the International Association for the Physical Sciences of the Oceans (IAPSO) to prepare the symposia and conduct their assemblies every two years. IAPSO is one of seven associations that make up the International Union of Geodesy and Geophysics. We worked closely with them all, but very closely with those associations that dealt with meteorology, atmospheric sciences, geomagnetics, aeronomy, volcanology, and hydrology. During those years, there was hardly a scientist or a scientific effort of any merit of which I was unaware.*

By now, he was also employed in briefing NASA's Apollo and Skylab space crews, training and briefing the astronauts in oceanography and surveillance techniques from orbit and in how to maximize the quality and usefulness of the photos they took as they swung around the planet. In 1978 he was joined in this task by an affable fellow oceanographer, Australian-born Dr. Paul Scully-Power, who worked at the Naval Underwater Systems Center in New London, Connecticut. The space agency now had two expert oceanographers engaged in training future space shuttle astronauts on this important facet of earth science.

By the time the first shuttle launch took place on 12 April 1981, Stevenson and Scully-Power had a regular set of ten lectures they would give to crewmembers preparing for their upcoming missions. The astronauts, in turn, would continue to take specific photos for the two oceanographers, enabling them to make important discoveries and dramatically advance their knowledge. During those early shuttle missions, the two of them would often sit in front of a control panel in Houston's Mission Control Center, advising crews on orbit what they should be looking for as their flight progressed. They found that this work occupied more and more of their time, but the results were certainly justifying their efforts.

Then, as Stevenson revealed, there was a huge push within NASA to have specialized oceanographers manifested aboard future spaceflights.

> One of the strongest advocates of this was Dick Truly, who flew on the second shuttle mission. While the first shuttle flight has only been a two-day proving mission, STS-2 was sent up for five days and carried the first synthetic imaging radar (SIR-A). Paul and I were the navy oceanographers assigned to that experiment.
>
> It was after that flight . . . that the thought of flying an oceanographer was expressed by Dick Truly to George Abbey, who was the director, Flight Crew Operations Division—an influential guy at NASA who had the final say on crew selections. The idea did not advance beyond the few of us until mid-1982 when the shuttle test program had been completed with the flight of STS-4 and the crews could then be expanded to four or five members.
>
> Had the problem of "space sickness" not begun to cause concern amongst NASA Headquarters people, then I would have flown on STS-7 with Bob Crippen and Sally Ride, and Paul would have flown on STS-8 with Dick Truly and his gang. The follow-on would have been for both of us to fly on 41G, as it was to be (and was) a high-inclination orbit, and carry the SIR-B and the large-format camera. It was not to be, however, as physician Norm Thagard was assigned to STS-7 and Bill Thornton to STS-8. At least they learned that space sickness could not be solved with a pill!

In planning its mission schedule, NASA designated the October 1984 shuttle mission to earth science rather than space science. Originally, NASA planned on using shuttle *Columbia*, but then a decision was made to fly *Challenger* instead. NASA then decided to add an additional payload specialist to the crew of six. *Challenger* was scheduled to circle the planet between fifty-seven degrees north of the equator and fifty-seven degrees south, and would fly over 75 percent of the oceans on an eight-day observation mission. This meant the flight was perfectly suited to ocean research. Consequently, NASA held discussions with the U.S. Navy's oceanographic committee and decided to place an oceanographer on mission STS-41G.

Due to the necessity for training the chosen scientist up to flight status in just three months, NASA recognized that there were only two suitable candidates. Both were men familiar with NASA's astronauts and procedures and could easily slip into the crew, which had already been in training since February of that year. They were Bob Stevenson and Paul Scully-Power.

As the senior member of the oceanography team, the spare seat on *Challenger* was first offered to Bob Stevenson by George Abbey, with Paul Scully-Power to act as his backup payload specialist. Had these plans gone ahead, Dr. Stevenson would have achieved a unique place in history. Not only would he have been the oldest space traveler to that time, but of more statistical significance, as he came into the world on 15 January 1921 (four months before cosmonaut Georgi Beregovoi and six months before John Glenn), he would today be recognized as the firstborn of Earth to have ever flown into space.

Initially, and with great anticipation for what he might be able to achieve, Stevenson accepted the assignment and underwent a full medical examination. When the results came in, he was advised to have a hernia operation if he wanted to fly on the mission. This he did, and everything now seemed to be in order. Then life delivered him a crushing blow.

His second wife Elizabeth had earlier been diagnosed with breast cancer and was bedridden. They were now told that the disease had spread and that she was terminally ill. It was obvious to him where his priorities should be, and after serious consideration, he asked to see George Abbey and told him he had to decline the offer. "I could not leave her," he stated. Later, after discussing the sad matter with Stevenson, Abbey phoned Scully-Power, who was aware of the domestic problems facing his fellow scientist. Abbey explained that he had already spoken with mission commander Bob Crippen, who said he would welcome the substitute oceanographer into his crew.

"I had no hesitation at all in accepting the flight," Scully-Power told the author. "In fact, it was something I'd dreamed about doing for years but never thought the chance would come. Life plays some pretty cruel and

weird tricks at times, and Bob told me that he'd decided his first duty in
life was to his wife. It was, of course, quite a devastating decision for this
wonderful man to make."

As it turned out, Stevenson's noble but heartbreaking decision to decline
the flight turned out to be the correct one, as his wife passed away on 26
September, just nine days before the 5 October launch, so he would not
have been able to fly after all.

The STS-41G flight went ahead as scheduled and would prove the worth
of having a trained oceanographer on board. Scully-Power's mission, and
the important discoveries he made, contributed greatly to advancing our
understanding of ocean phenomena such as spiral eddies, which would
allow Bob Stevenson to fine-tune his later briefings to other crews.

Following the *Challenger* mission, there were calls to reschedule Stevenson on another flight, as there was still much work to be carried out. One
of the biggest problems when Scully-Power flew was that his time on the
flight deck observing and photographing ocean phenomena was restricted.
The crew had designated sleep periods, and those who were rostered awake
had to be as quiet as possible in carrying out any duties, which made it
impossible for him to use his camera at those times. The camera he was
using had an automatic film advance, which would have made far too much
noise in the otherwise-silent spacecraft. When he learned that Stevenson
was being rescheduled onto a later flight, he recommended that he carry a
complete Hasselblad camera (including a full set of lenses) on his mission,
along with extra magazines of film and extra audiotapes to assist him in
documenting his flight and observations.

In February 1985 Stevenson received some very welcome news. NASA
administrator James M. Beggs and the secretary of the U.S. Navy, John F.
Lehman, had held discussions, one of the results of which was an agreement
that Stevenson should be given another opportunity to fly on a research-
suitable mission before the end of 1985. However, his flight kept being
rolled back due to satellite repairs and the decision, given under pressure
from above, to allocate shuttle seats to two elected political officials. In the
meantime, Stevenson was elected deputy secretary general of IAPSO. With
no further news of a mission for him, 1985 slipped into 1986.

Eventually, Stevenson was assigned a seat on mission STS-61K, then
scheduled for October 1986. It was further agreed by George Abbey, in

consultation with veteran astronaut John Young, then chief of the Astronaut Office, that after STS-61K, both oceanographers would fly together on a later, high-inclination Earth observation shuttle mission.

Then, on 28 January 1986, a catastrophic explosion took place seventy-three seconds into the launch of *Challenger* on mission STS-51L, which took the lives of the seven crewmembers. As an immediate consequence, the shuttle fleet was grounded while a thorough investigation was carried out, and technical, procedural, and management reviews also took place. The cause was traced to problems within the solid rocket boosters, and numerous changes were implemented.

One of the recommendations that came into force was to postpone indefinitely any flights by non-NASA astronauts—the payload specialists. This embargo included any scheduled or proposed flights for Bob Stevenson and Paul Scully-Power.

Two years after the *Challenger* disaster and with any thoughts of flying into space now gone, Stevenson retired from his job with the Office of Naval Research. Before he retired, however, he completed his seminal work, *Oceanography from the Space Shuttle*, a two-hundred-page book published the following year that contained approximately ninety high-quality color photographs of ocean phenomena taken during several shuttle missions. These phenomena included spiral eddies, solitons, suloys, and internal waves—all of which would have been near impossible to have detected and measured from an oceangoing ship.

"Over the years, my father received numerous awards for his enormous contributions to the field of space oceanography," his son Robert reflected. "Most notably, in January 1985 at a special ceremony in a packed auditorium at Scripps, Rear Admiral [John] B. Mooney, chief of naval research, acting on behalf of President Ronald Reagan, presented him with the Navy Meritorious Civilian Service Award—this being the highest award possible for a civilian to receive from the navy. He was the only Office of Naval Research employee to ever receive the award."

Robert also remembers being present when his father was proposing observation opportunities from the platform of the proposed space station along with John Kaltenbach, from NASA's Earth Sciences Division. Then going by the name of "Freedom," the massive orbiting station was a concept that ultimately folded into what later became the ISS.

13. At the Scripps Institution of Oceanography on 10 January 1985, Bob Stevenson was a surprised but proud recipient of the U.S. Navy's Meritorious Civilian Service Award. Shown wearing his award medal, he is flanked on the left by shuttle astronaut Bob Crippen and on the right by fellow oceanographer Paul Scully-Power. Photo by Damion Lloyd Photography, courtesy Robert K. Stevenson.

John Kaltenbach was in charge of earth observations. I recall him and my father discussing in the mid or late 1980s what would be the best way for the astronauts to observe the earth from the future space station. My father told Kaltenbach that the space station had to contain a large, facing-down-to-the-earth viewing window. He completely agreed with my father regarding the enormous value of having such an outstanding viewing window and was the one who saw to it that such a window was incorporated into the space station's design. As we know, this type of window—what's called the cupola—did, in fact, get built, and it's now the favorite place on the space station for the astronauts.

In June 1988 while still serving with IAPSO—now as their secretary general—Stevenson was married for a third time, to physical therapist Jeani Marie Wetzel. They lived for several years in Solana Beach, California, before moving in 1999 to the Hawaiian island of Kauai.

In 1995, soon after stepping down from his position with IAPSO, Stevenson was diagnosed with prostate cancer. To this time, he had written more than 130 scientific papers and books and had supplied factual information for textbooks, encyclopedias, and other compendia. Hormone therapy kept the cancer under control for several years, but eventually it began to spread throughout his body.

Following a lengthy battle against his illness, Dr. Robert Stevenson passed away on 12 August 2001, at eighty years of age. His widow, Jeani, who now worked in real estate, remained in their home in Princeville, Kauai, for several years, until she too succumbed to illness on 12 October 2012, at the age of sixty-four.

As Paul Scully-Power said in eulogizing his longtime friend and colleague, "He instructed each and every one of the astronauts in the greatest of all endeavors—looking at Mother Earth and understanding what they saw and recording that which was new. In this sense, he is singularly responsible for one of the greatest treasure troves of knowledge that we have today of the earth."

In summing up his father's prolific and prestigious life, Robert Jr. said, "When one discovers and works tirelessly to develop an entirely new field of science, as my father did, as well as vigorously defends and promotes throughout his career the values of ethical scientific conduct, few words can adequately describe the legacy left to us by such a man. Amongst all the accolades that could be made, probably the words that would satisfy him most to hear said of him are the following: the presence of Dr. Robert E. Stevenson, 'the Father of Space Oceanography,' made our planet a much better place—in short, his life was a success."

7. Test Pilot and Ex-Astronaut

Group 5 Astronaut Lt. Cdr. John S. Bull, USN

Mankind is drawn to the heavens for the same reason we were once
drawn into unknown lands and across the open sea. We choose
to explore space because doing so improves our lives and lifts our
national spirit. So let us continue the journey.

—President George W. Bush

For many people growing up in Great Britain, the only person they had
ever heard of named John Bull was a stout, imaginary figure with a top
hat and Union Jack waistcoat who personified England in much the same
way as his counterpart Uncle Sam represents the United States. The name
came to prominence once again on 4 April 1966 when NASA announced the
selection of its fifth group of astronauts, bringing on board another nineteen candidates to train for future spaceflights. Listed among those names
was Lt. John Bull, a determined and highly talented test pilot with the U.S.
Navy. Less than two years later a chronic pulmonary disease would sadly
result in his reluctant withdrawal from the astronaut corps.

Over later years, NASA's group 5 astronauts built up an incredible record
of achievement; nine of their number would travel to the moon, including three who would walk on its ancient surface. The remaining members
later flew on missions to the *Skylab* space station or in the early flights of
the space shuttle program. Had he not lost his chance to fly for NASA, John
Bull was well in contention as a frontline candidate to fly to—and perhaps
even leave his footprints on—the moon.

For devoted fans of the New York Yankees baseball team, Tuesday, 25
September 1934, was a day filled with mixed emotions. On that date, Lou

Gehrig slammed his forty-eighth home run of the year in his 1,500th consecutive game, while fans were still coming to grips with the news that
Babe Ruth, another legend of the game, had played his last-ever game for
the Yankees the day before. Meanwhile, down in Memphis, Tennessee,
Ruth and Charles Mayrant Bull, an engineer, were celebrating the birth
of a baby boy they named John Sumter Bull, a younger brother to Charles
and Lori. Another sibling, Steve, would be born two years later to complete the family.

Some three centuries earlier, the Bull and Mayrant families were among
the first settlers of South Carolina. Their family trees can be traced back
to such notables as William Bull, a governor of the province of South Carolina in the mid-eighteenth century; Gen. Thomas Sumter, a hero of the
American Revolution and later U.S. senator (and the source of John Bull's
middle name); and Capt. John Mayrant Jr., who served with distinction
alongside the legendary John Paul Jones, founder of the U.S. Navy, and
was one of the representatives who ratified the U.S. Constitution in 1788.
It was an impressive pedigree for young John Bull.

As they grew up, John and his older brother Charles shared a passion for
making and playing with model airplanes—an interest that later flowed on
to their younger brother Steve. This obsession with airplanes would remain
with Bull all his life, providing the spur that set him on the path to one
day becoming a naval aviator. He took his early education at primary and
secondary schools in Memphis, joined the Boy Scouts, and graduated from
Central High School in 1952.

Bull received his bachelor of science degree in mechanical engineering
from Rice University, Houston, in 1956, following which he completed a
year of study toward his master's degree in aeronautical engineering. He
entered active duty with the U.S. Navy in June 1957. On receiving his commission, Bull began his initial flight training as a naval aviation cadet at
Pensacola, Florida, later receiving advanced jet transition training at NAS
Kingsville, Texas. He was awarded his coveted wings of gold as a naval aviator in 1958. Then, from March of the following year until November 1960,
he flew McDonnell F3H Demons while attached to Fighter Squadrons VF-
121 and VF-92. In 1962 he was assigned to VF-114 based at NAS Miramar,
California, where he would fly both the Demon and F-4 Phantom II jets.
Altogether, he served three squadron tours on western Pacific (WESTPAC)

cruises aboard the carriers USS *Ranger* (CV-61), *Hancock* (CV-19), and *Kitty Hawk* (CV-63).

In June 1963 Lieutenant Bull was rewarded for his piloting work and skills with an assignment to the U.S. Naval Test Pilot School, located at Patuxent River, Maryland. It would prove to be both an extensive and intensive eight months ahead of the young aviator.

The school's curriculum at that time was divided into two principal areas of study—academic and flight. The former was comprised of classroom studies and lectures on such subjects as calculus, mechanics, aerodynamics, instrumentation, weapons systems, dynamic stability, and jet engines. The flight phase of the school dealt with both fixed-wing and rotary aircraft, in which they had to operate and evaluate a wide variety of vehicles, ranging from propeller-driven airplanes and high-performance jet fighters through to helicopters. It was an exacting course, but at the end of each one, the test pilot school graduated some of the best pilots in the sky. Many went on to become astronauts, including four of the original seven Mercury astronauts: Scott Carpenter, John Glenn, Wally Schirra, and Alan Shepard.

Eight months later, in February 1964, Bull graduated from test pilot school, having received the Outstanding Student Award in his eighteen-strong class 36. He was then assigned to remain at Patuxent River as a project test pilot in the Naval Air Test Center's Carrier Suitability Branch. In June of that year, he married Nancy Laraine Gustafson of Seattle, Washington. Their first son, Jeffrey Tyler Bull, was born in July 1965 while the family was living on the Maryland base. They would later have two more children: another son, Scott (born in 1968), and a daughter, Whitney (born in 1971).

On 31 August 1965 he suffered his first full-on emergency when the engines on his Douglas A-4 Skyhawk suddenly quit after taking off from NAS Lakehurst, New Jersey. Completely without power, he crashed into a marsh several hundred yards off the end of the runway. In a stroke of good fortune, a helicopter crew was practicing instrument approaches in the area and saw the A-4 go down. They flew straight across to the scene where Bull had managed to scramble free from the downed jet. After climbing into their rescue sling, he was hoisted clear of the accident scene before being transported to the station hospital. It was the first of three aircraft incidents in which he would be involved while flying with the U.S. Navy.

The following month, NASA announced that it would be recruiting a new group of pilot astronauts. Bull was one of 510 hopefuls who applied by the required date, and soon that number had been reduced to 158 who met the basic requirements. Out of that number, one hundred were military applicants and fifty-eight were civilians. As more rigorous medical and psychological testing and interviews took place, that number was culled even further until it finally reached thirty-five finalists. Grounded Mercury astronaut Deke Slayton was the director of Flight Crew Operations at the time, and when the selection panel asked him how many of the thirty-five he wanted to hire, he famously said, "As many qualified guys as you can find." The panel came up with nineteen names, and Slayton took the lot.

On 4 April 1966 NASA announced that it had selected its fifth group of astronauts. One of the nineteen names listed was that of U.S. Navy lieutenant John S. Bull. At the time of his selection, he had already amassed an impressive 1,634 flying hours, of which 1,424 hours were logged operating jet aircraft. At the press conference held to introduce the nineteen new astronauts the day after the announcement, his brief NASA biography noted that his hobbies included swimming, golfing, and, of course, flying. When asked by one reporter what he hoped to accomplish after his astronaut training, Bull responded, "I've watched all the shots on television, and I've wished it could be me, but I never thought I was that close to getting in. I certainly would like to be the first man on the moon. That's the big one!"

When asked by the author for any particular recollections of his father's time as a NASA astronaut, Scott Bull responded, "I recall he spoke about his days as a test pilot equal if not more than his astronaut training. He told me he crashed three times as a test pilot. He was very humble about being selected to the astronaut program, [but] he never spoke about his astronaut days unless asked." Scott then added that his father never wanted to talk about the past, and his passion was always in the present time.

Following introductory training, the newly selected candidates joined members of NASA's fourth astronaut group on 2 June 1966 to begin two days of geologic field training. Their first expedition was the beginning of an extensive course in geologic discovery to guide them in identifying the best samples to recover from the moon. Led by personnel from the U.S. Geological Survey's branches of Astrogeology and Surface Planetary Exploration, the twenty-four astronauts were taken deep into the Grand Canyon. Three weeks later they were given additional expert tuition and guidance

14. NASA astronaut Lt. John Sumter Bull, USN. Courtesy NASA.

in western Texas, while another geologic-training trip took them to Bend, Oregon, on 27–29 July. Bull participated in all three of these expeditions, as well as in later guided trips to Katmai, Alaska (21–25 August); Valles Caldera, New Mexico (25 September); and the Pinacates volcanic field in Mexico (29 November–2 December). For a week from 12 February 1967, he was a member of a combined group of fifteen astronauts from groups 4 and 5 who traveled to the Big Island of Hawaii to study a variety of volcanic features. They would return for a second, four-day study trip on 20 March 1967.

Having settled into his new and exciting career, Bull continued his astronaut training and associated duties. In November he received his first mission-related assignment as a support crewmember for the third planned Apollo mission, along with fellow astronauts Ken (T. K.) Mattingly and Jerry Carr. Their principal role was to assist the prime crew of Frank Borman, Michael Collins, and William Anders, as well as the backup crew of Neil Armstrong, James Lovell, and Edwin "Buzz" Aldrin. Plans then in place called for the third crewed Apollo mission to be launched into Earth orbit early in 1969.

In January 1968 John Bull and another group 5 astronaut, Jim Irwin, wore a newly configured A6-L pressure suit during a series of four-hour verification test runs in NASA's eight-foot altitude chamber, located in Houston's Manned Spacecraft Center's Crew Systems Division. The A6-L suit incorporated design and material changes recommended by a review board that had investigated the fatal Apollo 1 (AS-204) spacecraft pad fire in January the previous year. These tests marked the first use by astronauts of altitude chambers at MSC since the tragic accident that took the lives of three of their colleagues.

Included in the exhaustive reevaluation and redesign of the Apollo spacecraft was an immediate change from the 100 percent oxygen environment that was chiefly responsible for the deaths of the three astronauts. It had only taken what was believed to be an arc from some frayed wire insulation in the cabin to spark the ferocious fireball that engulfed the sealed interior of the spacecraft being tested on the launchpad that day. The cabin's environmental systems redesign included a change to the far less flammable nitrogen-oxygen mix that was only used in ground tests. The space suits would also undergo a change. The redesigned suits, in addition to being covered in nonflammable beta fabric fiberglass cloth, were far more comfortable and mobile than the original suits.

The altitude chamber used ambient air, and during the tests the two men's pressure suits utilized a 100 percent oxygen system at 3.7 pounds per square inch. The tests, conducted at simulated altitudes of up to 240,000 feet, were preparatory to trials of Grumman's Lunar Module Test Article 8 (LTA-8) in chamber B within the Space Environment and Simulation Laboratories (SESL). In these new tests, NASA wanted to simulate the space environment for both the command and service module (CSM) and the lunar module (LM). On 13 January the two men performed work tasks in chamber B during which they simulated a crew transfer from the CSM to the LM.

Irwin and Bull would later team up once again for the LTA-8 thermal-vacuum tests. This was a crucial checkout of the Lunar Module Test Article, which was scheduled for completion in June. In the April 2000 edition of the British Interplanetary Society's *Spaceflight* magazine, space historian Ed Hengeveld wrote about these tests and what they entailed.

> *The two LTA-8 crewmen would perform the full range of activities that would be necessary during a LEM's flight to and landing on the moon. They would simulate firing the descent and ascent stage engines. In addition they would practice unhooking their spacesuit umbilicals from the LM's Environmental Control Subsystem and switching to the Portable Life Support System (PLSS), the backpacks that contained the air supply and cooling to keep the astronauts comfortable while working on the lunar surface. Then they would depressurize the LM cabin, open the hatch, crawl out onto the porch and descend the ladder to simulate activities on the lunar surface.*

Ahead of the full commencement of the LTA-8 vacuum tests, Irwin and Bull performed a number of emergency-egress exercises in order to test evacuation procedures from the chamber. These crucial exercises required both men to don oxygen masks before exiting the Lunar Module Test Article through the hatch and making their way onto the tiny porch and down the lunar module's ladder before leaving the chamber.

It was during this time that Jim Irwin noticed a worrying change in the condition of Bull, which he later recorded in his memoir, *To Rule the Night*: "Before we did any thermal work, we had to run through some emergency egress tests. Just as we were getting involved in this, John Bull started developing curious symptoms. We played handball almost every day, and I could see that John was losing his stamina. Occasionally he would have coughing spells."

For Bull, the first inkling of a medical problem had occurred a few months earlier, in August 1967, when he sought remedial treatment for a case of sinusitis. Over the next three months, he began suffering from the recurring cough noticed by Irwin, and in January 1968 he experienced a severe asthma-like attack.

15. John Bull during tests of a newly designed Apollo pressure suit. Courtesy NASA.

While conducting the Lunar Module Test Article evacuation exercises, his sinus condition seemed to be aggravated by the constant changes in pressure. At first, the mystery illness had simply aroused the curiosity of the NASA doctors, but as it persisted, their concerns grew. He was placed on a course of aspirin, but this only seemed to make his condition worse.

If he took an aspirin, it would begin to constrict his lungs and he would no longer be able to breathe normally.

He continued to receive treatment for the unknown pulmonary condition, but by mid-May his condition had not eased and was actually getting worse. Based on the recommendation of their medical staff, the space agency had no option but to stand Bull down from participating in the LTA-8 tests. Deke Slayton was unable to spare any astronauts to take Bull's place, so it was filled by a nonastronaut backup, Gerry Gibbons, a consulting pilot with the Grumman Corporation. "He was almost the same size as John," Irwin wrote, "and since Gerry was a consulting pilot working on the LTA-8, he had been following all this stuff and had the procedures down."

In July an understandably anxious Bull reported to the National Naval Medical Center in Bethesda, Maryland, for an examination to determine whether he was medically fit to remain on active duty in the U.S. Navy. NASA also reluctantly announced that the well-liked astronaut's medical condition could possibly lead them to grounding him, "perhaps permanently." To his acute disappointment, when the test results came in, the navy doctors decided that he should be temporarily placed on nonflying duties.

Throughout his illness, no one was able to pinpoint the cause of Bull's disease. What they *did* determine was that it had no medical name and no known cure or effective treatment. In fact, it has only recently been defined and identified as alpha-1 antitrypsin deficiency. Until then, it was mostly referred to by physicians as aspirin asthma. The disease is actually characterized by three distinct factors: (1) chronic sinusitis, (2) chronic obstructive pulmonary disease, and (3) a marked sensitivity and intolerance to aspirin. It is a progressive disease, and while not a true allergy, it is far more serious than asthma, most frequently striking young men in their late twenties and early thirties. In the 1960s a lack of knowledge of the disease had restricted treatment to an alleviation of the symptoms.

On 16 July 1968 NASA announced with understandable reluctance that Lt. Cdr. John S. Bull would be withdrawing from the astronaut program. In qualifying the announcement, NASA's director of medical research and operations, Dr. Charles Berry, stated that Bull's condition "has not responded to treatment," adding that he "is a rather ill young man." Bull's departure from the space center would leave fifty-three astronauts still active in the NASA program.

"We found him a job at the NASA Ames Research Center in Palo Alto, California, where he did some research flying and went on to get a PhD," Deke Slayton later said of Bull in his posthumously published memoir. "He was a great guy and would have been one of my early picks for a lunar module pilot. I hated to lose him."

In 1971 Bull took leave from his work at Ames in order to complete his master of science degree in aeronautical engineering, this time at Stanford University, and in 1973 he was subsequently awarded his PhD, also in aeronautical engineering. He then returned to the NASA Ames Research Center, where, over the next twelve years, he conducted research in simulation and flight-testing of advanced flight systems both for helicopters and for fixed-wing aircraft. One of Dr. Bull's first assignments at Ames was to investigate the feasibility of landing a space shuttle without engines. Together with fellow Ames investigator John Foster, he developed the algorithms and successfully demonstrated them on a CV-990 aircraft. Following this work, Bull headed the Helicopter All-Weather Project, during which he conducted vital research that would eventually lead to the development of several innovative landing guidance systems.

Harry N. Swenson, now a NASA senior scientist at the Ames Center, recently recalled Bull's work on different research projects.

In the early 1980s, John was the helicopter group leader and assistant chief of the Aircraft Guidance and Navigation Branch. He managed, within his group, a series of instrumental advanced guidance and navigation helicopter research projects that were on the cutting edge of research at the time. This included numerous firsts—some of the first research in differential GPS for precision landing of helicopters; the first adaption of an airborne weather radar system to provide landing guidance for helicopters traveling in the Gulf of Mexico; development of an advanced precision tactical approach system that could be set up by a single person in remote areas, providing the army with an advanced new capability and providing the [Federal Aviation Administration with] the first data on the use of the microwave landing system focused on helicopter operations.

He led a group of young engineers to these firsts, several of which led to direct commercial and military applications that are commonplace today, with technical acumen and a managerial focus that challenged and encouraged these engineers to achieve these great things. As a fresh-out-of-college engineer, there was not a better place to have come to work at or a better leader to work with.

As I look back at my thirty-year career that has been labeled by others as highly successful, I owe a lot to John's early inspiration, especially when I would ask for too much permission to do or try things. I seem to remember him saying that it is better to ask forgiveness than permission when you are on the cutting edge [and to] trust your instincts and analyses. So I stopped asking permission and started just doing what led me to what I feel was a highly successful thirty-year NASA research career. So as a young guy that only worked for John for a couple of years, his mentorship has lasted for three decades.

The Bull family would be further touched by tragedy on 28 January 1977 when their older son Jeffrey passed away, aged just eleven years old. Totally unknown to anyone, their son had been suffering from a heart abnormality that finally resulted in a sudden, fatal cardiac arrest. His younger brother, Scott, remembers a devastated father who tried to be "very strong" during the difficult time. "I never recall seeing sadness in him, but I know how painful this must have been," he reflected.

John Bull may have been an astronaut, but according to Scott, he was also a loving father.

We always had paper airplanes all around the house that he would design for us. Model planes became a connection that I carried with my dad through college. We did a lot of family water ski trips before Jeff died. As well, Dad took me and my brother to Oakland A's baseball games and some high school football games. He once walked out of a meeting at the Johnson Space Center because he did not want to miss my high school football game. He also coached many of our sporting teams and would keep lots of team statistics, which I understand now because he had such a mathematical mind.

In late 1983 Bull became chief of Ames' Aircraft Systems Branch, where he managed the development of research flight control systems for rotor-craft and STOL (short takeoff and landing) aircraft. Then, from 1986 until his retirement in 1989, he managed NASA-wide research programs in autonomous systems technology for aeronautics and space applications.

Despite his retirement from NASA, Bull still remained close to the Ames family, providing technical support and consulting services for aerospace research and technology programs. Now employed by the CAELUM Research Corporation, he and his team made several important contributions in advanced flight control law design for the PCA (propulsion-controlled aircraft) program, which had applications to the MD-11 and Boeing 747 commercial aircraft. Spurred on by a number of airplane crashes caused by the loss of hydraulic flight controls, a NASA-industry team at Dryden began working with Ames in developing an effective method of safely landing an airplane by means of a computerized PCA system, which used only engine thrust to give the aircraft emergency flight control.

This team, led by Bull, successfully developed a computerized system demonstrating PCA on simulations for generic commercial airliner models. These tests proved that the problem could be solved by using the flight director needle in an aircraft's cockpit. This allowed the pilot to achieve effective lateral control by moving the throttles based on cues on the flight director needle. The aircraft would then stabilize and land through computer-driven engine thrust. Pilot evaluations later carried out at Ames in 1998 confirmed these results.

According to *Touchdown: The Development of Propulsion Controlled Aircraft at NASA Dryden*, "The engineers have shown how a commercial airliner without flight controls and without an operating engine on one wing can engage PCA by using fuel transfer to offset the center of gravity toward the operating engine. John Bull and his colleagues at NASA Ames have fashioned a brilliant sim demonstration: the Boeing 747 has its hydraulics fail at 35,000 feet, rolls until it is upside-down, and then the PCA mode is engaged. The airplane rights itself, levels its wings, and comes in for a safe landing nearly identical to a normal auto landing."

Bull often commented to his colleagues that this was probably one of the most rewarding projects in which he had been involved. As retired NASA Dryden program manager Frank W. Burcham remarked, "Our work with John Bull found him to be a unique asset to the science of aerospace: brilliant, practical, thorough, and always cooperative. No one will replace him."

Today, John T. Kaneshige is a research engineer at NASA Ames, and he added that Bull had a large impact on his life. "John Bull's experience as a pilot, astronaut, and researcher made him a truly unique individual. However, it was his kindness and unassuming nature that made him such an exceptional mentor to young engineers such as myself."

Similarly, Joseph J. Totah, the current associate chief of the Intelligent Systems Division at NASA Ames, offered his personal reflections.

It was truly a privilege working with John Bull. His technical expertise and wealth of experience were remarkable, and we all learned so much from him. John was eager to share the many successes he achieved in his research—he taught us how to analyze complex problems with simple yet elegant solution techniques.

He led by example and was a source of knowledge, insight, and inspiration that provided the foundation for our successes in both aeronautics and space technology projects and studies.

Prior to his final retirement in 1997, Bull's contributions extended to a number of other projects and studies. Among these were advanced flight control for lunar landing and autonomous docking applications, as well as conducting research and development in high-visibility NASA systems directed toward space missions and science operations, including the Access to Space initiative, the International Space Station, the space shuttle program, Mars Pathfinder, and Deep Space 1.

Apollo 15 CMP Al Worden had been selected in the same group 5 astronaut cadre as John Bull. Following his journey to the moon, he would also take on a position at the Ames Research Center. Worden told the author,

He was a great guy. John was very much like another well-liked astronaut named C. C. Williams—quiet and modest, a very competent guy who came out of the navy. But when he had his health problem, which is why he left the program, there was no place for him back in the navy. So he went out as a researcher to Ames.

I also went to work at Ames following my Apollo 15 *flight, and he was in their Aircraft Systems Branch. There was kind of a sense of "Hey, here we both are." But I only saw him every once in a while. We'd say "Hi" and all that, but we weren't really close. The fact that we were in the same group in Houston was kind of tenuous, as John wasn't there that long. So we never really got back together in any meaningful way at Ames or developed a deeper connection.*

Dave Anderson, now a pilot for a major American airline, began working at NASA Ames in 1979 after he was interviewed for the job by John Bull at the University of California. He recalled,

Whatever happened in that interview resulted in my starting my career in aviation at NASA working for John. When I arrived at Ames, I was given a tour of the facility by a fellow engineer who had started about a year before I did. He mentioned that John had been an Apollo astronaut, selected in the fifth group. John never said anything during the interview.

John was a very soft-spoken man and very intelligent. My life goal was to be a pilot, and I think that was possibly the reason that I was hired. There was a connection between us, and he literally took me under his wing and did whatever he could to help guide me in that direction. That included giving me his test pilot manuals from Navy Test Pilot School.

In the three and a half years I worked for John, he never talked about his time as an astronaut. He was very professional, and you would never, for a second, guess that there was any angst about being let go from the Apollo program due to health reasons. He never talked about it. He did talk about flying, though, and he would light up when talking to me about my dreams.

One story that was told to me by the secretary on the second floor of building 210 [she covered all the engineers on the floor] was on the twenty-fifth anniversary of the Apollo 11 moon landing, when she started to get letters written to John asking for an autograph. She asked John why he was getting these letters. It was only then—after twenty-five years—that he told her he had been an Apollo astronaut. She had never known. That was the kind of man he was.

At the time of his retirement in 1997, Bull was listed as a member of the Society of Experimental Test Pilots; the American Helicopter Society; the American Institute of Aeronautics and Astronautics; and Sigma Tau, Sigma Xi, and Tau Beta Pi (the oldest engineering honor society in America).

Having raised their family in the San Francisco Bay area, John and Nancy retired to South Lake Tahoe, California, in 1998. In the years prior to his death, Bull resumed recreational flying in his Piper Comanche 250, making short trips with friends and family to and from the local airport.

On 11 August 2008, at the age of seventy-three, John Bull died in South Lake Tahoe, following complications related to his long-term asthma. He was laid to rest at the Alta Mesa Memorial Park in Palo Alto, California.

In paying tribute, the Ames Research Center newsletter, *Astrogram*, said that Dr. Bull "was always thrilled to share his insights, and we all shared in the excitement of his amazing contributions. [He] was a mentor, a role model and an inspiration to all who had the privilege of working with him."

Dr. John Bull is survived by his wife Nancy, son Scott and his wife Ellen, daughter Whitney and her husband Jason, and four grandchildren.

In eulogizing her late husband, Nancy Bull said, "We will remember John as a loving husband, father, and grandfather who lived life to the fullest and always found the positive side of things no matter what the situation."

8. An Indonesian Flag in Space

Payload Specialist Pratiwi Sudarmono

Always remember, you have within you the strength, the patience,
and the passion to reach for the stars to change the world.

—Eleanor Roosevelt

Some lesser casualties of the 1986 *Challenger* disaster were those manifested for future missions as payload specialists. Among them were two candidates from Indonesia, whose dreams of flying in space subsequently fell into an indefinite limbo, although their expectations of ever flying into space sadly dissipated many years ago.

There exists an understandable misconception that space shuttle *Challenger* was blown apart by the massive explosion witnessed by millions on live television coverage, but that is not the case. When the venerable orbiter was launched into the skies for the tenth time, there were pools of ice covering the ground on that freezing-cold January morning, and lance-like clusters of icicles hung from the rust-red launch tower. In hindsight, *Challenger* should never have left the launchpad under those terrible conditions.

Even as the glistening orbiter was sitting on the launchpad during the final countdown, two O-rings used in the lowermost field joint of the right-hand solid rocket booster became stiff due to the extreme cold and lost their ability to completely seal a critical joint. As *Challenger* blazed a fiery trail into the Florida skies, first a puff of black smoke and then a thin stream of superhot propellant gas began to escape from the joint at the bottom of the booster. Acting like a blowtorch and growing rapidly in intensity, the white-hot plume of gas soon burned through one of the steel struts holding the booster rockets against the huge orange external tank, filled in that area with liquid hydrogen. Once the strut had burned through, aerodynamic forces caused the booster to sever and swivel around, slamming into the massive fuel tank, which ruptured. A huge fireball ensued, almost instantly consuming 2 million liters of fuel. Despite how it appeared to shocked onlookers and television viewers, the shuttle was actually lost when it was torn apart by the force of the air.

As NASA shuttle astronaut Don Peterson once explained,

When that vehicle turned sideways, the wind force just ripped it apart. When we launch the shuttle and we light all five engines, we're burning ten and a half tons of fuel per second. That's the weight of three full-sized automobiles every second being burned up. The amount of energy and the force and the power that's in that vehicle is gigantic . . . and when you're boring through the atmosphere at high speed, the wind force is tremendous. The shuttle is not designed to stand big side loads. You've got to keep it pointed exactly properly. Once that rocket came loose and pushed the stack sideways, it just came apart. It just literally disintegrated.

The loss of *Challenger* and its crew of seven, including a much-loved teacher named Christa McAuliffe, had an immediate impact on the American space agency. For far too long, NASA's management had grown dangerously complacent as the shuttle program continued to send astronauts into space in its fleet of four orbiter vehicles, and this complacency would become their worst enemy. Despite concerns expressed by the engineering community, an impatient NASA forged ahead with the shuttle program, in spite of technical and other delays, as well as damage sustained to critical areas and components on returning orbiters. The space agency was living on borrowed time as it remained intent on maintaining a demanding and unrealistic mission schedule.

Then, on the morning of 27 January 1986, seven lives were lost in front of horrified family members, friends, and millions of television viewers, including schoolchildren right across the nation. Encouraged by their teachers, the students had been eager to follow the launch and on-orbit exploits of Christa McAuliffe, who was going to run an ongoing educational program from space. In just a few seconds, everyone's excitement and celebrations turned to horror and bewilderment, and NASA would pay a terrible price for its collective impatience and arrogance.

Pratiwi Pujilestari Sudarmono first heard the tragic news of the *Chal-*

lenger disaster on a local radio station. The thirty-three-year-old microbiologist was staying out of her populous home capital of Jakarta at the time, giving lectures to the health staff of a police station. Newspapers later confirmed that *Challenger* and its STS-51L crew of seven had been lost when the space shuttle was torn apart seventy-three seconds after liftoff. The news for Sudarmono was particularly devastating; she had been undergoing preliminary training for a shuttle flight into space later that year.

Pratiwi (which translates to "earth woman") was born 31 July 1952 in Bandung, West Java. She modestly claims an aristocratic background, as her grandfather was a regent for the sultan of Solo. She took her early education at St. Joseph Elementary School and recalled that when she was in grade 2, her teacher asked the class what they wanted to be when they grew up. Her hand shot up and her answer came quickly: "I want to be an astronaut!" She would graduate from St. Angela High School in Jakarta in 1971.

When asked about early influences in her life, she responded, "The one who inspired my life the most was my father. My father was a researcher. So if I cried when I was little, he could show me that he could transform white liquid in the test tube into pink liquid; then he added something to make it become white again. So it made me astonished. And because I liked it, I often went to the lab with my father. Since then, I have fallen in love with research."

Following her graduation, Pratiwi attended the University of Indonesia, achieving a degree in medicine in 1976 and a microbiology degree four years later. She then attended the University of Osaka in Japan, researching and writing in Japanese and receiving her doctorate in molecular biology and biotechnology in 1984, following which she returned to Indonesia. The following year she traveled to the Walter Reed Army Research Institute in Washington DC for postdoctoral work in enteric (or intestinal) bacteria research, working with the genomes of bacteria and studying how they evolve and what part they play in transmitting diseases to humans.

In July 1985 a NASA team visited Jakarta to discuss and supervise the selection process for an Indonesian payload specialist who would fly aboard shuttle *Columbia* on mission STS-61H, slated for a 23 June launch the following year. On 1 November the chairman of the Agency for the Assessment and Application of Technology appointed members of a steering committee to determine and oversee the selection criteria in choosing the most suitable candidates for that role. The following month the Indonesian government formally accepted the U.S. offer to allow an Indonesian astronaut to join the shuttle mission in order to assist in the launch of another Indonesian communications satellite.

The satellite in question, Palapa B-3, would replace the US$50 million Palapa B-2, which had strayed from its projected orbit in February 1984, rendering it useless. In carrying out a dramatic and spectacular salvage mission, NASA astronauts had retrieved the wayward satellite on shuttle mission STS-51A. During this tricky operation, spacewalkers Joe Allen and Dale Gardner gave NASA one of its finest moments with their daring manhandling of the giant Palapa B and Westar 6 communications satellites into the vast payload bay of shuttle *Discovery*. Both satellites were returned to Earth, where they were each refurbished for a shuttle journey back into space.

Having accepted with enthusiasm NASA's invitation to fly their own national astronaut, the Indonesian government hurriedly arranged a selection process. They were keen to not only have an Indonesian astronaut aboard the shuttle and assist in the deployment of Palapa B-3 but also take part in a biological program called Indonesian Space Experiments (INSPEX), which would be conducted during the flight.

With a preliminary selection completed, there were 207 candidates, including twenty-five women, out of which only four were nominated as the finalists. Following further evaluation, and in consultation with NASA, the names of the prime and backup payload specialists would then be announced.

Eventually, four names were submitted to NASA, including Pratiwi Sudarmono. The other candidates were Taufik Akbar, an engineer working with the state-owned telecommunications company Perumtel; Bambang Harymurti, son of an air force pilot and a reporter (and now editor in chief) for *Tempo*, an Indonesian weekly newsmagazine; and Capt. M. K. Jusuf, a test pilot at the government-owned Nurtanio aircraft company.

Following a meeting with President Suharto at the president's Jakarta office, Ahmad Tahir—the minister for post, telecommunications, and tourism—announced the names of the four finalists. He said that NASA would put the four through a series of tests and send the results back to the Indonesian government, which would then make the final decision as to who would be the prime and backup candidates.

I asked Pratiwi if she had ever imagined as a youngster that she might one day fly into space and why she had put her name forward as a candidate.

I have never been interested in rockets or astronomy as my prime study, except for reading as an addition to my knowledge. My background of education is doctor in medicine and a PhD in microbiology. So I had no thoughts of flying into space, not until the head of my department asked me to join the team to design the Indonesian space experiments. My research proposal was about the monitoring of the growth of micro-organisms in space, those able to cause a disease.

As the proposal was accepted and was being promoted to become one of the INSPEX, *I became more interested in conducting the research myself in space. That was the reason I applied.*

After all the tests and medical examinations had been concluded and scrutinized by certain members of the Indonesian government, Pratiwi Sudarmono was announced as the prime candidate payload specialist for the flight, with Taufik Akbar to act as her backup. At the time of her selection, she was busy experimenting in genetic engineering and lecturing in microbiology at the University of Indonesia.

"I felt very happy and excited to be selected," she stated. "The Indonesian astronaut in space program became a source of national pride, providing good inspiration to the young generation."

INSPEX eventually comprised a package of five experiments, which ranged from monitoring the growth of human pathogens in space to research on cell differentiation using tadpoles, soy beans, and corn roots. As well, there were experiments on red blood cells and remote sensing of what Sudarmono called an "exotic spot" in Indonesia's Wallace Strait. On a lighter note, she said she was also planning to perform a classic Indonesian dance while weightless in the microgravity of space.

Pratiwi's backup, Taufik Akbar, was born in Medan, Indonesia, on 8 January 1951. He attended the Bandung Institute of Technology, the oldest technology-oriented university in Indonesia, graduating with a telecommunications degree in 1975. While working as a Telkom telecommunication engineer, he was involved in the development of the Palapa satellite system and subsequently worked at Hughes Aircraft in the United States and at the University of Concordia in Montreal, Canada.

16. Taufik Akbar and Pratiwi Sudarmono with a model of the space shuttle. Courtesy NASA.

Space shuttle mission STS-61H was scheduled to be operated by orbiter *Columbia*, with a projected launch date of 24 June 1986 and a landing seven days later on 1 July at the Kennedy Space Center's runway 15. The mission was to have been commanded by Capt. Michael Coats, USN, making his second flight into space, along with rookie shuttle pilot Col. John Blaha, USAF, and three mission specialists—Robert Springer, Anna Fisher, and James Buchli. Pratiwi Sudarmono was one of two payload specialists manifested on the seven-person crew; the other seat on *Columbia*'s middeck would have been occupied by Sqn. Ldr. Nigel Wood, RAF.

Like Sudarmono, Nigel Wood had been one of four final candidates chosen to operate as a payload specialist on STS-61H and received the news that he was the prime candidate for that flight on 25 April 1985. In December 1983 Britain had booked slots in the shuttle timetable for the deployment of a pair of Skynet 4 communications satellites on two separate flights. Wood, who would have become the first Briton in space, was assigned to monitor the deployment of the first satellite, Skynet 4A, from *Columbia*'s payload bay on mission STS-61H. Another member of the Skynet astronaut team, Peter Longhurst, would fly on a separate mission (STS-71D, then scheduled for December 1986) to observe the launch of the second communications satellite, Skynet 4B. His backup was named as Chris Holmes.

With the loss of *Challenger* and its crew in January 1986, four of the five NASA astronauts who were to have flown on STS-61H remained as a crew and would eventually fly as the crew on STS-29 in March 1989, with Anna Fisher being replaced by fellow astronaut James Bagian. However, Sudarmono and Wood both lost their chance to fly, with the loss of *Challenger* and a resultant embargo by NASA on future flights by payload specialists.

The Palapa B-3 satellite also lost its chance to fly aboard the shuttle. Because of lengthy posttragedy delays, it was renamed Palapa B-2P and was reallocated to an unmanned booster, successfully launched into space atop a Delta 3920 rocket on 29 March 1987. Britain's Skynet 4 satellites were shifted over to the European Ariane expendable launch vehicle, and Skynet 4A was launched on 1 January 1990 on a Titan III rocket.

Despite the loss of the shuttle *Challenger*, Sudarmono and Akbar still traveled to Houston as scheduled and underwent payload specialist training from February to May 1986 before returning to Indonesia. During this time, they did not have their own blue flight training suits, so Taufik wore one he borrowed from NASA astronaut Hank Hartsfield, while the one Pratiwi wore (along with her training helmet) had once belonged to Christa McAuliffe, who had been an identical build to her. They had been roommates during Pratiwi's initial visit to Houston to undergo selection tests.

These days Taufik Akbar is still in the space business. After his time as a candidate payload specialist, he continued to work for Telkom, and from 1990 to 1992 he was appointed general manager telecommunication planning. The following year he took on the role of executive general manager for Palapa satellites operation. In 1994 he became president director of Aplikanusa Lintasarta and six years later was announced as its director of human resources.

After returning from Houston, Pratiwi Sudarmono resumed her work as a microbiology researcher, and in 1992 she attained recognition as a clinical microbiology specialist. As a World Health Organization grantee, she was involved in researching the molecular biology of *Salmonella typhi*. In 2001 she worked for a year at the Johns Hopkins University in Baltimore, Maryland, under a scholarship provided by the Fulbright New Century Scholars (NCS) program, which is sponsored by the United States Department of State, Bureau of Educational and Cultural Affairs. Here she conducted collaborative research into tropical diseases. In 2007 she was appointed professor of microbiology in the University of Indonesia's faculty of medicine.

Currently, professor Dr. Sudarmono is the vice dean for education, research, and student affairs at the University of Indonesia and chairperson of the Indonesian Committee on Infectious Disease, Emerging and Reemerging, with a ministerial decree. This includes her responsibilities related to biosafety and biosecurity capacity building in the research institute and university laboratories in Indonesia. She is also a steering committee member of the Indonesian Research Partnership on Infectious Disease (INA-RESPOND) and an executive committee member of the South East Asia Infectious Disease Clinical Research Network (SEAICRN). These days she continues to focus on her career as a microbiologist, primarily studying the causes and effects of typhoid fever and tuberculosis. She also gives lectures, edits three scientific journals, and is frequently asked to attend seminars abroad. As well, she is chairman of the executive board of Himpunan Karya Wanita (the Association of Women's Work), a cross-country co-op that educates and trains women who live in rural Indonesia. Despite her ongoing studies and numerous, nonstop involvements, Pratiwi still manages to maintain a fulfilling home life and today has three grandchildren through her only son, Pandito.

Although she lost out on her ambition to fly into space when that exciting challenge was lost forever in the clear Florida skies on that cold, tragic day in 1986, Dr. Sudarmono realized a much more stellar and important career.

Some years ago, in 1999, I asked Professor Sudarmono when she realized, or was officially informed, that her spaceflight had been canceled, and she responded, "We just knew it—there was no formal letter to the government of Indonesia." In fact, there was nothing until 1997, when the long-held plans were officially abandoned due to the global financial crisis.

In addition, on the question—now moot—as to whether she would still be keen to fly into space if NASA made the call, she responded, "Yes—even though the chance is small now."

9. Countdown to Skynet

Britain's First Astronaut Candidates

We want to explore. We're curious people. Look back over history,
people have put their lives at stake to go out and explore. . . . We
believe in what we're doing. Now it's time to go.

—Eileen Collins

In the latter half of the twentieth century, the word *Skynet* came into prominence through two very different reasons. For movie fans across the planet, Skynet was a rogue computer system utilizing artificial general intelligence in the 1984 blockbuster *The Terminator*, starring Arnold Schwarzenegger. In this popular science fiction thriller, Skynet was developed for the U.S. military as a digital defense system and was eventually given autonomous control over America's entire nuclear weapons arsenal. However, instead of maintaining a defense network, it deliberately initiated a thermonuclear war coupled with killer robots that came close to wiping out all human life on the planet.

By way of contrast, the Skynet military communications satellite system was a very real program developed in the early 1960s on behalf of the British Ministry of Defence (MOD). The first of these military satellites, Skynet 1A, was built in the United States by Philco Ford–Ford Aerospace and launched on a Delta M on 22 November 1969 from Cape Canaveral's Eastern Test Range. The 975-pound satellite was inserted into a geostationary orbit over the Indian Ocean to provide secure and strategic services such as voice, telegraph, and fax communication to the three branches of the British Armed Forces and to NATO forces engaged in coalition tasks in the Middle East.

Over the years, larger British-built Skynet satellites would follow their predecessors into orbit. Then, in January 1984 (coincidentally the same year in which the first *Terminator* movie was released), the MOD announced that it had secured a contract with NASA to launch the Skynet 4A and 4B communications satellites on two separate space shuttle missions. NASA also agreed to train four MOD service candidates to act as prime and backup payload specialists on the two spaceflights. The following month, the MOD formally announced the names of four finalists who would undertake payload specialist training. One was a squadron leader in the Royal Air Force; another, a weapons engineer with the Royal Navy; yet another was an officer of the Royal Signals in the British Army; and the fourth worked as a civilian physicist within the MOD. One of those men, it seemed, was destined to become the first Briton to fly into space.

Britain's Skynet satellite system was conceived during the Cold War years of the 1960s, with the first in a series of military communications satellites, Skynet 1A, launched in November 1969. Nine months later Skynet 1B was similarly launched atop a Delta M rocket from Cape Canaveral, but a failure in the apogee motor left the satellite in a highly elliptical transfer orbit. The next two satellites, Skynet 2A and 2B, were developed and built by Marconi Space and Defence Systems at their plant in Portsmouth, becoming the first satellites built outside the United States or the Soviet Union. Unfortunately, Skynet 2A was lost in an unsuccessful launch attempt atop a Delta 2313 rocket in January 1974. However, the spin-stabilized, 530-pound Skynet 2B was successfully placed into a geosynchronous orbit in November that year and was still operating twenty years later. A further satellite upgrade, Skynet 3, was abandoned due to budget restrictions and decisions to rely on allied assets.

In 1981, British Aerospace had been awarded a $100 million contract to build two larger Skynet 4 satellites (4A and 4B), which would serve a widely dispersed array of stations located on land, on sea, and in the air. These ranged from small man-portable radio sets and aircraft terminals to rugged systems on naval vessels and submarines, as well as large anchor stations on land. Each Skynet 4 satellite had a design lifetime of seven years and a planned weight of some 13,800 pounds at launch. They were equipped with two solar arrays spanning 52.5 feet, giving the spacecraft power equal to 1.2 kilowatts. The communications payloads included three X-band transponders and two UHF transponders.

At first, it was planned that a European Ariane rocket would propel the huge Skynet 4 satellites into a geostationary orbit over the Atlantic, some twenty-two thousand miles above the equator. Back then, however, all the major launchers were suffering from failures and setbacks, and occasionally some extremely valuable and important payloads were being lost. With the recent and successful advent of space shuttle operations, the United States and NASA had mounted a massive drive to impress on potential customers the reliability and cost-effectiveness of the crew-tended, winged orbiters. Once in orbit, fully trained NASA mission specialist astronauts could manually deploy satellites from the shuttle's cavernous payload bay, keeping careful watch until they had been propelled away and into the planned orbit.

Britain's MOD tended to agree that this was the way to go. The Falklands War the previous year had highlighted to defense chiefs the importance of maintaining good communications. The previous Skynet satellite, launched back in 1974, could no longer be relied on to give full service, and Britain had been forced to "borrow" radio channels on an American military satellite in order to stay in touch with its forces in the South Atlantic. The situation was becoming critical. It was therefore felt that the shuttle was a far less risky option for the launch and positioning of crucial payloads into orbit, and a dialog began on the possibility of launching the two Skynet satellites on shuttle missions. Much to the reported chagrin of the Ariane consortium, an agreement to move ahead with the shuttle-based launch was eventually locked in between NASA and the MOD.

On 20 December 1983, well after this launch agreement had been reached, NASA contacted the MOD with an interesting proposition. On the STS-9 mission launched the previous month, two non-NASA crewmembers were aboard shuttle *Columbia*—an American and a German. They were the first to fly in a whole new category of space travelers known as payload specialists, technical experts chosen to accompany specific payloads such as commercial or scientific satellites. There was no requirement for them to be American citizens, and once their participation had been approved by NASA, they would commence mission training, including spacecraft familiarization. Now NASA was looking to extend the payload specialist program.

There was a fundamental difference between the full-time NASA astronaut and a payload specialist. NASA's astronauts were selected as either a pilot or mission specialist and then undertook long and extensive training as they waited—sometimes several years—for assignment to a mission. The payload specialist, on the other hand, started with a specific payload and mission and perceived the shuttle as a launch platform. For them, knowing how to live and operate on the winged spacecraft was a fascinating part of their training, but it was only a part.

Following discussions with the MOD, NASA was now prepared to train and fly British national payload specialists on two separate shuttle flights, primarily to assist in the deployment of the Skynet satellites. This arrangement would include two PAM-D2 upper-stage rockets, intended to boost Skynet 4A and 4B into their geosynchronous orbits. One flight was planned to take place in 1986; and the other, possibly later that year. With those flight reservations in mind, each of the British military forces would be represented in the astronaut selection process, and they began the task of assembling their own shortlist of candidates.

The selection criteria for candidates included an appropriate degree, physical fitness, a mature and stable personality, and "the capability of working as a team member in close confines under the unique stress of space flight." Overall, the pair of candidates chosen for the first mission would spend a total of seventeen weeks at the Johnson Space Center in Houston, Texas. By agreement, this would be completed on a part-time basis over a two-year period of project work, as they were also busy people with duties to attend to at home. While at the Johnson Space Center they would undergo basic training and familiarization with the space shuttle and its many systems. They would also experience the incredible sensation of weightlessness in NASA's KC-135 jet airplane and be fully trained in emergency procedures.

One person who had been heavily involved in the negotiation process with NASA from the outset was Peter Longhurst, a commander in the Royal Navy, who would become a leading candidate for one of the four available positions as a payload specialist.

Peter Longhurst was born in the Middlesex town of Staines on 8 March 1943. Deciding to join the Royal Navy, he spent his midshipman year at sea before attending the Royal Naval Engineering College in Plymouth. After receiving his bachelor's degree, he became a member of the Institute of Electrical Engineers. He was then assigned as a weapons engineer specialist aboard the frigate HMS *Tenby* for two years until 1969. After additional training, he served from 1971 to 1973 aboard another frigate, HMS

Gurkha, and then worked on the Sea Dart program. Later in his career, in 1981, Commander Longhurst joined the MOD's Directorate of Naval Operations Requirements, where he became involved in the Skynet program. Along with his other duties, Longhurst was asked to explore all the possibilities associated with using British payload specialists in the deployment of the Skynet communication satellites and how this development might apply to the operational needs of the Royal Navy.

With the two satellites to be deployed on separate shuttle missions, it was recognized that each flight would require a prime payload specialist and a backup, who would take over in the event of illness or other factors. Therefore, a suitably qualified team of four seemed a good approach. It was then determined within the MOD that each military service should provide one candidate, with the fourth coming from the civil service. The Royal Air Force, Royal Navy, British Army, and civil service were subsequently each handed the responsibility of selecting one of their own for their respective position. The navy chose Peter Longhurst as their representative on the candidate team.

As one of those later selected, RAF squadron leader Nigel Wood said, "I don't know whether the Royal Navy actually ran a selection process or whether they just let Peter get on with it. Either way, he ended up transferring to the Skynet project office in Turnstile House, High Holborn (now a hotel) as the leader of the Skynet payload specialist team."

Somehow, London's ITN Media Company were able to delve into this story, and in January 1984 they reported that Commander Longhurst would be Britain's first person in space. This report did not go down well with the other military services, especially after a Sunday newspaper article presumptuously stated that he had actually appointed himself to the role of astronaut.

In its 22 March 1984 issue, *The New Scientist* magazine also proclaimed Longhurst to be their candidate of choice: "Barring upsets, it is clear that the Navy's man, Cdr. Peter Longhurst, will have the first flight. Apart from anything else, he has been training since 1981, while the other three learnt only weeks ago of their selection."

The British Army's Royal Signals had officially announced their candidate as Anthony Hugh (Tony) Boyle on 6 March. Born in the Worcestershire town of Kidderminster on 18 January 1941, Boyle was commissioned into the Royal Signals from the Royal Military Academy Sandhurst in 1961 and went to St Catharine's College, Cambridge, gaining a first in engineering. As a young officer, he commanded a signals troop on operations in North Borneo. After completing staff training, he joined the MOD in 1973 as a communications and IT expert and was assigned to the development of the army's computer-controlled battlefields communications system. In 1981 he was appointed to command the Ninth Signal Regiment in Cyprus, a radio-monitoring outpost of the Government Communications Headquarters (GCHQ). In March 1984 he was serving as an instructor at the Royal Military College in Shrivenham, Oxfordshire, when the army selected him to participate in the Skynet 4–space shuttle satellite project.

Three years earlier, on 14 April 1981, a thirty-one-year-old British pilot with the Royal Air Force was close to bursting with undisguised excitement as he and his family sheltered underneath the wing of a B-1 bomber jet at the end of a long lake bed runway, trying to avoid the unrelenting heat of the Californian desert. Nigel and Irene Wood and their two daughters, Melanie and Katherine, were standing amid a small gathering of base airmen and other spectators, all eagerly searching the bright-blue skies over Edwards AFB for that elusive first sight of a piloted vehicle returning from space. Two days earlier, *Columbia*, the first space-rated shuttle orbiter, had rocketed into space with NASA astronauts John Young and Robert Crippen on board on the maiden flight of the winged spacecraft. Now, after thirty-six orbits of Earth, it was on its final, unpowered descent, heading for a landing on the dry salt lake bed at Edwards, ready to announce its pending arrival with a double sonic boom.

"Nobody before had ever flown a genuine spaceship and landed it under proper control," Wood later reflected. "We knew it was either going to be a huge moment in history, or a massive disaster." He was not to know it, but in the not too distant future, he would be chosen to fly aboard that same returning shuttle as the first Briton to venture into space.

Nigel Wood was born in Clifton, on the outskirts of York, on 21 July 1949. As a youngster, he went to junior school in Ripon, North Yorkshire, and then completed his schooling at Brockenhurst Grammar School in the New Forest, Hampshire. He was keen to follow the example of his father, Donald, who had served a full career as a pilot in the RAF, including notably flying, in the rank of warrant officer, in the first wave over the English Channel as a glider tug pilot on D-day in 1944.

17. The original Skynet astronauts. *From left*: Nigel Wood (RAF), Tony Boyle (Royal Corps of Signals), Christopher Holmes (Ministry of Defence), and Peter Longhurst (RN). Courtesy NASA.

My dad actually flew two missions on D-Day. On the first, they took off shortly before midnight to tow gliders across the channel to capture the bridges that the Germans might have used to reinforce the area. The weather was very bad, and they were forced lower and lower under the cloud but managed to find the target, and the mission was a success.

On return, they went into the main D-Day briefing but found other crews in their place. On asking what these guys were doing there, they were told that these were the replacement crews—because it was assumed that the first wave would not make it back! Later in the day, the main armada took off in much better weather. This time they climbed up to altitude, and Dad said it was amazing. There was a whole queue of aircraft flying across to France, "and we just joined in behind." He also flew missions into Arnhem during that historic siege—very scary indeed!

When he left school in 1967, Wood was accepted into the RAF's graduate entry scheme on the proviso that he went to university. He applied to the University of Bristol and was accepted on an aeronautical engineering course, winning an open scholarship. On his twentieth birthday, while serving with the RAF, Wood watched in wonder as Neil Armstrong and Edwin "Buzz" Aldrin walked on the dusty surface of the moon. It was a time of amazing advances in spaceflight achievements and technology, as he acknowledged: "I was a Royal Air Force pilot at the time. I'd followed in my father's footsteps and had a pilot's license before I could even drive a car. I never dreamt of being an astronaut. The *Apollo 11* mission happened while I was at Bristol, and I was just as in awe as everyone else. It was the pinnacle of aerospace engineering—and adventure—at the time, but too far removed from life as a student for me to imagine myself there."

In June 1971 Wood was awarded his bachelor of science degree with first-class honors. "I was lucky to have Dr. David Birdsall as my tutor," he later reflected. "He encouraged us to look beyond the confines of the syllabus and the limitations of our work."

The following year, Wood received his wings as an RAF pilot in a ceremony at RAF Cranwell, Lincolnshire. Then, from 1974 to 1976, he completed his first operational tour with the Ninety-Second (East India) Squadron at RAF Gütersloh, then located near the border between East Germany and West Germany, flying the supersonic English Electric Lightning interceptor jet fighter along the edge of the so-called Iron Curtain. He also took part in skillful aerial formation flying with the squadron's Cobra Five at air shows around Germany and Denmark. He was then selected for test pilot training and served as an exchange officer at the French test pilot school at Istres, near Marseilles. While there, he had the chance to fly the Dassault Mirage and SEPECAT Jaguar attack aircraft. In 1978 he received the French test pilot's diploma. Over the next two years, back in England, he served as a test pilot with the Royal Aircraft Establishment at Farnborough, Hampshire, involved in research and development projects.

In October 1980 Flt. Lt. Nigel Wood was selected to take part in another exchange program, this time with the U.S. Air Force. Assigned to the Air Force Flight Test Center at Edwards AFB for the next three years, he brought his wife, Irene, and his daughters, Melanie and Katherine, on this latest adventure. Over the next three years, he would work closely with U.S. Air

Force personnel in advanced aircraft programs and with a number of air force pilots later selected as astronauts. He also became project pilot and project manager for the A-7D Digitac II program. Later, as a squadron leader assigned to the McDonnell Douglas F-15 Eagle Test Force, he flew on and managed several test programs in the all-weather tactical fighter.

Altogether, during his exchange tenure at Edwards, he would manage to watch six shuttle landings, but the first, to him, was always the most memorable.

In 1981 my young family and I watched the first space shuttle land on Earth. It was so tense and dramatic, it's hard to explain. Suddenly, way up in the sky, there was this tiny white triangle. It was the most moving moment. Suddenly we knew they were okay. It came down in an arc and performed this perfect landing right in front of us. It was one of the most emotional moments in my life . . . people were hugging each other, people were in tears. You knew right then that aviation history had been made in front of your eyes.

We were at Edwards from October 1980 to the end of '83 and so had seen the first shuttle landing (and Young and Crippen's endless practices in the shuttle training aircraft beforehand), the first runway landing, first night landing, and so forth. It was all happening right there in front of us on the base. The chance of me ever being involved was, of course, zero.

Then, just as he and his family were preparing to return home to England, he received a telephone call that would change his life forever.

One morning at breakfast towards the end of 1983, the phone rang at home, and this voice said that he was a group captain from the RAF Personnel Management Centre near Gloucester and they were looking for volunteers to go on a shuttle mission. Not having been born yesterday, I didn't believe a word of it and thought it was a windup (not uncommon in the military). But I didn't recognize the voice, and nobody was due to visit us, so I couldn't figure out what the game was. Eventually I told the good group captain that I was highly suspicious, and he understood and took it all in good humor. I asked him to give me his name and office title and then hung up. I called the Personnel Management Centre and asked the operator if there was such a person and then to put me through. They did. "Okay," I said, "now I'm listening!"

The group captain told Wood that a formal agreement had been reached to fly British astronauts on two space shuttle missions, possibly in 1986 and 1987, and wanted to know if he was interested in becoming a candidate. Almost in disbelief, he listened to the details before being asked for his response.

"I said yes! For an aviator it was the most fantastic opportunity you could imagine. When someone says, 'Do you want to go up in the space shuttle?' you don't say no. I put the phone down, looked at Irene, and said, 'They want somebody to fly in space!'"

Wood was now faced with a happy but difficult dilemma. He already had a posting back to RAF Binbrook in Lincolnshire to refresh on Lightnings and become a flight commander on the Fifth Squadron. He knew this was an exceptionally good posting and career opportunity and would have put him back into the operational world after two tours of test flying. "I was very reluctant to give that chance up. Irene and I discussed it over and over, but inevitably, in the end, I could hardly say no to a shot at space!"

While waiting to hear further news, the family finished their packing at the end of his tour at Edwards and headed back to the United Kingdom and his refresher work at RAF Binbrook.

Wood (nowadays a retired air commodore) told the author,

At this time, the RAF was working through its selection process, and I was just one of the candidates. The selection was done with a degree of secrecy, to avoid any public knowledge of who had turned down the offer (if anyone did) and who had not been selected. The idea was that there would just be one announcement from the RAF—with a single name.

The RAF selection went along these lines: The Personnel Management Centre identified likely candidates and called them privately on the phone to see if they were interested. If they said no, that was it and nobody was any the wiser. From this process, a shortlist emerged and was staffed further up the RAF chain of command. As I understand it, there was some debate about whether we were looking for an engineer or aircrew—were we looking for a satellite engineer or an astronaut? So candidates with both backgrounds were considered. I never knew who else was on the shortlist. The final step was a selection board in MOD Whitehall, chaired by no less a figure than the chief of the air staff, Sir Keith Williamson, himself.

I had to go to a number of interviews at MOD in London, so was away from Binbrook from time to time. The RAF senior staff informed the Binbrook station commander what was going on, but no one else knew and the commander told everyone not to ask questions. In fact, my nickname at Binbrook became "Knotty" Wood, because whenever someone asked for me, the reply was usually, "Oh he's not 'ere." But by March 1984 my name came out of the hat, and I left Binbrook and headed to the Skynet office in London.

Nigel Wood does not know why he was the one ultimately selected to represent the RAF, but he feels that he was a low-risk choice. He was both an engineer, with a bachelor of science degree in aeronautical engineering, and a pilot. He had just completed two tours as an experimental test pilot, flying (and in some cases managing) high-tech systems projects. As well, he had just returned from Edwards AFB, where he had been working within the U.S. Air Force. Everything, he assumed, seemed to fit.

On 15 March 1984 British defense minister Michael Heseltine announced the names of the four shuttle-Skynet candidates. They were (as expected) Cdr. Peter Hervey Longhurst, forty-one, of the Royal Navy; Sqn. Ldr. Nigel Richard Wood, thirty-four, of the Royal Air Force; Lt. Col. Anthony Hugh Boyle, forty-three, of the Royal Corps of Signals; and Christopher John Nicholas Holmes, thirty-three, a career civil servant then working in the Skynet office and serving as deputy project manager of the Skynet 4 project. Holmes was very much the right person in the right place at the right time.

The defense minister also stated that the candidates would begin training for the Skynet 4A deployment mission, first in the United Kingdom and then at NASA's Johnson Space Center. Two would then be selected for the first of the Skynet deployment missions, while the two remaining candidates would be assigned to a later space shuttle mission involving the supervision and deployment of the Skynet 4B communications satellite, possibly in late 1986. It was an amazing and interesting time, as Wood recalled.

So we all turned up at Turnstile House into an office within the Skynet program and the MOD Procurement Executive. Peter Longhurst was the senior officer and leader of the team and was therefore very familiar with the satellite project. Chris Holmes was already working within the project, so he just changed desks to join the team and brought a lot of knowledge with him. Tony Boyle and I were the new boys starting from scratch. However, as regards the role of a shuttle payload specialist, we were all starting from scratch.

This was only three years after the first flight of the space shuttle, so the program itself was new—and the concept of payload specialist (PS) even newer. As we came together in '84 to form the Skynet PS team, we all had little knowledge of what the PS role entailed. We realized that, at least in part, it was up to us to define our role. As team leader, Peter was in pole position but we all knew that there was a long way to go before any down-select decision was made. We all took the view that our goal was a successful deployment from shuttle, and as a team, we were all pulling in the same direction. Of course, there was a certain amount of competition and interservice rivalry, but we never let that get in the way.

One of their first actions was to fly to the United States and familiarize themselves with what was expected of them. An exciting facet of this was the chance to play VIP tourist and be shown over the facilities at the Kennedy Space Center and Houston. In Florida they viewed the gigantic Vehicle Assembly Building (VAB) and were fortunate enough to see a shuttle perched on the launchpad. They were permitted to ascend the launch gantry up to the entrance gangway but were not allowed to enter the orbiter itself.

"This made a huge impression on me," Wood revealed. "From the gangway, you could look down the entire length of those two huge rockets and the massive external tank. It seemed vaguely alive. There was no doubt in my mind that this was one serious and very high stakes business. I had flown some of the highest-performance fighter aircraft in the world—but this was on a different scale."

They would also visit Houston to view the facilities available at the Johnson Space Center's Payload Specialist Office and meet many of the support staff there before flying back to England.

Then, on 15 June 1984, the MOD made the dramatic announcement that Tony Boyle had been withdrawn from the astronaut selection process and replaced by Royal Signals major Richard Farrimond, thirty-six, another army communications officer, who flew from his base in Northern Ireland with less than twenty-four hours' notice of his appointment.

"I'd done at least eighteen months of a two-year tour in Londonderry,"

Farrimond told BBC science correspondent Jonathan Amos, "when I got a call from the postings branch to ask me, was I interested in going to the moon?—in those words. The chap probably knew less about space than I did, but it was soon made clear to us what we really had to do."

Tony Boyle had been replaced in the astronaut program due to his former army unit, the Ninth Signal Regiment, being involved in an investigation of a possible Soviet spy ring. According to a United Press International (UPI) report at the time,

> *Eight members of Boyle's former signals unit based in Cyprus, a strategic Western listening post for the Middle East and the Soviet Union, are currently before London courts charged with breaching the Official Secrets Act. Two of the accused served in the regiment while Boyle was commanding officer. Few details of the charges against the soldiers have been disclosed in public. But London newspaper reports early this year [1984] said British intelligence believed a Soviet spy network had used sexy female agents in Cyprus to try to blackmail young soldiers into divulging secret information.*

Nevertheless, MOD officials were quick to emphasize that Boyle himself was not personally involved nor under investigation over this serious matter and had only been withdrawn as investigators felt that rather than have him begin a nine-month training period in America, he should be readily available for close consultation in the subsequent investigation.

Although the sudden loss of Boyle came as a real shock, the other three candidates now welcomed Lieutenant Colonel Farrimond to the team. Like Wood, he was starting from scratch but was keen and willing to learn.

The four candidates were then dispatched to the Johnson Space Center in Houston to undertake extensive and intrusive psychological and medical tests prior to beginning their payload specialist training. "I spent three hours with a psychologist asking all kinds of funny questions," Richard Farrimond recalled, "and it was the first time I have ever had a camera up my backside."

Back home, a good deal of time was spent with the Skynet satellite's manufacturer, British Aerospace, at Stevenage, Hertfordshire. Wood said the people there

> *were immensely helpful and set about teaching us in great detail about the satellite as it would be configured in the payload bay. We had access*

18. The final makeup of the British Skynet astronaut team. *Top row*: Peter Longhurst (*left*) and Richard Farrimond. *Bottom row*: Chris Holmes (*left*) and Nigel Wood. Courtesy NASA.

to the design engineers and so were able to develop a very thorough and accurate understanding of the satellite and its interactions with the shuttle during the trip into orbit and during the deployment. We also spent some time with Marconi, who designed the communications systems for Skynet. Although communications was the raison d'être of Skynet, it was of less relevance to us because we were focused on the launch, not the in-service use of Skynet.

Meanwhile, the first Skynet launch was scheduled for mission STS-61H on 24 June 1986, and the normal procedure for NASA was to form a crew about twelve months ahead of the launch. Working as a team, the Skynet astronauts proposed to the MOD that the selected British crews should be publicly revealed at about the same time. This would allow the first Skynet crew—prime and backup—to begin working with the NASA astronauts from the outset. It would also eliminate the uncertainty within their team as to who was assigned to which flight, to assist in their preparations. The MOD saw the sense in this and agreed.

A decision on the selection of the first Briton in space had been expected to be made public in December 1985, but the announcement now came a lot earlier, on 25 April.

As Nigel Wood recalled, it was a difficult day for the Skynet team: "We were to present ourselves in best uniform to the secretary of state's office to be informed of the decision and then immediately go downstairs for the press conference where we all sat on the stage with Michael Heseltine while he made the announcement. We would then be interviewed by the press."

Just ten minutes before Heseltine made the announcement, he informed Squadron Leader Wood that he had been chosen as the prime payload specialist for the first Skynet deployment mission. Richard Farrimond was named as the backup PS to Wood on STS-61H. Meanwhile, Peter Longhurst was named to fly as the second British astronaut aboard the shuttle *Atlantis* on the STS-71C mission, with Chris Holmes acting as his backup. That flight had a provisional launch schedule of December 1986 or January 1987. After his initial disappointment at not being selected for the first flight, Longhurst was nevertheless happy to know that he was one of the two candidates who would actually get to fly into space. Wood recalled,

> *Needless to say, there were some strong emotions in the room when Michael Heseltine gave us the decision. There was no time to absorb this news or reconcile the changed status of each of us in the team before we were in front of the press. It was fantastic, but it was also kind of an odd moment. We had been a really tight-knit team—all for one, and one for all. And suddenly two of us were going to fly and two weren't, and we hadn't even had a chance to talk to one another before the press conference. This must have been particularly hard for Richard and Chris, who were both disappointed but had to smile for the cameras. Only afterwards were the four of us able to go down to the pub for a few beers and come to terms with the new batting order.*

As Nigel Wood began training for his shuttle mission, so too the publicity surrounding his upcoming flight into space began. Following his selection as the prime payload specialist, television crews started setting up in the back garden of the family home in Fleet, Hampshire, and his family was often asked to take part in interviews. While the four men had previously dealt with any media requests on an ad hoc basis, they now had two full-time public relations officers and were each spending about one day a week on public relations duties.

"My dad was very proud," Wood recalled of that time. "It was all happening, and I was the guy at the tip of the spear." In one such interview with Yorkshire's *Evening Press* newspaper, he said, "I wish the shuttle was outside now and I could go right on to the launch," adding that he was hoping to see the North York Moors from orbit. When asked by a reporter from the *Evening Press* if he would be doing a space walk, Wood laughingly stated that it was unlikely, "unless they throw me out!"

Then the training for the two men began in earnest. Nigel Wood was excited to be in Houston and was impressed by what he saw and experienced there: "In 1984 the space shuttle was still new. I have never seen such focused engineering talent—these guys could literally fly you to the moon. I had twelve months to train and prepare."

The STS-61H crew would be led by mission commander Mike Coats of the USN. John Blaha, USAF, on his first spaceflight, would be the pilot, and the three mission specialists would be two U.S. Marine Corps colonels, Bob Springer and Jim Buchli, together with a medical doctor, Anna Fisher. There would also be another payload specialist who would prepare for the flight—Pratiwi Sudarmono from Indonesia. Wood reflected,

Anna Fisher was the mission specialist assigned to deploy Skynet, and I asked her to think of Richard and I as the Skynet satellite main points of contact. She could call us twenty-four hours a day with any questions or concerns, and we would go find the appropriate design engineer, get the technical facts, and respond in terms of how that affected the shuttle. So to the crew, we were the satellite engineers, and to the British Aerospace team, we were the crew.

Months later, as we worked towards launch date, Anna remarked to me that although she would actually operate the control panel to deploy the satellite from the payload bay, she wanted me to be right behind her in case anything went wrong. That gave me some satisfaction.

Wood recalls that it only took about seventeen weeks in all to learn how to live and work on the shuttle and that he spent some of the rest of his time preparing secondary experiments from UK research establishments. These included a series of six British experiments focusing on the effects of cosmic radiation; changes in hand-eye coordination and adaptation to weightlessness; studies of adhesive bonding; the ability to estimate mass in microgravity; motor skills, including postural control; and ergonomics.

Additionally, Wood and Farrimond received instruction in human physiology, the effects of cosmic rays on equipment, and such things as the shuttle's tricky vacuum toilet and food preparation aboard the shuttle. As described by Wood, "It was mainly about things like how to cook, how to sleep, how to go to the loo, [and] how to use the fire extinguisher."

They also had to learn how to cope with living and working in a weightless environment. Part of this involved taking dizzying parabolic flights on NASA's KC-135 jet aircraft, which gave them bursts of weightlessness sometimes lasting up to nearly a minute within the heavily padded fuselage. "The best fun was our zero-gravity training," Wood stated, "experiencing how to work in weightlessness." It may have been fun for some, zipping like Superman from side to side and performing aerial somersaults, but for others the rollercoaster ride soon caused feelings of nausea. "People were going to the back of the plane and sitting there with a sick bag," he said.

The space shuttle program continued at a furious pace, and all too soon, the calendar clicked over to 1986. In the United Kingdom, excitement began to grow as the flight of Britain's first astronaut, and possibly even the second, drew ever closer. On 12 January, shuttle *Columbia* lifted off from Kennedy launch complex 39A, carrying a crew of seven on what was scheduled as a four-day mission. However, continuing bad weather around the Edwards landing site caused the STS-61C flight to be extended by two days, and it finally touched down at Edwards on 18 January at the end of a highly successful mission, readying the way for the postponed next flight, STS-51L, now scheduled to begin just ten days later.

On that mission, the crew of seven aboard shuttle *Challenger* would include two payload specialists: a dedicated young teacher by the name of Christa McAuliffe, who planned to give educational talks to school students across the United States from orbit, and Greg Jarvis, a spacecraft engineering manager from Hughes. Wood and Farrimond had trained with both of them and their backups, and all had become friends with one another.

It was Tuesday, 28 January 1986, and it seemed likely that shuttle mission STS-51L would face another launch postponement. It was bitterly cold that early morning over Florida, with the temperature reading just 27°F. There had already been calls to delay the launch, with lingering concerns in such freezing conditions about the integrity of the solid rubber O-rings located in the two solid rocket boosters and their ability to guard against dangerous exhaust gas leaks. By midmorning, as the crew began preparations to board *Challenger*, the temperature still hovered just a few degrees above freezing, and they were prepared for yet another postponement of their flight.

Despite the chill and with icicles covering the launch tower, the countdown proceeded. By 11:30 a.m. the temperature had crawled up to 38°F, which was still 13°F below the coldest temperature at which a shuttle had been launched. The crew, now firmly strapped into the orbiter, were ready to launch.

Just eight minutes later *Challenger*'s main engines burst into life, followed shortly after by the ignition of the two solid rocket boosters. Within moments, the veteran shuttle had broken free of the launchpad and was climbing steadily into the bright-blue Florida skies. Then, seventy-three seconds into the flight, the unimaginable happened when *Challenger* was torn apart following a massive explosion in the fuel tank. In the most dramatic and public fashion, the crew was lost in front of television cameras and in full view of millions of viewers at home and in schools across the nation and around the world.

Back home in England, both Wood and Farrimond were shocked when they heard the news. "We lost personal friends, colleagues in other astronauts, and suddenly this marvelous endeavor had come to a horrendous end," Wood later told reporters. "There was the human loss—you knew your mates had been killed. And it was one of those moments, too, when you knew that history had changed dramatically. Not just for me, but for NASA, for the United States, for the space program."

Just days after the loss of *Challenger*, Nigel Wood and Richard Farrimond were flown to the United States for the final stages of shuttle training. With heavy hearts, the Skynet astronauts continued their mission training and remained hopeful that their June flight might still go ahead, although as the weeks went by, it became evident that it would be a long time before the next shuttle left the launchpad. Then flights began to be canceled. In late March came the expected news—the entire space program had been placed on hold, and it would likely be some two years before the shuttle program resumed.

"We carried on preparing," Wood said of that terrible time, "but our mission was put on hold and eventually canceled. It just kind of floated off. Nobody ever said, 'Sorry mate, it's gone.'" At the end of the month, Wood and Farrimond returned to Britain.

In May an MOD spokeswoman said of the Skynet astronauts, "They are returning to military duties since we do not have a firm date for the shuttle launch and the astronauts do not embark on specific mission integration training—how to live aboard the shuttle—until about four or five months before shuttle launch."

On Friday, 3 October 1986, NASA finally announced that its first post-*Challenger* shuttle flight was scheduled for 18 February 1988 and issued a cargo manifest that did not accommodate a paying satellite-launch customer for two and a half years beyond that date. It meant that the first Skynet satellite would not be launched until July 1990.

Still recovering from the tragic loss of the shuttle *Challenger* and its crew, as well as the cancellation of his own spaceflight, a disappointed Squadron Leader Wood resumed his service in the RAF, eventually becoming the RAF's chief test pilot. In 2003 he retired from the RAF in the rank of air commodore.

Following the disbanding of the UK astronaut group, Richard Farrimond returned to active duty with the British Army, commanding a Royal Signals regiment in Germany. Then, after leaving the army, he joined the commercial space industry, initially working as a general manager for British Aerospace Space Systems in Bristol. Later he had key involvement in the Skynet 5 program and was much involved in his company's Australian subsidiary, Auspace. He retired in 2010, stepping down as the United Kingdom's military marketing director at Astrium, Europe's biggest EADS (European Aeronautic Defence and Space) company. He then embarked on a postgraduate master's degree in world history and cultures at King's College, London, titling his dissertation "The History of the U.K.'s Involvement in Human Space Flight." He has also written a book, published by the British Interplanetary Society (BIS) in 2013, similarly titled *Britain and Human Space Flight*. He is now pursuing a history PhD.

Christopher Holmes returned to his duties as Skynet 4's deputy project manager with the MOD. It must have been difficult being so closely involved with the Skynet program—being swept up in all the excitement of training as a payload specialist and the tantalizing prospect of possibly flying into space—and then having to return to desk duties.

Cdr. Peter Longhurst returned to the sea with the Royal Navy. After retiring from the service in 2006, he took up farming in the Somerset village of Seavington St. Michael, where he was an active and popular resident and a valued member of the parish council. He passed away in Taunton, Somerset, on 25 May 2010 and is buried in the grounds of Seavington St. Michael village church, which dates back to the late twelfth century.

Another member of the original Skynet astronauts was lost the following year, when Maj. Gen. Anthony Boyle passed away from cancer in Hereford on 25 October 2011, aged seventy. He was highly regarded throughout UK defense and industry circles for his leadership and knowledge in the field of military communications. From 1992 to 1995 he was the last officer to hold simultaneous appointments as signal officer in chief and director general of communications and information systems. In the New Year's Honours list in 1996, his tireless work was rewarded with his appointment as companion of the Order of the Bath. A funeral service was held in St. Mary's Church in Hay-on-Wye, Herefordshire. Major General Boyle is survived by his wife, Ann, and by their son and two daughters.

Decisions also had to be made on the future of the Skynet 4A and 4B satellites, especially in light of NASA announcing that it would be at least July 1990 before either of the communications satellites could be carried or launched from its orbiters. In the meantime, a rush had begun for companies to build expendable launch vehicles as an alternative for the MOD and other satellite customers. With the shuttle program in its enforced hiatus and Skynet 4A already configured for launch from the shuttle's payload bay, it now had to be adapted for launch atop a Titan III, which took considerable time. As Skynet 4B was still undergoing modifications at the time of the *Challenger* tragedy, it was more easily converted and was actually launched ahead of 4A, on 11 December 1988, aboard a French Ariane rocket. Skynet 4A was finally placed into orbit atop an expendable Titan III rocket on 1 January 1990.

As history recalls, the first Briton in space was a woman, a chemist named Helen Sharman, who was flown to the Russian space station *Mir* aboard the *Soyuz TM-12* spacecraft on 18 May 1991. However, the program in which she was involved, Project Juno, was a commercial enterprise paid for by the Soviet government and a consortium of private companies and was neither backed nor financed by the British government.

Three British-born NASA astronauts would make various journeys through space on both the shuttle and Soyuz spacecraft, joining crews occupying *Mir* and the ISS. Michael Foale, born in Louth, Lincolnshire, carried dual U.S. and British citizenship, with an American mother and a British father, but this meant he could not legitimately claim to be the first Briton in space. This also applied to several spacefarers from other nations holding dual citizenship. Foale managed to journey into space six times, the first as a crewmember aboard STS-45 in 1992. British-born shuttle astronauts Nicholas Patrick and the late Piers Sellers had to take out U.S. citizenship in their preastronaut careers. All three played a part in encouraging UK participation in human spaceflight. Gregory H. Johnson, born in Greater London, England, flew into space twice on shuttle missions in 2008 and 2011, but as his parents were both American citizens, he is not normally included with the above three. Richard Garriott (born in Cambridge and the son of Skylab astronaut Owen Garriott) and Mark Shuttleworth (who held dual British and South African citizenship) also flew to the ISS, but like Helen Sharman, they flew into space as private individuals, having paid to occupy Soyuz seats on their respective spaceflights.

The title of Britain's first-ever *official* astronaut would eventually be claimed by Maj. Timothy Nigel Peake of the British Army Air Corps. On 15 December 2015, after traveling into orbit aboard the Russian *Soyuz TMA-19M* spacecraft, he boarded the ISS after a six-hour flight from the launchpad in Kazakhstan. He had been recruited into the European Space Agency's astronaut team five years earlier. In fact, Wood remembers meeting a young Tim Peake when he joined the British Army Air Corps as a test pilot. "He seemed really pleasant—everything you see on television," he said. But having watched Peake's journey into space on TV, he added that it also brought back some personal sadness: "It's very odd because there are so many flashbacks. You see pictures of Tim and think, 'Crikey, thirty-odd years ago that was me.'"

These days, Nigel Wood runs his own photography and design business. Sadly, his wife, Irene, died of cancer in 2003. He still believes strongly that all manner of benefits—chiefly scientific—are derived from space exploration and that it needs to continue, to inspire and ignite the imaginations of young people, especially scientists and medical professionals. "It gives them something to aspire to," he says with obvious feeling. "And a nation needs to do that—to give people something to aspire to."

As a young man, he certainly saw space travel as the greatest of all opportunities: "It is a frontier of human endeavor. When I was at university, men were going to the moon. And to me, to do things like that, to go and physically walk on the moon, to tackle that final frontier, it was just . . . wow!"

10. Patience, Persistence, and Guts

The Extraordinary Story of Frank K. Ellis

> You will never do anything in this world without courage. It is the
> greatest quality of the mind next to honor.
>
> —Aristotle

For an energized NASA, 1965 was a pivotal year in space exploration, one in which they would finally achieve a technical ascendency over the Soviet Union. In June that year, Maj. Edward White II carried out the first U.S. space walk—or extravehicular activity (EVA), in the NASA lexicon—but was beaten by mere weeks to the honor of being the first person to leave an orbiting spacecraft by cosmonaut Alexei Leonov, drifting around while tethered to his *Voskhod 2* spacecraft. Although the public perception might have been that the United States was trailing Russia in the race to the moon, 1965 was the year in which NASA's Gemini astronauts began carrying out complex rendezvous and docking techniques, crucial in accomplishing President John Kennedy's pledge to land an American astronaut on the moon by the end of the decade. At that time, the Soviet Union did not possess the technical expertise or equipment to match these critical tasks and did not send another cosmonaut into space for another two years.

In the fall of 1965, NASA confirmed that several more astronauts were required to ensure that an adequate number of flight crews were available for the upcoming and projected Apollo missions, as well as other Earth-orbiting missions envisaged in the years beyond the first moon landings. As a result, on 10 September 1965, NASA issued a call for qualified applicants wanting to join the space agency's fifth group of astronauts.

The cutoff date for applications to join NASA's latest astronaut corps was 1 December 1965, by which time 351 suitably qualified aspirants had applied, including six women. One interesting application arrived from a determined young U.S. Navy lieutenant named Frank King Ellis. Aged thirty-two, he was a double amputee who had lost both legs following the crash of a Grumman F-9 Cougar jet fighter that he was piloting three years earlier, on 11 July 1962. Ultimately unsuccessful in his attempt to become a NASA astronaut, his remarkable story is one of indomitable courage, persistence, and sheer defiance and bears similarities to that of the legendary legless British fighter ace, Douglas Bader, whose accident and the loss of his legs did not prevent him flying and leading RAF fighter squadrons over Germany during World War II.

Born in Painesville, Ohio, on 26 July 1933, Frank Ellis was the second oldest in a family of four born to Frances Louise (née King) and James Delmont Ellis. Frank spent his preschool years in Hudson, Ohio, before attending grade school in Clearwater, Florida, and then high school in Oberlin, Ohio, where the family finally settled.

With the draft board breathing down his neck, Ellis decided to join the naval ROTC program at the University of Colorado and hitchhiked his way across to Boulder. After graduating in 1956 with a bachelor of science degree in civil engineering, he also received his commission as a navy ensign on 6 September that year. Ellis had already decided to defer a possible career in engineering, preferring instead to take on flight training, in which he had developed a strong interest. This began on 23 September 1956 at NAS Pensacola, Florida, and he later completed jet fighter training at NAS Memphis, Tennessee.

During this period of his life, he met his future wife, Christine Cecile Robarts; was awarded his wings as a naval aviator on 6 December 1957; and received a promotion to lieutenant (junior grade). In 1958, while serving as an instrument flight instructor on Northrop T-28 jet trainers at Whiting Field in Milton, Florida, he and Chris were married, and their first child, David Alan, was born in July 1959.

Ellis's first fleet duty began in September 1959, taking the young family to San Diego and Hayward, California, where he had been assigned to an all-weather night fighter squadron, VF-21, flying F3H Demons from the carrier USS *Midway* (CVA-41). He received a further promotion to full lieutenant, and the couple celebrated the birth of their second child, Debra Ann, in July 1960.

On his next assignment, Lieutenant Ellis flew a variety of jet aircraft, including the F4H-1 Phantom and the Grumman F-9 Cougar, as a pilot with Aircraft Ferry Squadron 32 (VRF-32), based at NAS North Island, Coronado, San Diego. He was now thinking seriously of ways he could obtain orders to attend the navy's coveted test pilot school based at Patuxent River, Maryland. Beyond that, as it did for any red-blooded jet pilot, NASA's astronaut program beckoned. He dared to dream that one day he might qualify to follow in the footsteps of the Mercury astronauts. It was an exciting and appealing prospect.

On the afternoon of 11 July 1962, following a delivery flight from Norfolk, Virginia, Ellis was commencing a routine landing approach at the naval air station located at Point Mugu in California in an F9F Cougar. His last stop along the way had been at Kirtland AFB, New Mexico, and he was enjoying the last leg of his flight. Being straight out of overhaul and repair, the Cougar he was delivering was flying like a dream. This was supposed to be his last flight until after the birth of their third child, which was imminent. "I felt on top of the world," he reflected. "All of those dreams, however, were about to explode in jet fuel and F9F pieces."

At 3:43 p.m. he contacted the tower at his destination: "Mugu tower, this is navy jet 28229 over Los Angeles for landing. Over." Some eight minutes later he lowered his landing gear, set the flaps, and went to call the tower again, but as he did so, he noticed that the jet's nose had begun dipping down. He called it in: "Mugu tower, 229 at the 180 with gear down and a slight trim malfunction but am under control."

It was then that everything suddenly went bad, and his life was about to change forever. Ellis was calmly adjusting the trim with his control stick when the Cougar suffered a crippling failure in the elevator trim system. Almost instantly, the jet heeled over and began to hurtle nose-down to the ground. Ellis desperately hauled back on the stick, but to no avail, and a crash seemed inevitable. He was still at three hundred feet—high enough to have safely ejected—and he reached for the ejection seat face curtain above his helmet, ready to pull it down to cover and protect his face during the ejection. As he did so, he noticed to his horror that some on-base housing and a trailer camp filled with civilians was directly in the jet's downward flight path. He knew he could not allow an unpiloted airplane to hit this populated area.

Despite the imminent danger to himself, Ellis took his hand away from the face curtain, electing instead to try to steer the wayward jet to a safer region. Reacting instinctively, he raised the landing gear and threw on power, gradually banking away from the trailer park. Following a mighty effort, he finally managed to maneuver the Cougar toward a lemon grove, and only then did he prepare to eject. Unfortunately, he was at an extremely low altitude when he triggered his ejection, later judged to be only 65 feet off the ground, well below the 325-foot minimum point for a safe ejection. As he was jettisoned out of the cockpit, he had a momentary sensation of being hurled into a massive fireball created when his jet slammed into the ground and exploded.

As he flew through the air, still in his ejection seat, hurtling shards of wreckage thrown up from the explosion struck his lower legs. Then the seat finally separated, but even as the parachute streamed out, it quickly collapsed due to the shock wave of the explosion. He finally smashed into a row of eucalyptus trees, which broke his fall somewhat, before tumbling forty-five feet to the ground and landing unconscious in the lemon grove.

The high-speed impact with the trees and ground caused Lieutenant Ellis several severe injuries. His lower back was broken, he had three fractured ribs, and there were minor burns on his face and hands. A rescue helicopter and NAS crash crews were quickly on the scene and attended to the shocked and barely conscious pilot. They saw that his left leg was badly mangled (it was broken in three places), while the right leg had been sliced off some nine inches below the knee. His courageous and selfless actions had undoubtedly saved many lives, but he would now face the fight of his young life to survive.

Ellis said that his first recollection after being transported under police escort to St. John's Catholic Hospital in Oxnard, California, was a Catholic sister in the emergency operating theater asking him for his religion: "I was awake enough to realize the 'last rites' reason behind her question, for without hesitation I replied, 'I'm Protestant, and I'm not going to die anyway!'" Meanwhile his heavily pregnant wife, Christine, was being rushed to the hospital to be by his side.

Although the doctors and surgeons at the hospital early on held out little hope of saving him, Ellis's mighty courage and excellent physical condition saw him through the immediate recovery period, but he admits to wondering why his bed sheet sloped so much from left to right. One day his curiosity got the better of him, and he raised the sheet, only to discover the reason—his right leg was completely missing below the knee. It took a while to sink in, but he later reasoned that a lost lower right leg seemed a relatively small price to pay for his life, when by all rights he should have been killed in the accident.

Two weeks later Ellis's name was removed from the critical list, and there was a reasonable chance his badly damaged left leg might be saved. Now deemed fit enough to travel and accompanied by his pregnant wife, he was taken by ambulance to Point Mugu for air evacuation to San Diego. In the aircraft parking area, his wire stretcher was transferred from the ambulance to a forklift that raised him into the cargo bay of a navy transport aircraft. Ellis recalled, "As the pilot added power for the takeoff roll with me secured in the stretcher lashed to the deck, I looked up at Christine, buckled up in a seat beside me. 'Gee, honey,' I exclaimed, 'it's great to be flying again—even in this capacity.' I suppose that was the first hint of how I would spend the next six years of my life—fighting to return to an unrestricted flight status as a naval aviator."

The thought of one day becoming an astronaut seemed extremely remote and—in the words of the popular song—an impossible dream. Nevertheless, Frank Ellis was a man who dared to dream, and despite the odds, he resolved to overcome his handicap and fly again. Beyond that, given the chance, he was determined to one day ride a rocket into space.

Upon his arrival at Balboa Naval Hospital—again by ambulance—he was greeted by a doctor who had been through his medical records and casually asked what he intended to do now that he could no longer fly. Annoyed, Ellis responded with, "I'm going to be a navy astronaut!" The doctor frowned and said, "Look, Lieutenant, I want to set your thinking straight. You may never walk again." Ellis stiffened at this, looked the doctor straight in the eye, and said with great conviction, "Doctor, with due respect for your rank and your knowledge, I'll walk again. I'll even fly again!"

Just two days later Christine called from her own hospital bed with the happy news that there had been a small but welcome increase in their family, with the birth of a daughter they named Dana Angela. As thrilled as he was with this news, Ellis was becoming increasingly concerned, as the infection in his badly damaged left leg was spreading, causing considerable pain, fever, and weight loss. He knew that the fight to save his leg had likely been lost. "Penicillin injection needles bent on my leathery skin at the rate of five in a row," he reflected. "A body cast had to be cut from me so towels soaked in ice water and alcohol could be placed on my stomach and chest to reduce a 105-degree fever."

At first, Ellis steadfastly refused to take any pain-killing drugs, even though the pain in his left leg was acute. However, he relented after one night when the pain became so intense that he was found repeatedly banging his head against the pillows in agony. The damage to his left leg was now deemed irreparable, and he was advised that it had to be amputated. The operation took place on 14 September.

Charles Jennings was a U.S. Navy corpsman on duty at the time in the Sick Officers Quarters, Surgical Specialties, at the hospital when Lieutenant Ellis had first been admitted. "He still had his left leg in a cast," Jennings said, "but severe staph infection required guillotine amputation and subsequent daily debridement [removal of dead tissue], irrigation, and wound dressing. We called the open wound 'the whale' due to the gaping appearance of the wound as he held it up so I could work on him. Eventually, surgical closure was achieved."

Once his left leg had been amputated, Ellis's physical pain and emotional trauma quickly began to recede. "The amputation itself came as quite a relief after so much fever, loss of weight, immobility, and pain," he later stated.

Following the amputation, the stoic aviator started out on a steady path to recovery, both physically and mentally. "I was just so grateful to be alive," he reflected. "I should have died in the crash, no question." He did not wait for his prostheses to be manufactured; instead, with the help of two hospital corpsmen, he fabricated peg leg pylons made of felt, plaster gauze, sponge rubber, straps, and crutch tips, in order to begin the long, arduous, and painful path to walking again. Once he was allowed to return home, with "some luck, perspiration, and determination" he began training himself to walk on his pylon leg using crutches. In December he was fitted with his first pair of prosthetic artificial legs, carved out of willow.

Two years after the accident, Ellis was awarded the Distinguished Service Cross "for heroism," with the presidential citation reading, "Although sustaining serious injuries, Lieutenant Ellis, by his selfless and decisive action, undoubtedly prevented loss of life and property in the housing area."

Then came his next battle—to regain flight status with the navy. "The navy trained me to be a winner, not a loser," he told *Listen* magazine reporter Eloise Engle. "I only want to serve my country. I'll prove I can do it, too." Not for him was the grim prospect of leaving the navy, giving up flying forever, and living an uncertain future life supplemented by a disability pension. He not only would walk again, he resolved, but would one day take to the skies again.

As he also revealed in a 1963 article for *Life* magazine, "I realized the burden of proof was on me, and that I was going to have to give the brass some pretty dramatic proof before they would let me fly again." A year after the crash and despite being a double amputee with new artificial legs, Frank Ellis began an intensive physical training course. Refusing to bow to his severe handicap, he took up swimming, underwent a tough water survival test, ran obstacle courses, scaled ropes, and even made a demonstration parachute jump from 2,500 feet with the San Diego Sky Divers. "I twisted my 'right ankle' about forty-five degrees on impact," he told *Life*, "but I just took the leg off, twisted the ankle back, and was in business once again."

His determination soon won over understandably cautious navy brass, and he was granted temporary flight status in Service Group 3, albeit only flying dual-control aircraft and only if accompanied by a qualified copilot. He was then assigned to return to duty with VRF-32. One person who knew Frank Ellis well in this period was fellow naval aviator Jack Ferrell. He recalled,

> I was in VRF-32 with Frank in 1963 and 1964. First day that I checked into the squadron, Frank came up to me and introduced himself. He said, "My name is Frank Ellis, and I would like to welcome you to VRF-32. I lost my legs in an aircraft crash a few months ago." Then he turned and walked off without a limp. I said to myself he must have said he had broken his legs. As time went on, I heard the full story and that he was awarded a Distinguished Flying Cross for his courage in staying with his jet fighter until the last second, thus saving countless lives.
>
> My best memory of Frank is when I volunteered to take him as my copilot in a TC-45J (a twin-engine airplane used for training and transportation). Frank and I left NAS North Island on June 12, 1963, bound for NAS Pensacola, where Frank would be evaluated as to whether he

was capable of flying as pilot in command of naval aircraft. The trip was uneventful until we left El Paso and our right engine stared to overspeed. We shut down the engine, feathered the engine, and made a one-engine landing at Midland, Texas.

At Midland, no one knew how to fix the overspeeding propeller. We finally decided to make a normal takeoff putting a load on the right engine, thus keeping the RPM limits within the green lines. When we reached cruise altitude, the engine again oversped. We again shut down the engine and feathered the propeller. We could not hold our altitude, so we would drift down to a lower altitude, restart the engine, put a load on the propeller and climb back to our cruise altitude. We did this until we reached Barksdale AFB and landed. We decided not to write up the airplane, because Frank [was scheduled] to be evaluated at NAS Pensacola. That afternoon, we checked into the BOQ [Bachelor Officer Quarters] and decided to go for a relaxing swim in the base swimming pool. As we arrived, Frank took off his artificial legs and walked out on the diving boards, with his hands and arms doing the walking, and dove off into the water. Needless to say . . . all mouths were gaping open.

The next day, we went out to the TC-45J expecting to do our same routine to NAS Pensacola, and for some reason, the propeller had fixed itself, and we had a normal flight into NAS Pensacola.

As indicated by Jack Ferrell, Ellis was aeronautically evaluated by the Special Board of Flight Surgeons in Pensacola. Following a grueling week of extensive survival, medical, and flight tests in a T-28 Trojan, C-45 Expeditor, and the F-9, the special board recommended that he be returned to flight status in Service Group 2, which only restricted him from aircraft carrier flying. At the end of his report, the board chairman, Capt. Clifford Phoebus, added a two-page addendum. It said, in part,

Lt. Ellis is a truly unique individual in terms of his motivation, his determination and achievements in preparing himself for any and all duties of a Naval Aviator in spite of his amputation handicap and last, but far from least, his superior physical condition. From the physical examination viewpoint, the testimony presented to the Board indicated that Ellis, in spite of his handicap, is a superb pilot. His performance is above average in every respect, and there seems to be no reason to anticipate

*that he would be unable to carry out all the duties of a Naval Aviator
in any kind of aircraft.*

The other good news in his life was the birth of their son Daniel Andrew
in September 1963, rounding out the Ellis family. Apart from the birth of
his baby son, the report gave him the most joyous moments he had known
since his crash sixteen months earlier. At the time, a navy spokesman stated
that if Ellis was successful in his bid, it would be the first time a legless
American pilot had been given flight status. The recommendation of the
board was subsequently sent to the U.S. Bureau of Medicine and Surgery
in Washington DC, where a board of inquiry would adjudicate on the case
for his reinstatement to flight status. Following this, the chief of navy personnel would make a final decision.

For a while, everything seemed to be going well, and then it all began to
unravel once again. In January 1964, along with Lieutenant Commander
Imming, Ellis delivered a Lockheed P-2F Neptune to NAS Jacksonville, Florida, where a message was waiting for him, requiring his immediate return
to NAS North Island. Once there, he was told that not all the hurdles had
been cleared, and he was to report back to Pensacola to go through all the
fitness tests again.

This time the testing would last for a grueling seventeen days and was
far more extensive and demanding. "The flight portion included seven day
and one night flights, netting 10.5 day hours and 1.3 night hours, plus thirty-
eight day, seven night, and four carrier landings," Ellis recalled. "In addition, the survival testing was both more involved and realistic." This time,
as it happened, the results were even more favorable.

In his report, the chief of orthopedics, Lt. Cdr. Edwin M. Hemness, MC,
changed his original recommendation of "not fit for duty involving flying,"
to "fit for flying in Service Group I," which meant solo flying.

As well, Ellis received supportive reports from the investigative pilots.
Concerning his formation flying, check pilot Lt. Jeryl D. Funderburk wrote,
"Lt. Ellis encountered no difficulty with any phase of this flight. As compared to instructors under training, he displayed above-average ability to
control relative motion. The aircraft was well trimmed. He makes nice,
smooth corrections. In short, I consider him a fine aviator in all respects."

Concerning his carrier landings, safety pilot Robert G. Carlson wrote,

19. Lt. Frank Ellis as a bicycle-riding student at Naval Postgraduate School in Monterey, California, and proving that being an amputee did not exclude him from flying high-powered aircraft such as the McDonnell F3H Demon. Courtesy Frank Ellis.

"Prior to qualifying on the carrier, Lt. Ellis received only two periods of practice landings on the field [versus] the normal five periods given to instructors under training. In my opinion, Lt. Ellis' performance both on the field and on the ship was at least as good as that of the average instructor under training, and in many cases superior."

Feeling confident in his abilities and performance, Ellis waited patiently as the board deliberated in an adjoining room. He was then called in to hear the decision, and it was definitely not what he was expecting to hear. Although sympathetic, the chairman said, "Lieutenant Ellis, the board recommends you be returned to a flight status in Service Group 3." As before, this meant only flying dual-control aircraft together with a qualified copilot. On the commercial flight back home to San Diego, he was awash with a range of emotions: anger, frustration, disbelief, doubt, and anxiety over his future.

The final decision, based on the board's recommendation and other factors, was due to come from Washington. Eventually that decision came through in a phone call from Paul Fay Jr., the supportive undersecretary of the navy. It brought the worst possible news; Ellis's temporary Service Group 3 flight status had been made permanent.

Ellis was bitterly disappointed, as he had been striving hard for a solo certification, with the navy's test pilot school as his next goal, followed by trying for NASA's astronaut corps. Nevertheless, he was determined not to give up or to simply accept that he had done his best but fallen short. Looking ahead, his next step was to attend the U.S. Naval Postgraduate School in Monterey, California, undertaking a three-year course in order to achieve his master's degree in aeronautical engineering. He was accepted into the school and commenced his studies in the summer of 1964. He and Christine had purchased a family home in an attractive area of Monterey called Fisherman's Flats, where he could ride a bicycle to and from postgraduate school every day. Undersecretary Fay subsequently wrote to him, saying,

Your recent progress report sounds like the same old Frank Ellis—tenacious, tigerish and talented. As you well know, I admire all your efforts to become restored to full flight status and I sincerely hope that you make the grade. . . . Since postgraduate school puts everyone in a proficiency flight status and you will be there for a couple of years, I think your best move would be to continue in your present status—impressing as many people as you can with your flight abilities—and try for a reclassification of your flight status as you approach the end of your schooling. I have prepared a memorandum for the record, which endorses your return to Group II status upon completion of your postgraduate schooling, providing your flight abilities and physical condition remain what they are. Best wishes for continued successes. I'm confident that your ability and determination will get you into space sometime.

While still undertaking studies at postgraduate school, Ellis—by now something of a minor news celebrity due to his desire to regain his solo certification and one day fly into space—applied to NASA for consideration as a group 5 astronaut. It would have been considered ambitious enough for the young naval aviator to want to return to solo flying, but here was a man who, despite the odds, continually set his sights ever higher. As far back as when he was recovering in a hospital bed, he had resolutely mapped out his future, both in the skies and among the stars. Now it was time to press on to his next goal. After obtaining a copy of the requirements and qualifications for astronaut selection, he found he met them all. There was no mention of the eligibility of amputees.

Observing military protocol, he then called his assignment officer at the navy's Bureau of Personnel (BUPERS) to see if any rules existed that might preclude him from applying. The officer was stunned when he heard what Ellis was planning but promised to make enquiries. The following week, when Ellis checked back, he was told to go ahead—there was no known impediment to prevent him from submitting an application form.

Taking his time, Ellis carefully prepared his application to NASA. Where it asked for his height, he wrote, "Adjustable," and added, "My height is adjustable from four feet eleven inches to any height desired. This depends on the length on my below-knee prostheses. My weight is also adjustable for the same reason, with the minimum value being 135 pounds. This I feel is a highly advantageous feature when considering height and weight limitations for occupants of space vehicles. . . . I have over 2,700 hours of pilot time in 24 different aircraft. I have over 1,000 jet hours in 13 different aircraft including the F-4B [Phantom] and I am presently flying the T-2A [Buckeye]."

In support of his application, Ellis also received a written endorsement from the navy's rear admiral Edward J. O'Donnell, who stated, "Forwarded, highly recommending approval. . . . Lt. Ellis is a highly motivated aviator and his temperament is well suited to the rigorous requirements of an astronaut."

Once the media got wind of his application to NASA, it became an even hotter news story. As he told one reporter at the time, "I heard on the radio the other day that the space agency is looking for qualified aviators under five feet, seven inches. I'm the only pilot who can vary his height from five feet, four inches, to six feet, one inch." He also pointed out that the loss of his legs did not impair his flying ability, and there was no need for legs in the weightlessness of space. "Maybe NASA has a small capsule just big enough for the navy's shortest pilot," he joked in one interview. "I could leave my legs behind on the launching pad."

For the group 5 astronaut intake, NASA required the U.S. Navy to submit the names of aviator applicants they felt were qualified to undergo initial scrutiny and medical clearance.

"I learned that I was one of the 50 pilots selected by the Navy," Ellis later wrote in an article for the spring 1996 edition of *Foundation* magazine. "However, when the list was sent to the Chief of Naval Operations, my name was no longer on it. A letter sent with the list to NASA [by Adm. David L. MacDonald] stated that I was not technically qualified for the astronaut program; but from the standpoint of motivation, background, training and experience, would have ranked number five on the list."

Now that the nation's newspapers were discussing Frank Ellis's bid to become an amputee astronaut, he wanted to assure NASA that his application was genuine: "I flew to the Manned Spacecraft Center in Houston to tell the staff how much I wanted to become an astronaut, but only on my own merits. They were receptive, familiar with my campaign, and willing to consider me just like any other applicant, but only if the navy would return me to Medical Service Group 1. That ended the matter right there, but it sure was worth the try."

One man who did succeed in becoming a group 5 astronaut is retired USAF colonel Al Worden, and he read the book Frank Ellis wrote on his life and experiences, *No Man Walks Alone*. Afterward, Worden, who flew to the moon as the command module pilot on the *Apollo 15* mission, wrote that he was in awe of the man. "Quite a guy," he said. "He is certainly an inspiration; but I can understand why NASA did not take him, with all the other highly qualified guys also applying. There is lots of evidence that a person could function well with no legs. It could be an advantage in space for certain operations but handicapped if doing a space walk because you would need the four-point suspension for stability. So some operations would be okay, but not all required for a flight."

Dee O'Hara had been appointed nurse to the NASA astronauts in the early days of NASA's space program, and she too was mightily impressed with Ellis's courage and tenacity. When asked how she thought he might have fared as an astronaut, she replied, "There is no question being an amputee would not be a problem in space. You don't really need your legs except to push off from the walls and propel yourself. In fact, Joan Vernikos [her former boss] and I talked a number of times about this very same thing. Back then, the term 'outside the box' wasn't part of the NASA lexicon. Perhaps the only issues that might arise would be regarding emergency-egress situations. This guy certainly had the right stuff and more."

Frank Ellis did try on two more occasions—in 1963 and again in 1968—to have his flight status upgraded to solo operation, but the final response came in a letter dated 9 May 1968 from Charles F. Baird, undersecretary of the navy. By this time, Ellis had been elevated in rank to lieutenant commander.

Dear LCDR Ellis,

Your recent visit once again impressed everyone with your conviction and your sincere determination to be placed back on an unrestricted flight status. This impression is certainly consistent with those of many people who have known you throughout your naval career. Your courageous belief that you can overcome your handicap has earned you admiration from many sources, sources that have championed your case.

In the face of such support, it is difficult to again deny you unrestricted flight status. In doing this, the Navy has weighed your personal conviction that you could handle any contingency while flying in an unrestricted status against the measured view of the Bureau of Medicine and Surgery that occasions may well arise that will confront you with unmanageable odds.

The Navy has responsibility for you as a Naval Aviator and in exercising this responsibility, it must consider all risks relevant to you as a person and to the Navy overall. In denying you Service Group I status, it does so because of that responsibility. The Navy has decided that it must lessen the risk by maintaining you in Service Group III. I am sincerely sorry that I could not provide you the answer you so hoped for.

Sincerely,
Charles F. Baird, Under Secretary of the Navy

Frank Ellis would later serve as a management services officer and comptroller at the Naval Air Rework Facility, NAS Jacksonville, Florida, before retiring from the U.S. Navy on 31 October 1968. He then worked in civilian life as a financial planner and later in real estate.

"If I had to give a one-word answer describing why all of this has been so relatively easy for me," he later ventured, "that word would be faith—faith in myself, faith in my family, faith in my friends, faith in our American heritage, and most important, faith in God. No man walks alone."

On Tuesday, 27 December 2016, just six months after I had conducted my long-distance telephone interview with Frank Ellis, he passed away. He had been amazed to hear from someone as far away as Sydney, Australia, and some weeks later, having read my draft article, he sent me a marvelous letter in which he gave his approval with a few minor changes and permission to quote from his published story. A memorial service was held at NAS Pensacola, Florida, two weeks after his passing, on 6 January 2017.

The *Pensacola News Journal* newspaper recorded his many wonderful achievements and renowned tenacity in their unaccredited obituary, which in part stated,

> *As the U.S. Navy's first double amputee to return to active flight status, Frank Ellis is the true epitome of a faithful man. . . . His faith and indomitable spirit touched everyone he knew and his infallible sense of humor and duty guided his actions throughout his life. Frank lived to help others and no task was too much of a burden for him.*
>
> *Frank is survived by his wife [of sixty years], Christine Cecile, who has courageously and faithfully loved him beyond description; his children, David, Debbie, Dana and Danny, and six grandchildren.*

11. Vostok Lady

Pilot and Parachutist Marina Popovich

Without women, we stood in space on one leg only.

—Vladimir Dzhanibekov

At 11:02 a.m. Moscow time on 12 August 1962, a Soviet-built R-7 rocket carrying the *Vostok 4* spacecraft thundered into the sky and ripped a path toward the heavens from a remote launch complex in Tyuratam, carrying thirty-one-year-old Ukrainian-born cosmonaut Maj. Pavel Romanovich Popovich into an elliptical orbit above Earth. He became the eighth person to fly into space and the fourth Soviet cosmonaut. For the very first time, however, a spaceman was not alone in space; less than twenty-four hours earlier Maj. Andrian Grigorievich Nikolayev had been launched into orbit from the same launchpad aboard *Vostok 3*.

Having achieved the desired orbit, Popovich began circumnavigating the globe every 88.5 minutes. Although the two spaceships would never come any closer than three miles before inexorably drifting apart, the world nevertheless stood in awe at this tremendous feat of unmatched precision, at a time when the United States had only just begun launching solo astronauts into orbit.

Three days later the Soviet space spectacular came to a successful conclusion when both cosmonauts fired their retrorockets six minutes apart, reentered the atmosphere, and landed safely south of the town of Karaganda in Kazakhstan, in southern Russia. Even as the Soviet people erupted in joyful celebration at the successful dual spaceflight, the wife of the *Vostok 4* pilot, Marina Popovich, was already making plans of her own. She was a renowned, record-breaking aviator in her own right, and this would soon lead to well-founded speculation that she was about to become the first Soviet woman—indeed, the *first* woman—to travel into space.

Marina Lavrentievna Vasilyevna, the eldest child of a peasant woodcutter, was born on 30 July 1931 in the village of Leonenki, situated within Russia's Smolensk region. In June 1941 her father was ordered to the war front to fight against invading and powerful German forces, tearfully leaving his wife to look after their four children. Following two months of heavy fighting, rapidly advancing enemy forces moved into and occupied the Smolensk region. "The Fascists continuously bombed us," she recalled. "When the Germans invaded the village on motorcycles, [they] fired machine guns at every living thing. Children were burned in the barn." Desperate to escape the invading forces, families hurriedly packed their meagre belongings and evacuated the area. Marina's family moved to Novosibirsk in Siberia, in southern Russia.

Over the next four years, her youthful desire to become a pilot would be fueled by witnessing fierce air battles above her town, intermittent reports of bombings of Smolensk, and her horror at hearing reports of how German troops on the ground were said to be shooting unarmed Soviet pilots parachuting to the earth after their aircraft had been shot down.

When the Great Patriotic War ended and a relative peace reigned once again, Marina was still determined to learn how to fly. After completing grade school in 1947, she applied several times over the next three to four years for a commission in the Soviet air force. Meanwhile, she joined the parachute section of an amateur flying club in Novosibirsk.

At that time, she recalled, the Soviet air force had only three female pilot regiments: one for fighters, one for bombers, and one for transport aircraft. Finally, in desperation after all her applications to join the air force had been flatly rejected, Marina made her way to Moscow and appealed directly to Marshall Kliment Voroshilov, chairman of the Presidium of the Supreme Soviet. He was greatly impressed by her drive and enthusiasm, even though he rightly suspected she was much younger than she claimed to be. A letter was subsequently written to Lt. Gen. Nikolai Kamanin, then the chairman of DOSAAF (in English, the All-Union Voluntary Society for Assistance to the Army, Air Force, and Navy), asking him to give her application a far better hearing and, if he found it suitable, to find a place for her on a flying course.

Kamanin agreed, the application was approved, and Marina was finally permitted to become a trainee pilot. In 1951 she graduated from the Aviation Technical School in Novosibirsk and would later serve in what became the Seregin Regiment, where she piloted Ilyushin Il-14 and Antonov An-26 aircraft, the type from which the first cosmonauts would carry out parachute jumps.

It was at her graduation dance that she first met her future husband Pavel Popovich, who was stationed at a nearby air force station in Siberia. While there was a definite attraction, they drifted apart. By the time they met up again in 1955, she had also graduated from the DOSAAF technical school in Saransk, the Moscow branch of the Kiev Aviation Institute, and the Leningrad Academy of Civil Aviation (Higher Aviation School). There was no separating them this time, and the happy couple were married later that same year. In July 1956 they celebrated the birth of their first child, a daughter they named Natalya Pavlovna.

In a 2007 interview, Marina Popovich recalled that when her husband Pavel was selected for cosmonaut training in 1960, the news not only was a pleasant surprise but also came to them very quickly. So quickly, in fact, that they had to pack their belongings in a matter of minutes, following which the still-bewildered couple were transported to their new living quarters. The cosmonaut trainees and their families were housed initially at the Frunze Central Airfield in Moscow and later in a Moscow apartment block located in nearby Chkalovsky. The accommodation proved to be a great disappointment for many of the fledgling cosmonauts, especially those with wives and young children. When they finally entered their living quarters, they found them bare and unwelcoming; Marina saw no beds nor any other furniture. Here, temporarily, Pavel and Marina had to share a two-room "apartment" with fellow cosmonaut trainee Gherman Titov and his wife, Tamara, while other trainees and their families began occupying other rooms in the Chkalovsky complex.

In her interview, Marina smiled as she recalled that another cosmonaut, Yevgeny Khrunov, did not even have a place to hang his jacket in their allocated space, so he managed to find two nails and hammered them into the wall. Problem solved. Alexei Leonov once described the living quarters allocated to him and his wife, Svetlana, as "bunk beds in the corner of a volleyball court." He said they had to drape newspapers over the net in order to get some privacy, "because another pilot and his wife were sleeping at the other end of the court." They knew better than to complain but were told that things would soon improve.

20. Marina and Pavel Popovich. Author's collection.

At first, there seemed to be no visible glamor attached to the men's selection in the first group of Soviet cosmonauts, which of course—unlike their Mercury astronaut counterparts—was a state top secret. While their husbands went off for initial parachute training in the port city of Engels on the Volga River, Marina Popovich and Tamara Titov decided to team up and earn a little money for domestic necessities. They managed to obtain a floor-polishing machine, which they used to clean other people's floors for a fee of twenty rubles. In this way, they were able to prove their independence to their husbands when they finally returned. Marina would also take the opportunity to enroll in a Moscow flying club and renew her proficiency in aviation. Eventually they would all move into large, individual furnished apartments within the newly constructed cosmonaut training center known as Zvezdny Gorodok, or Star City.

As history records, on 12 April 1961 the first of the cosmonaut group, Yuri Gagarin, became the first person to fly into space when he completed a single orbit of Earth in a flight lasting 108 minutes, before safely parachuting to the ground. Then, on 6 August that year, Gherman Titov was launched into space aboard the *Vostok 2* spacecraft, completing seventeen orbits of Earth before he, too, landed safely. The one serious problem he encountered during his flight was falling prey to what later became known as space adaptation sickness, an embarrassingly common occurrence experienced by many subsequent space travelers, but at the time, it was an unknown ailment. Titov would never fly into space again, although this was also for disciplinary reasons. Some years later it was revealed that he had been involved in a motor accident while driving intoxicated, in which his female passenger was killed. He is said to have fled the scene in a taxi and gone to bed. The whole incident was covered up, but it's true to say that anyone but an extremely famous cosmonaut would have ended up serving a very long jail sentence.

Sometime around December 1961, now swept up in the excitement of space travel, Marina Popovich heard through her husband of a top secret quest to find a suitable female to fly into space and immediately applied for cosmonaut training.

The first mention Nikolai Kamanin made in his diary regarding the possibility of selecting female cosmonauts was dated 24 October 1961. In this, he wrote that following the flight of Yuri Gagarin, he tried to convince Konstantin Vershinin (commander in chief of the Soviet air force), Sergei Korolev (the Soviet space program's legendary chief designer), and Mstislav Keldysh (president of the Soviet Academy of Sciences) to train a group of women for a Vostok mission. In order to justify this, he stated,

1. "Women will definitely fly in space, which is why we already should start preparing for [such flights].
2. We cannot allow that the first woman in space will be American. This would be an insult to the patriotic feelings of Soviet women.
3. The first Soviet woman cosmonaut will be as big an agitator for communism as Gagarin and Titov have turned out to be."

Accordingly, on 30 December 1961, the Central Committee of the Soviet Communist Party approved a proposal from the MOD to select around sixty new cosmonauts the following year, which was to include five women. It later transpired that the selection of the male cosmonauts was deferred until

1963, and the number selected was reduced to just fifteen. But the selection of the five women went ahead as a matter of urgency.

As explained by Tony Quine, a British researcher into early Soviet space activities,

> *The task of finding female candidates was given to* DOSAAF . . . *which was instructed to focus on unmarried women aged under thirty with some aviation experience, but not necessarily pilots. In the event, some candidates were married, or older than thirty, reflecting the difficulties which would be encountered finding enough suitable women. The records of hundreds of parachutists, flying instructors, sports pilots, aerobatic pilots, and the entire national skydiving team were scrutinized. In addition,* DOSAAF *"spotters" were sent to visit aero clubs to identify possible candidates from local records and interview them— presumably without giving too much away. Kamanin hoped to find one hundred candidates, but by mid-January they had only fifty-eight names to consider.*

On 16 January 1962 Kamanin wrote in his diary that "we will consider the files of 58 candidates identified as possible female cosmonauts and select 30–40 whom we will bring to Moscow to place before the Medical Commission and for other tests." Three days later he wrote

> *Yesterday I considered the files of 58 female candidates. Generally disappointed and dissatisfied. Majority are not suitable for our requirements and have been rejected. Only 23 will be brought to Moscow for Medical Tests.* DOSAAF *did not examine their credentials correctly. I told them I needed girls who were young, courageous, physically strong and with experience of a field of aviation, whom we can prepare for a spaceflight in no more than five or six months. The central objective of this accelerated preparation is to ensure that Americans do not beat us to place the first woman into space.*

Tony Quine's deep and ongoing research led him to understand that "of the 23 women brought to Moscow in two groups, either four or five failed the initial medical, and so only 17 (or 18) went forward for further tests. Most of the candidates who remained at this stage have now been identified [see table 4]."

Table 4. First Soviet women cosmonaut candidates

Group 1	Background
Valentina Tereshkova	Club parachutist—Yaroslavl
Irina Solovyeva	National parachute team, USSR
Tatyana Kuznetsova	National parachute team, USSR
Vera Kvasova	Club parachutist—Yaroslavl
Tatyana Yfremova	Not known
Rita Sokolova	Not known
Ludmilla Solovyova	Not known
Valentina Daritcheva	Club parachutist—Yaroslavl
Tatyana Morozitcheva	Club parachutist—Yaroslavl
Anya Pivovorova	Helicopter pilot
Valentina Myzdrikova	Club parachutist—Kursk
Alla Malysheyva	Club parachutist—Kursk
Ludmilla Nikitina	Club parachutist—Kursk
Galina Mosolova	Club parachutist—Kursk
Group 2	**Background**
Valentina Ponomaryeva	Academy of Sciences candidate
Zhanna Yorkina	Club parachutist—Ryazan
Marina Popovich	Test/aerobatic pilot
Valentina Borzenkova	Club parachutist—Orel
Galina Korchuganova	Test/aerobatic pilot
Rosalie Shishina	Test/aerobatic pilot
Inga Ivanova	Club parachutist—Orel
Guinara Berdnikova	Club parachutist—Orel
Alla Ledovskaya	Club parachutist—Orel
Unknown Candidate	Not known

Source: Tony Quine, email correspondence with the author, 9 July 2017.

For the record, there was another female candidate, thus far unidentified, making twenty-four names in all. It is believed she was another member of the parachute group from Orel who failed to turn up for her medical tests. Once the two groups of candidates had undergone extensive medical testing at the Air Force Central Aviation Science Research Hospital in Sokolniki, Moscow, several were deemed unsuitable for further consideration. Others failed the probing physical and psychological tests or did poorly at their interviews. All these failed candidates were told to return home.

The pace with which the process moved forward demonstrates the pressure Kamanin was under to complete the selection process quickly. A diary entry, which Quine cites, was written on 22 February 1962 and reads, "Nine girls from the first batch have passed the tests and we will interview them on the 26th at 1400, and select four or five. . . . It is necessary that they commence training by 1 March if we are going to be able to prepare one for a spaceflight by mid-August."

Eleven candidates, including Popovich, made it through to the next phase, which meant an appearance before the Credentials Commission, the top government commission for cosmonaut selection. It is now known that Popovich was eliminated from the selection process at this stage, with five of her fellow candidates subsequently approved by the commission: Tereshkova, Solovyeva, Ponomaryeva, Kuznetsova, and Yorkina. The following year, on 10 May, Tereshkova would be selected as the prime pilot for the *Vostok 6* mission, with Irina Solovyeva as her backup and Valentina Ponomaryeva filling the role of reserve pilot.

To Popovich's dismay, she firmly believes she was excluded from cosmonaut suitability testing as Col. Nikolai Nikitin, then head of cosmonaut parachute training, was only interested in having proficient parachutists in the squad.

In 2007 Marina talked with some bitterness about the selection process to find the first female cosmonaut and said that Valentina Tereshkova, who eventually launched on the historic spaceflight, had only made twenty-eight parachute jumps when selected out of the five women finalists as the prime candidate. She asserted that Tereshkova might have had an unfair advantage over the other women, as she was by then Colonel Nikitin's lover. In her opinion, another of the five candidates, Irina Solovyeva, would have been "a far better candidate."

If Tereshkova and Nikitin were romantically involved (which Marina's daughter Oksana also regards as true), one can only ponder how the death of Nikolai Nikitin in a parachuting accident on 28 May—his own fault— would have affected Tereshkova. Together with Valeri Bykovsky (*Vostok 5*), Tereshkova attended his funeral on 30 May, and just two days later they were flown to the Tyuratum cosmodrome to begin final launch preparations. As Tony Quine observes, "Kamanin makes a reference to it in his diary and wonders about the effect on Tereshkova's composure, which might have been a veiled reference to the relationship."

Nikolai Kamanin, by now the head of cosmonaut training in the Soviet space program, would later write in his memoirs of Marina's passionate desire to become a cosmonaut, but he commented that her flying seemed to cause some problems for her husband, who was in deep training for the all-important *Vostok 4* mission. Marina said that according to Kamanin, her husband was fully prepared for his mission, but he was having a "difficult time" because she was flying again. As a result, "he screwed up a test and asked to be allowed to repeat it, but that was refused." Consequently, she was virtually ordered to cease her flying activities until after Pavel's spaceflight, "in order not to disturb his concentration." As time went by, there would be further conflicts resulting from her flying activities and his role as a cosmonaut.

Despite these domestic problems, Pavel Popovich was launched aboard *Vostok 4* on 12 August 1962, just a day after his so-called space twin, Andrian Nikolayev, lifted off from the Tyuratam launchpad in his *Vostok 3* spacecraft.

Following the successful tandem mission and with Soviet leaders exultant over the positive propaganda it created, the two cosmonauts were feted around the world. Everyone was eager to know what the next Soviet space spectacular might be, especially as there was a continual and compelling buzz that a woman might be launched within months aboard a Vostok spacecraft. On a trip to Cuba in January 1963, Popovich provoked global interest when he talked to the Havana press before boarding a Soviet airliner bound for Moscow, revealing that everyone would soon know about the first female cosmonaut. However, he refused to be drawn further on his tantalizing statement.

Speculation was now rife as to the identity of this mystery female cosmonaut, and then, on 13 June 1963, informed sources began reporting that a spaceflight by a female cosmonaut was imminent. Further fueling this speculation was an article in *Pravda*, the official Soviet newspaper of the Communist Party, quoting Yuri Gagarin and Gherman Titov as saying that "both sons and daughters of the Soviet Union" were trained and ready to fly into space.

Amid mounting interest, newspaper articles in Western countries even described the woman as "good looking, short, strongly built and in her early twenties," who might even be romantically linked with Andrian Nikolayev, at that time the only bachelor among Russia's four known cosmonauts. Some Western newspapers even announced the mystery cosmonaut candidate as Anna Massevitch, who was at that time the vice president of the Aeronautic Academy of Science in Moscow. A head-and-shoulders photograph of Massevitch accompanying the articles in some global newspapers certainly showed an attractive woman matching that general description. Other speculation then turned to an obvious candidate—a woman known to have strong aviation credentials who just happened to be married to a flown cosmonaut—Marina Lavrentievna Popovich. It seemed to the media the perfect choice for the job.

On 14 July, a day after those speculative reports were published, the world woke to the news that Lt. Col. Valery Bykovsky had been launched into orbit aboard the *Vostok 5* spacecraft. Eleven minutes after leaving the launchpad, he calmly reported to ground control that he was "feeling fine." As the Soviet people cheered this latest space mission, they assumed that something spectacular, akin to the tandem flight of Nikolayev and Popovich some months earlier, was in store. They did not have to wait long; two days later the Tass News Agency proudly announced that "on 16 June 1963, at 12:30 p.m. Moscow time, a spaceship, *Vostok 6*, was launched into orbit . . . piloted, for the first time in history, by a woman citizen of the Soviet Union, Communist Comrade Valentina Vladimirovna Tereshkova."

Tereshkova would complete forty-eight orbits of Earth over three days, although for much of it she felt nauseous and physically uncomfortable. At the end of her journey, she ejected as planned from the *Vostok 6* spacecraft and landed by parachute. The feat was hailed across the world as a great step forward for women in the Soviet Union. Sadly, despite the euphoria her flight created, it would be another nineteen years before another Soviet woman—Svetlana Savitskaya—flew into space.

In 1964 Marina enrolled in the military flight test school in Akhtubinsk, situated by the Volga River in the southeastern Russian Republic. At that time, even though it was informally called a flight "school," military test pilots were trained there via the mentor system, and a formal academic program did not commence operation until the 1970s. In Marina's case, she began her flight training under the guidance of Stepan Anastasovich Mikoyan, the renowned pilot nephew of aircraft designer Artem Mikoyan (the "Mi" in MiG). At that time, Stepan Mikoyan was the commander of Soviet aviation at the Research and Flight Test Institute of Chkalovskaya and Akhtubinsk.

Also in 1964 Marina stubbornly applied once again to become a cosmonaut, in a group aimed at recruiting experienced test pilots to the cosmonaut team. At that time, the qualifying criteria required that an applicant be less than thirty-five years of age, have logged over 1,500 hours flying time, and hold a degree in higher education—all of which she met. The candidates had to complete twenty crucial exams, nineteen of which required a passing grade of five out of five. The other subject, meteorology, only required a passing grade of four. Next followed forty days of grueling tests. Marina felt as though she had done exceptionally well throughout the test period, but when she presented herself for notification, she was told—without any explanation—that she had been unsuccessful in her application. Later, having requested a reason for her exclusion, it was revealed that she had not been considered because she had a child, Natalya, then eight years old. Her husband Pavel was furious when he heard this and demanded to know why she had gone through forty days of difficult testing if it had already been decided beforehand that this was a disqualifying factor. Given this disappointing news and following the advice of academician Boris Rauschenbach, a prominent Soviet physicist and rocket engineer, she felt that it was time to abandon her dream of flying into space like her husband and instead devote her life to military aircraft testing.

In October 1964 speculation grew once again about another Soviet space spectacular, especially gaining momentum after Andrian Nikolayev was quoted in the government-run newspaper *Izvestia* as saying, "A group of cosmonauts are ready for a flight and we will not delay it." Rumors began to strengthen that the next flight might once again involve a woman cosmonaut, and yet again the name of record-breaking aviator Marina Popovich came to the fore. Pavel, probably quite bored with this renewed speculation surrounding his wife, decided to tantalize everyone by saying, "The machine with which she is now familiarizing herself is considerably more powerful than the one in which she set a new speed record two months ago."

In the end, there were no women on the following space mission involving a three-person Voskhod spacecraft, with the crew squeezed into an uncomfortably cramped cabin so small that they did not even wear protective space suits. The highly touted one-day mission in this so-called new-generation spacecraft (basically a gutted Vostok) was an extremely hazardous attempt to overshadow America's upcoming Gemini two-man program for propaganda purposes and could so easily have cost the lives of all three unprotected cosmonauts had there been a mishap.

Marina would go on to fly MiG-15, MiG-17, and MiG-21 fighters and even flew as commander of the Antonov An-12, a four-engine turboprop aircraft. On 19 June 1964, with the rank of first lieutenant, she set a new Fédération Aéronautique Internationale (FAI) closed-circuit class record in a Czech-built L-29 Delfin jet trainer. Flying over a triangular circuit from an airfield near Moscow, she recorded an average speed of approximately 373 mph at an altitude of 16,400 feet.

By now Pavel Popovich was becoming increasingly annoyed and perhaps even a little jealous of his wife's flying aspirations (she actually had more flying hours than he did when he became a cosmonaut). This not only began to cause domestic disputes, but he was also making his strong views on the subject known in the cosmonaut community. Trouble finally erupted on the evening of 11 April 1966 when four cosmonauts—Gagarin, Nikolayev, Popovich, and Viktor Gorbatko—went out for an evening with their respective wives and some family members to entertain a number of delegates to the Twenty-Third Party Congress from Kiev. During the evening, Marina noticed her husband in an unacceptably close embrace with Gorbatko's wife and angrily confronted him. Heated words were exchanged, and then Popovich, possibly a little drunk by this time, allegedly angrily lashed out at his wife. Her brother happened to see this, rushed over, and punched Pavel in the face, giving him a black eye. There was a strong sense of community among the wives of the cosmonauts, and when they heard about this incident, they banded together and wrote a letter of condemnation to Pavel's superiors, strongly denouncing him for striking out at his wife and for his continued efforts to force her into abandoning her own career in aviation. "While I was flying," she admitted, "Pavel Popovich flew out of my life."

Eventually, despite the birth of their second daughter Oksana Pavlovna in 1968, the marriage completely broke down and the couple divorced. Pavel continued with his cosmonaut career and later married Alevtina Oshegova, an economics engineer. In June 1974 he completed a second journey into space along with fellow cosmonaut Yuri Artyukhin aboard the *Soyuz 14* spacecraft, which achieved a successful docking with the *Salyut 3* space station. The two cosmonauts spent two weeks working aboard the orbiting station before undocking and returning to Earth.

For her part, Marina continued to fly and break aviation records. In 1972 she set ten world aviation records as commander of the huge Antonov An-22, a heavy military transport aircraft. On this flight, she piloted the An-22 at just over 368 miles per hour around a 1,240-mile closed circuit, with a 110,000-pound payload. She then flew the aircraft a second time two days later around a 620-mile closed circuit at a speed of just over 378 miles per hour, with the same payload.

Now bearing the rank of colonel in the Soviet air force, Marina Popovich finally left Moscow in 1979 after being invited to join the design bureau of legendary aircraft designer Oleg Antonov as a test pilot in Kiev. In this capacity, she went on to hold 101 world flying records (the vast majority of which she still holds today) and log over six thousand hours flying time in forty different types of aircraft (including helicopters), six of which she flew as a test pilot. She said that she flew all types of Antonov aircraft during her seven years with the design bureau, except for the massive An-124 Ruslan and the An-225 Mriya. The latter aircraft, also a strategic jet cargo plane, is the largest airplane in the skies today, and she had to admit that it was beyond her capabilities. Trying to fly this beast, which required a force of 75 pounds for steering, while the foot pedals required a force of 220 pounds, was something she just could not manage. In her seven years with the Antonov design bureau, she would also walk away from six bad crashes.

Marina was the first Soviet woman to fly faster than Mach 1, reaching a speed of 1,119 miles per hour, becoming the third woman in the world to reach that supersonic milestone, after Jacqueline Cochran and French aviatrix Jacqueline Auriol. In achieving this feat, the foreign press dubbed her with the nickname Madame MiG. At one time, she said her name was put forward to be awarded the Gold Star for Hero of the Soviet Union. But this never materialized, and she said the reason was unknown to her. Like Pavel, she would also marry again, this time to Boris Aleksandrovich Zhikharev, a major general in the Soviet air force and deputy chairman of the Central Committee of the Union of Soviet Officers.

With a PhD in flight technology from Leningrad University and nine published books to her name, Marina traveled the world giving talks as a self-proclaimed expert in unidentified flying objects (UFOs) and related paranormal subjects, in which she had a passionate belief. In her talks, she stated that Russia's military and civilian pilots were covering up over three thousand sightings of UFOs, while the air force and KGB were in possession of pieces of five crashed alien spacecraft that have visited our planet since 1908. She added that analysis of the debris concluded that it was not manufactured on Earth using terrestrial technology.

On 30 November 2017 eighty-six-year-old Marina Popovich died in a hospital in the Krasnodor region of southern Russia. She was buried with full military honors in the Federal Military Memorial Cemetery in Moscow.

Among her numerous awards and accolades, she was made a Hero of Socialist Labor, received the Order of the Red Banner and the Order of the Red Star, the S. P. Korolev Gold Medal, the Fédération Aéronautique Internationale's Great Gold Medal for the distribution of aeronautical knowledge, and was personally presented with her Order of Courage Medal by Vladimir Putin in 2007.

A star in the Cancer constellation also bears her name.

12. With Stars in Her Eyes

Group 19 Mission Specialist Patricia Hilliard Robertson

To be inspired is great, but to inspire is an honor.

—Stacey T. Hunt

Most NASA astronauts, when asked, might easily recall how and when they first developed an abiding interest in airplanes and flying. As well, they can often nominate an inspirational person behind their decision to consider aviation as a career choice. For Patricia Hilliard Robertson, one person stood out above all others in having such an influence in her life. "My father is my hero," she wrote in August 1999. "A hero inspires others. My father inspired me. When we lived in Thailand, my father took us to a B-52 bomber base regularly. I loved to watch those enormous planes take off, but the noise scared me to death. I'm not even sure why I looked forward to those trips. Maybe because my dad loved those airplanes so much. And maybe that's why I love airplanes so much today. My father inspired my love of aviation, my love of space, and my drive to succeed."

Harold Hilliard lived long enough to see his beloved daughter Patricia achieve one of her country's highest honors in June 1998 when the civilian space agency NASA selected her as a mission specialist in the thirty-two-strong astronaut group 17. She would commence her ASCAN training in August that year. To her immense sorrow, her father passed away at the age of seventy-one just a year after she had begun that astronaut training. In hindsight, this turned out to be something of a blessing, as he would never know the heartache of a parent losing a daughter in a tragic accident two years later, just as she was on the verge of achieving her childhood dream.

Patricia Consolatrix Hilliard was born in Indiana County, Pennsylvania, on 12 March 1963 to Harold C. and Ilse Trouda Wilson Hilliard. She would grow up in Homer City, six miles from of the county seat of Indiana, along with her three male siblings: older brother Tim and younger brothers Scott and Keith.

Their father, Harold, had learned courage at the early age of eight when he lost his own father, Heath Hamlyn Hilliard, a mining official who died in a hospital at the age of forty-eight a day after suffering a cerebral hemorrhage. Harold's mother, Elizabeth Mae, now had the daunting task of raising their eight children during the grim and poverty-stricken years of the Depression. "By her example," Patty recalled, "my father learned the importance of hard work, of never letting your cards down, and of never giving up. As a boy of nineteen with no money and no opportunity for further education, he left behind all that was familiar and comfortable, in search of a better life. He traveled to Alaska without a penny in his pocket to work on the Alaska Railroad. He spent the next several years sleeping in a boxcar, working twelve-hour days. He never complained, because the money was good, and he sent money home to his mother regularly."

Later, Harold became involved in the business of international construction and worked most of his career on postings outside of the United States, which involved temporarily living and working in such countries such as Canada, Brazil, British Guiana, Australia, Thailand, and Indonesia—Ilse's homeland, where she and Harold met and were married. This constant travel gave their children a wonderful opportunity to experience the cultures of many different countries, and Patty was happy to spend time living in her mother's native Indonesia.

In 1972, nine years after the birth of their daughter, Harold finally returned to Homer City, where he worked for the Indiana borough as a code enforcement officer, became president-elect of the local Kiwanis Club, and was an active leader in the Boy Scout movement. He was also a member of the Homer City Parks and Recreation Advisory Board.

As they grew up, brothers Tim, Scott, and Keith Hilliard said they always looked up to their sister while at the same time tormenting her. Patty's life was "part hard work, and of course play as hard as you can, and the more the better," Scott Hilliard recalled.

In January 1978 an event took place that aroused significant excitement in Patty, when NASA selected the first group of astronauts specifically tasked with one day crewing missions on the innovative winged space shuttle, which was still in its construction stage. Two things about the selection caught her attention. First, for the very first time, NASA had chosen a number of candidates who were neither professional pilots nor test pilots. They were the trailblazers in a new category of astronaut known as mission specialists, who would carry out a mission's flight plan, including a wide range of experiments, medical studies, and technical operations while in orbit. The second part of the announcement was certainly compelling news for any fourteen-year-old student interested in medicine and aviation, in that six of the selected mission specialists were women, with greatly diverse backgrounds in geology, engineering, chemistry, and biochemistry, while two were physicians. It was a deliciously tempting glimpse into the future of space travel and definitely something to aim for.

Patty graduated from Homer Central High School in 1980. Her cousin Bernadette Hilliard happened to be an English teacher at the high school and recalled that her young relative was a popular and ambitious but modest student. Hilliard was also Patty's cheerleading coach and said that when the squad performed pyramids, Patty always insisted on supporting the other cheerleaders instead of climbing to the top of the pyramid. "She didn't want to go up, and that's kind of ironic, because her love was planes," Bernadette Hilliard said. "She never wanted to go up in cheerleading, but she wanted to fly. After that, she just kept on going higher and higher."

For someone growing up in an era in which the conquest of space was a popular and enthralling topic of conversation and interest, Patty Hilliard was no different than millions of others across the United States as she followed NASA's preparations to launch the first space shuttle into orbit, carrying a crew of two astronauts. On 12 April 1981 she was excited beyond words to watch the shuttle *Columbia* roar away from the launchpad at Cape Canaveral and achieve orbit. A little over fifty-four hours later, having completed thirty-seven orbits of Earth, *Columbia* successfully reentered the atmosphere and glided down to a perfect touchdown on runway 23 at Edwards AFB, California. The two astronauts, John Young and Bob Crippen, were widely praised for their boldness and courage in flying a NASA spacecraft that had not been previously launched on an unmanned test flight. It was an enthralling event in spaceflight history. More than ever before, Patty's youthful dream of one day flying into space began to grow and evolve into a determination.

Completing her undergraduate studies at Indiana University of Pennsylvania, Patty was awarded her bachelor of science degree in biology in 1985. Fellow medical student Beth Shepherd first met her when they enrolled at the same time at the Philadelphia College of Osteopathic Medicine, a private, nonprofit graduate college, in the spring of 1985. They got on well and agreed to look at an apartment that day, becoming roommates for the next four years. This remained the situation even when Patty transferred to the Medical College of Pennsylvania. "Patty and I studied hard, but let me tell you, we also played hard," Shepherd said, recalling that her friend taught her to windsurf and the basics of downhill skiing, even taking her home to Homer City for a ski trip in western Pennsylvania. Keith Hilliard remembered his sister honing that love of skiing in Indiana, saying he learned the sport from her at the College Lodge slope in White Township. He even said the bumper sticker on her car read, "Don't postpone joy." And that, he reflected, was the motto by which she lived.

While studying at the Medical College of Pennsylvania, Patty was a member of the American Medical Student Association and the American Medical Association.

On receiving her degree from the medical college in 1989, there were new worlds to conquer for the keen twenty-six-year-old student, and she began a three-year residency in family medicine. In 1992 she was awarded her certification from the American Board of Family Practice. Now, having achieved her medical degree, she also earned her pilot's license from Dr. David Dulabon, a urologist who also happened to be a flight instructor.

It was during this time that Patty met real estate agent Greg Gordon. They were married on 19 September 1992, but it turned out to be a short-lived marriage, ending in divorce. There was no animosity involved; they simply fell out of love and agreed to go their separate ways. She subsequently worked as a family practitioner in Erie, Pennsylvania, became a member of the staff of nearby St. Vincent Hospital, and served as the clinical coordinator for medical student training. Patty was also involved in training and supervising resident physicians. Then, until 1995, she was a family practitioner at the Elk Valley Medical Center in Girard, Pennsylvania.

After being awarded a two-year space medicine fellowship at the University of Texas Medical Branch in Galveston, Patty finally left her home state. She was one of only two students selected for the fellowship. During her time at the university, according to her May 2001 NASA profile, she studied "eccentric and concentric resistive exercise countermeasures for space flight," on which her research project was based. She also worked on staff as a member of the Departments of Family Medicine and Emergency Medicine.

The space medicine fellowship, which included an aerospace medicine primary course at Brooks AFB in San Antonio, Texas, ended in 1997. Patty then joined NASA's Flight Medicine Clinic at the Lyndon B. Johnson Space Center in Houston. Here she provided health care for the astronauts and their families and served as chairperson to the Bone, Muscle, and Exercise Integrated Product Team. In May of that year, she became engaged to Scott Robertson, a Houston-based commercial pilot with Continental Airlines.

Knowing she now had a reasonable chance of being selected as a mission specialist in NASA's astronaut corps, Patty waited until the space agency issued a call for a new class of astronaut candidates, which came about early in 1998. She immediately posted in her application, meticulously listing all her medical and flight qualifications and experience. Detailed background checks, extensive interviews, and medical checkups ensued, and then it was time to wait for the result.

"My father is not a religious man, but he is a spiritual man," she once said of the anxious time she spent hoping for a life-changing call from the space agency. "As I waited for what seemed an eternity to hear from the astronaut selection board at NASA, my father would offer me this: 'Pat, I'll send a prayer that you get selected. He doesn't hear from me often, so he may just answer this time.' Well, God answered, and my dream to become an astronaut came true."

In June of that same year, her telephone did indeed ring, and it was the best possible news. NASA had selected her as an astronaut candidate to become a mission specialist, and she would begin her training in Houston in August. Her fiancé, Scott, was elated, and her mother, Ilse, recalls Patty calling her and screaming with joy into the telephone after receiving the news of her selection. "Mom—I made it!" she cried. "It was just so exciting," Ilse Hilliard said. "I could see her jumping up and down."

Dr. Patricia Hilliard was now a member of the seventeenth group of NASA astronauts chosen by the civilian space agency since 1959. In a tradition handed down from one astronaut group to the next, they were quickly

21. Patty Hilliard's official NASA portrait, taken after she had commenced her astronaut training. Courtesy NASA.

and whimsically dubbed "the Dodos" (as extinct flightless birds) by the previous large astronaut group, who had themselves been saddled with the name "the Sardines." The new group of thirty-two astronauts—also a large increment to astronaut numbers—rebelled against their given nickname, however, and humorously rebranded themselves "the Penguins," after a flightless bird that eats fish.

Patty was one of just four women in her astronaut class of thirty-two when they all came together for training. The other three were Suni Williams, Tracy Caldwell, and Barbara Morgan, who had once served as the teacher backup to Christa McAuliffe, lost in the *Challenger* tragedy in 1986. "All three of us got a lot of strength from Patty," Caldwell once recalled, "because she grew up with three brothers," adding that Patty drew from her roots to fill the familiar role of big sister to them. The four women decided to call themselves "the Spice Girls," with forty-six-year-old Barbara Morgan grudgingly accepting the dubious title of Old Spice.

During her early astronaut training, Patty also became good friends with Indian-born mission specialist Kalpana Chawla, who was affectionately known to everyone as KC. Prior to her selection for astronaut training, Patty had provided medical care for the astronauts and their families, and this involved being KC's physician. Chawla held a certificated flight instructor rating for airplanes, gliders, and commercial pilot licenses for single and multiengine airplanes, seaplanes, and gliders, so she and Patty had much in common and quickly became good friends. Chawla had joined the astronaut corps in March 1995 and flew into space for the first time as a mission specialist on STS-87 aboard the shuttle *Columbia* in November 1997. Less than six years later she would meet a tragic death along with six fellow astronauts aboard the ill-fated STS-107 flight of *Columbia*, which was torn apart during a fiery reentry in February 2003.

Once she began her orientation and mission specialist training, Patty's days were comprised of scientific and technical briefings, as well as lectures and hands-on instruction pertinent to life and work aboard the ISS and space shuttle systems. There was much to learn and prepare for, but one facet of being an astronaut that she thoroughly enjoyed was the chance to receive instruction in the renowned jet-powered steed that other astronauts had jockeyed across the country for several past decades—the nimble, supersonic Northrop T-38 Talon. Physiological training was also covered, and in the event of a problem during launch and landing, the new astronauts had to learn wilderness and water survival skills.

Among her technical assignments, Patty served as the office representative for the Crew Healthcare System and as crew support astronaut for the ISS Expedition 2 crew of mission commander Yuri Usachev, from the Russian space program, along with U.S. astronauts James Voss and Susan

Helms. This assignment meant attending meetings to represent all three members of the Expedition 2 crew and coordinating their activities, as well as assisting with communication between the astronaut crew and NASA's staff and technicians.

At the completion of their twelve-month ASCAN program, Patty and her astronaut class had qualified to become regular members of the astronaut corps. The pilots in her group and all the mission specialists were now eligible for an assignment to future shuttle and ISS missions. Some would even get to fly to the ISS aboard Russian Soyuz spacecraft. In her role as a mission specialist on a future crew, she would be responsible, among numerous other duties, for coordinating onboard operations such as crew activity planning and the monitoring of the shuttle's consumables such as food, water, and fuel. She would also perform a number of experiments, be responsible for handling functions involving payload support equipment, and might even one day venture outside the ISS on a space walk.

In June 1999, following her graduation to astronaut status, Patty married Scott Robertson. By this time, in addition to being a medical doctor, she was a multiengine-rated flight instructor and keen aerobatic pilot with more than 1,500 hours of flight time. In her free time away from NASA, she enjoyed flight instructing, aerobatics, and flying with her husband. Scott Robertson told one reporter that he regarded her as a "wife, homemaker, pilot, mentor, and hero." A commercial pilot himself, he mentioned a potentially awkward occasion when he had a meeting with a crop duster, and while they were discussing flying matters, Patty joined them. The crop duster turned to her and asked in all innocence, "Well, little lady, what do you do while your husband is out flying the friendly skies?" Scott's astronaut wife merely shrugged and laconically replied, "Of course, I sit at home, bake cookies, and wait on my husband." It is a fond memory that still brings a smile.

During her time with NASA, Patty Robertson received the NASA Performance Award and the Young Investigator Award from the Aerospace Medicine Association. She was also involved with the Aircraft Owners and Pilots Association, the American Association of Family Practice, the Experimental Aircraft Association, and the International Aerobatic Club.

In 2000 Dr. Patricia Hilliard Robertson was honored to be the recipient of the Indiana University of Pennsylvania Distinguished Alumni Award.

On 3 June of that year, she was the featured speaker for the Stand for Children event at the Indiana County Court House. In her inspirational talk, she said her success should serve as an example for young people to pursue: "The sky's the limit. If *I* can do it, *anyone* can. Hang tight to your dreams; believe in your dreams."

Informally, it seemed as if Patty Robertson was going to fly to the ISS in 2002, although an official crewing manifest and launch schedule had yet to be announced by NASA. Family members understood that she had been unofficially assigned to a spaceflight mission, and everyone was just waiting for confirmation.

It was Tuesday, 22 May 2001. That afternoon, Patty Robertson was at the Wolfe Airpark (Federal Aviation Administration identifier 3T2) in Manvel, Texas, about twenty miles south of Houston. She was preparing to take a flight aboard a two-seat, fixed-wing, single-engine Gideon Wittman Tailwind W8, an experimental, amateur-built monoplane, registration number N3GJ. Patty and Scott were in the middle of assembling one of the lightweight, two-seat aircraft for their own recreational use, and that day she was looking forward to a test ride in a similar airplane in order to check its flying characteristics along with the owner, forty-six-year-old Roy Mack Paul Adams from Alvin, Texas.

According to the airplane's maintenance records, Adams's Tailwind had journeyed to the United States from Canada in July 2000, with an accumulated flight total of 358 hours. That same month, the airframe and engine had undergone a detailed inspection. On 8 August the Federal Aviation Administration issued the airplane with a special airworthiness certificate.

In its later accident report, the National Transportation Safety Board stated that by this time, Patty Robertson "had accumulated a total of 1,652.7 flight hours, of which 319.2 were in tail wheel equipped aircraft, and 356.4 were as a flight instructor." This compared with Roy Adams, who only had "94.9 flight hours of which 2.0 hours was in the accident aircraft."

Scott Robertson told the author that he disputes the wording of the National Transportation Safety Board accident report, which wrongly stated that his wife was acting as a flight instructor on that fateful day. "There was *no* flight instruction being given by Patty to Roy," he stressed. "It was simply a familiarization ride in his airplane, which was the same type of Tailwind that we were building."

Weather-wise, it was a perfect day for flying—warm and sunny with clear conditions, visibility up to ten statute miles, and a light, ten-knot wind blowing out of the north. Late that afternoon, according to later witness reports, the airplane executed several touch-and-go landings on runway 2. In this exercise, the airplane would land, accelerate for takeoff, and lift off the ground some 600–700 feet from the departure end of the 2,190-foot grass runway.

At approximately 6:00 p.m., central daylight time, the airplane rose once again from the grass runway on its fourth takeoff run and began flying just twenty feet above ground level. According to the Texas Department of Public Safety, Adams was flying the airplane. Witness accounts later stated that the right wing "dropped slightly and corrected back to level." The airplane was then heard throwing on additional power, at which point "the right wing dropped to about a forty-five-degree angle, stopped slightly, and then continued to drop to a full ninety-degree down position."

Moments later, the right wing clipped the ground, and the airplane immediately began to cartwheel, coming to rest against a tree forty feet beyond the departure end of the runway, in a near ninety-degree nose-down attitude. The fuel tank ruptured, and the airplane, with its wooden wings and fabric covering, was rapidly consumed by fire.

Incredibly, the two pilots managed to scramble out of the burning airplane, although their clothing was alight. A nearby witness ran over with a fire extinguisher and quickly doused the flames on their clothes. Soon after, the Manvel Fire Department arrived on the scene. Incredibly, it was reported that after their flames had been extinguished, Robertson and Adams were alert and talking to each other, even though they may have been suffering deep shock in addition to their terrible burns. One report even stated that Patty gave the witness her husband's telephone number to call.

Both pilots were in a critical condition and had sustained multiple injuries, with Robertson suffering second- and third-degree burns over 90 percent of her body. Roy Adams was airlifted by helicopter to the Memorial Hermann Hospital in downtown Houston, while Patty was loaded into an ambulance and transported to the same hospital for emergency treatment.

Meanwhile, Scott Robertson was enjoying a break between flying duties and was out in his garage happily working on the wing of their own Wittman Tailwind. Earlier that day, Patty had been involved in some local proficiency flying in a T-38 with fellow astronaut Frank Culbertson. After signing off, she had picked up some lunch items from a restaurant on the way home, which she and Scott had shared. She then left for Wolfe Airpark to meet up with pilot Roy Adams. Sometime later that afternoon the phone rang.

It was a gentleman at the airport, and once he made sure I was Scott Robertson, he told me there had been an accident and fire, and the pilot was being taken to hospital by helicopter, while my wife was being transported by ambulance to Memorial Hermann Hospital. Being an eternal optimist, I figured that if she was in an ambulance, perhaps things might not be that bad. I just didn't know at the time. After I'd hung up, I ran to the end of our driveway and flagged down a car driving down the street. The lady kindly gave me a ride to a friend's place where I knocked on the door and said there'd been some sort of accident at the airport and we needed to go downtown to the hospital.

We actually got to the hospital ahead of the ambulance. As I'm sitting in the waiting room, who should show up as the trauma doctor in charge but Dr. "Red" Duke, who had found fame on television for his ten-minute health segments, which I had often watched. I knew that if he was in attendance, anyone's chances of survival had to be much better, because by now I had also realized just how serious the situation had become. I was also introduced to the doctor who would be dealing with the burns Patty had suffered, plastic surgeon Dr. David Wainwright. He had been playing a game of rugby when the urgent call came in, and he was still wearing his rugby outfit.

Eventually I was allowed to spend a couple of minutes with Patty in the emergency room, and the only part of her body that was exposed was her head. I was so shocked and afraid that I don't even recall what we said to each other, but it was obviously not about the accident. It was tough—very tough—trying to discuss things and come to some resolutions in just two minutes before I had to leave her in the hands of the doctors. It was all so sudden—going from a wonderful married life to suddenly living through this horrible thing. It was devastating—at best, a very, very bad day.

Two days later, on 24 May 2001, Patty Robertson finally succumbed to the shock associated with her terrible burn injuries. Scott was alone at her bedside, and he knew that the end was near. She was unconscious and slowly slipping away. His tears were flowing freely as he whispered to her that her family and friends were all right there with him. "In our last moments together, I told her she was ultimately in command and we all agreed that if she felt like she needed to go, then we all supported her decision. Within five minutes she had gone."

The following day, the space agency was in mourning for the much-loved thirty-eight-year-old astronaut, whose enthusiasm and friendship would be sorely missed by everyone. That morning, the flags at the Johnson Space Center were flown at half-mast. "We're grieving at the loss of one of our own. It's a sad day," NASA representative John Ira Petty stated. "We're still praying for the health of the pilot that was flying with Patty."

Roy Adams, also critically burned in the accident, later died as a result of his horrific injuries. Of necessity, he had been transferred from the Hermann Hospital burn ward to the University of Texas Medical Branch in Galveston as a result of Tropical Storm Allison, which had dumped torrential rain over several days and caused flooding at the Houston medical center.

On Tuesday, 29 May, a week after the crash, a somber memorial service was held at Ellington Field, close to the Johnson Space Center. This was followed by a tree-planting ceremony at the center's memorial tree grove, observing a NASA tradition whereby a live oak tree is planted for each fallen astronaut. During the memorial service, NASA astronauts in four glistening T-38 jets performed an overflight above Ellington Field, breaking into a missing man formation in homage to the nation's latest lost astronaut.

A private family service for Patty followed on 19 June at the St. Thomas More University Parish, Indiana, Pennsylvania. Among the space agency's representatives at the family memorial service were female astronauts Laurel Clark and Kalpana Chawla. Sadly, both women would die in the loss of the shuttle *Columbia* in February 2003. During the memorial service, on behalf of herself and Kalpana Chawla, an emotional Laurel Clark read out the wistful poem "Do Not Stand at My Grave and Weep" by Mary Elizabeth Frye.

Fellow astronaut Frank Culbertson was also at the family memorial service and told reporters that he had attended both as a friend and to represent NASA management in Houston. "I have a third purpose," he said, "and that is to represent Patty's male friends." He mentioned that even though men tended to dominate the astronaut ranks, Patty Robertson continually proved herself an equal. Culbertson said that those at NASA who had selected Robertson to be an astronaut felt her loss deeply. "Of course, they had big plans for her in flying in space," he added. She was a flying partner, and Culbertson spoke of one shared trip in a T-38 jet in which they played among the clouds at fifteen thousand feet, treating them "like mountains, valleys, dragons, whatever you want." On the morning of the accident, Culbertson said Robertson had a "tremendous flight" in a T-38. "Every time I fly a T-38, I think of Patty," he said, "and when I fly to the International Space Station, I'll take a bit of Patty with me."

Similarly, fellow flight surgeon and astronaut Mike Barratt later put his feelings to paper.

> *I was on the interview committee when Patty came through as an applicant to the Space Medicine Fellowship in 1995. She was a clear top choice with all the academics, clinical experience, aviation background and genuine affability and warmth. I was only sorry we could not hold on to her longer; however, Patty took the pride of Medical Operations to the astronaut corps when she was selected to the 1998 class.*
>
> *There has been no one I have known with such a passion to fly as Patty; she had said many times that she would rather fly than do almost anything else. Whether aerobatics in her Pitts, bag rides in the T-38, or taking a new student for an intro flight, Patty lived on life and airspeed.*

Prior to the NASA memorial service, NASA administrator Daniel Goldin and Rep. John Murtha (D-PA) cowrote a letter to the editor of the *Indiana Gazette* newspaper, adding their praise for Patty's contributions to her community, country, and fellow citizens.

> *Every community in America has people who are able to dream big dreams and fulfill those aspirations to the pride of their family, friends and community. These people inspire us, lead us and teach us more about the people we can all be. Homer City's Patty Hilliard Robertson was one of those people. A physician, aviator and NASA astronaut, Patty was a unique breed among her peers. The poem "The Road Not Taken" by Robert Frost contains the words, "Two roads diverged in a wood, and I, I took the one less traveled by, And that has made all the difference." With technical and scientific gifts that enabled her to follow any road, she took the road less*

traveled and made all the difference to those who knew her. Skill, proficiency and balance are a challenge for anyone in professional life, but to combine the talents she possessed takes a unique person.

As a flight surgeon at NASA's Johnson Space Center, Patty demonstrated her gifts with pilots and astronauts by preparing them for physical challenges that would test their bodies' limits. She understood that for a shuttle crew to do its job and for the National Aeronautics and Space Administration to fulfill its space-flight ambitions, you had to be prepared to accept challenges in every form. Such care and competence instill comfort and confidence in patients, and flight crews knew Patty had their every interest at heart.

As much as she enjoyed preparing our nation's space pioneers for flight, her love of aviation took her quest for challenges to new heights. An accomplished aerobatic pilot, her greatest talent and reward came from teaching people how to fly. Her patience with her flight students, as with her patients, helped to instill in them confidence to reach for new heights, not just in an aircraft but also within themselves. When you merge the love of medicine with a quest for flight and choose to take those talents beyond the Earth, it becomes apparent how unique Patty was. Astronaut physicians are unique people. Patty and her colleagues are the people who will make it possible for future space flight crews to stay aboard the International Space Station for long duration missions. They make it possible for us to travel one day back to the moon and stay there. More importantly, they make the first step on Mars possible within the next two decades.

Patty's work with her fellow physicians and astronauts has helped NASA to begin these paths and her passing leaves America's space efforts with a void that will be difficult to fill. There is no one legacy for people such as these. Patty accomplished all of these feats not because they were her job or she was trained to do them, but because they were a part of her. Her quiet poise and focused spirit for sharing the next great challenge serve as a tireless inspiration to all. There will always be people among us who reach for the stars. Others, by nature of who they are, bring the stars into our lives and help us to reach them along our way.

Patty Hilliard Robertson achieved many goals by nature of who she was and what she did with her talents. By taking the road less traveled she made a difference here on Earth and beyond. [Signed] Daniel S. Goldin, NASA administrator, [and] U.S. Rep. John Murtha, D-Johnstown

22. Taken aboard the International Space Station on 18 August 2007, STS-118 mission specialists Barbara Morgan (*left*) and Tracy Caldwell pose with a photo of fellow group 19 astronauts Clay Anderson and Sunita Williams. A photo of their lost classmate Patty Robertson, along with the name badge from her flight suit, adorns the wall behind them. Courtesy NASA.

Following her loss, several institutions recognized Patty's life through a number of programs. In May 2003 the Graduate School of Biomedical Sciences at the University of Texas Medical Branch in Galveston posthumously awarded her a master of medical science degree in preventive medicine and community health. Her husband, Scott, gratefully accepted the degree on her behalf.

The Indiana University of Pennsylvania now awards an annual Patricia Hilliard Robertson Memorial Scholarship for Outstanding Female Science Student at the university. The scholarship was established by Ilse Hilliard as a living legacy for her daughter and provides financial support to a full-time student who has earned at least forty-eight credits toward a degree in the natural or physical sciences. Like her daughter, Ilse Hilliard is a person who follows her dreams. Today she is a retired professor of sociology at Indiana University of Pennsylvania, where she earned her bachelor's and master's degrees, and received her master of arts degree at Pennsylvania's St. Vincent Seminary in 2006.

Also in her memory, the Patricia Hilliard Robertson Center for Aviation Medicine was formally dedicated at the Indiana Regional Medical Center. Operated by the Indiana Regional Medical Center's Occupational Health Department, the center is staffed by a team of clinical secretaries, nurses, and a Federal Aviation Administration–certified aviation medical examiner. It provides pilots and aircrews access to flight physicals and health education required either by the Federal Aviation Administration or by corporations. During the opening service on 15 January 2007, Ilse said of her daughter, who had been born at the hospital, "She would be just so humbled. She would be honored because she was a part of both. She was a physician and she loved flying, and for all of this to be integrated, she would be in tears."

Today, Scott Robertson still talks in glowing terms of his lost wife and the life they had shared all too briefly. "She was a wonderful person, and I am so absolutely grateful that I had the opportunity to spend some of our lives together," he reflected. "She was such a kind and understanding and extremely passionate person when it came to helping others. She cared deeply about everyone and had no preconceived notions or expectations about anyone. She was just the most wonderful, loving person you could ever come to know. More than sixteen years have passed since that terrible day, but I will always cherish her memory and all that she meant to me and so many others."

Just as her father was a hero to her, so Patricia Hilliard Robertson will always remain a much-loved hero and inspiration to all those who knew her, not only for all that she had accomplished in her tragically shortened life, but for all that she might have achieved as one of her nation's finest and most talented and beloved astronauts.

13. New Hampshire to the New Frontier

Payload Specialist Candidate Robert J. Wood

People do not decide to become extraordinary.
They decide to accomplish extraordinary things.

—Sir Edmund Hillary

A dramatic headline in the 25 February 2009 issue of Missouri's *St. Charles Journal* newspaper stated that a local man, driving at high speed while heavily intoxicated, had caused and been charged over a fatal automobile accident that took the life of another driver. It referred to the innocent victim of the car crash as fifty-one-year-old Robert J. Wood, an engineer with Boeing and a triathlete. The accompanying photograph showed a young helmeted cyclist with determination written all over his face competing in the August 2008 Ultramax Who Tri's Harder Triathlon in Innsbrook, Missouri. As reported by staff journalist Kalen Ponche, the event included a five-hundred-yard swim, a seventeen-mile bike ride, and a three-mile run. Wood came in twenty-sixth place overall and in first place for his age group.

What the newspaper failed to comment on was the fact that Robert Wood had once been a corporate payload specialist, selected in 1985 to participate as an alternate payload specialist on space shuttle mission STS-61B and subsequently as a flight payload specialist on mission STS-61M, which was canceled following the loss of the shuttle *Challenger* and its crew in January 1986.

Robert Jackson Wood was born in Fitchburg, Massachusetts, on 26 June 1957, as the third child of Dorothy (née Arnold Van Iderstine) and Eugene Jackson (Jack) Wood Jr. Robert and his two older sisters, Leslie and Diane, spent their early years living in Brookline, Massachusetts, before the family moved to the small town of Lyndeborough in southern New Hampshire, which he always regarded as his hometown. Although the town was always Lyndeborough, its name was abbreviated by many (including Robert) to Lyndeboro in the 1960s through to the 1980s. Here they lived in a country home outside of town, sitting on what was once described by his sister Leslie as sixty acres of hilly land.

Following their move, Robert entered second grade at Lyndeborough Central School. Then, in 1969, he commenced his seventh grade studies at the Wilton-Lyndeborough Cooperative Junior-Senior High School. He graduated on 15 June 1975, just prior to his eighteenth birthday, as class valedictorian (first in his class of fifty-five students) with a 4.0 grade point average.

As his sister Leslie reflected, "He was in the seventh grade when I was a senior in high school, and after my graduation he announced that he would be the valedictorian of his class—and he was. I recall that in his valedictory speech he encouraged his classmates to go in search of their dreams but to never forget their roots and where they came from."

"Robert grew into a fine young man," said his mother. "I have fond memories of him hunting and fishing with his father and grandfather. He always treated his firearms with love and respect and passed these attributes on to his own children, as well as his passion for snowboarding."

Having grown up in an exciting era of rockets and astronauts, Wood was in constant awe of his nation's space program. He had early plans of becoming an astronaut and even considered joining the U.S. Air Force in order to achieve that goal. There was a problem, however; he had to wear glasses. Knowing that pilots needed nearly perfect eyesight, he reluctantly abandoned that particular cherished dream and decided instead to devote his studies to becoming a physicist.

He then took up studies at Ohio University, with the aim of achieving a bachelor of science degree in physics. While there, Wood found himself attracted to fellow student Alicia Angell. But for quite some time, he could not work up sufficient courage to introduce himself and was a little dismayed that she seemed to be ignoring him. But there was a good reason for this, as Alicia explained.

I was very nearsighted and too vain to wear glasses. As a college student,
I couldn't afford contact lenses, and apparently Robert—who was quite

shy—had been hanging about the periphery hoping to catch my attention, thinking I was playing hard to get. He didn't realize I couldn't see him. So one day, after about two years of me being absolutely oblivious of this, we were in volleyball class together, and he greeted me by name. I was very flattered that he pronounced my name correctly, as many people don't, and I could now see that he was extremely handsome. I have to admit I was quite surprised that this handsome man had introduced himself to me, and very soon we started dating.

A romance developed and grew, and soon they were inseparable.

Wood was finally awarded his bachelor of science degree (summa cum laude) from the Honors Tutorial College on 10 June 1978. Two months later he and Alicia were married in a small church in his hometown of Lyndeborough, where his parents still lived. He entered MIT, intending to pursue his lifelong goal of earning a PhD, but after a year of studies, he and Alicia realized that it was not going to work as they had hoped. While Robert was paid a small stipend by MIT, it was a stressful time, and Alicia was not coping with the pressure and expense of putting him through graduate school, projected to be for the next six years. As well, they were keen to start a family, so after talking it over, he transferred across to the master's program. Then, in 1980, he was awarded his master of science degree in physics (once again summa cum laude).

In his time as a graduate student, Wood also worked as a research assistant at the Bates Linear Accelerator Center, an MIT-owned facility in Middleton, Massachusetts. Located within Bates was a 500 MeV (megaelectron volt) linear accelerator that provided beams of electrons for a wide range of scientific experiments performed by users from around the world. Wood's work there involved studying neutral particle currents.

After leaving MIT, he became a senior research assistant for the Jarrell Ash Division of Fisher Scientific Company in Waltham, Massachusetts, which was developing automated laboratory instruments. According to his sister Diane, "He always wanted to understand things at a deeper level, and he had a passion for excellence."

In January 1983 Wood became a lead software engineer with the McDonnell Douglas Astronautics Company in St. Louis, Missouri. He enjoyed working for the company, and Alicia remembers him constantly seeking out a new task to tackle. "He was always looking for a new challenge, and when he did, he would dive straight into it. He was always early to work and often worked overtime, and I remember he was forever campaigning for new assignments. Once that assignment was well in hand, he would empower and delegate authority to someone else and move on to a completely new challenge. It was an exciting and fascinating time."

One role in which he participated was developing controlling software needed for the early versions of pharmaceutical processing systems being tested in a space, carried in the crew compartment middeck of NASA's fleet of space shuttle orbiters. As well, he was involved in developing all process controls and product design logic as a leading architect of the computer network that controlled the follow-on large-scale pharmaceutical production prototype equipment being built for spaceflight in a shuttle orbiter's cavernous payload bay. This became the Electrophoresis Operations in Space (EOS) semiautonomous payload. The commercial project of the same name, EOS, was a joint venture between McDonnell Douglas and the Ortho Pharmaceutical Division of Johnson & Johnson.

As explained by Douglas B. Hawthorne in his 1992 book, *The Men and Women of Space*, "The EOS unit takes advantage of the space environment to separate and purify biological materials in the manufacturing of unique drugs. . . . Wood managed all EOS flight-system software development, including flight and ground software for the space factory and modifications required to convert the middeck unit from the research to the production mode."

The maiden spaceflight of the shuttle *Challenger* on mission STS-6 took place in early April 1983. The middeck configuration of the EOS system—termed the continuous flow electrophoresis system, or CFES—made its second flight to space at that time. In preparation for the five-day mission, Robert Wood began serving as a support engineer for the CFES flights, working out of the Johnson Space Center's Mission Control Center in Houston.

An early advanced version of the unit would later be operated by Charles D. Walker, another McDonnell Douglas engineer, as a corporate payload specialist on three shuttle missions. Walker had originally begun working for the company in 1977 as a test engineer on the aft propulsion subsystem for NASA's space shuttles. He then joined the company's space manufacturing team as one of its original members, involving himself in applying a laboratory process known as the continuous flow electrophoresis to industrial developments based in space.

"In medical research, as well as medical pharmaceutical production, there is a need to achieve high purity," Walker explained of this work. "A process widely used is electrophoresis. McDonnell Douglas pursued the concept that the environment of orbital flight—microgravity—would improve the purification of these materials one hundred times better than could be done on Earth."

On his first shuttle flight, STS-41D in 1984, Walker was able to purify a gram of a hormone. When it was returned, however, McDonnell's experts found that a microorganism known as pseudomonas had contaminated the sample. On STS-51D in April the following year, Walker flew on his second shuttle mission. This time, as on his earlier flight, he did not have an alternate payload specialist from McDonnell Douglas. Robert Wood's first participation in this capacity would only come on Walker's third mission. On STS-51D Walker flew with equipment that allowed him to check on the purity of the sample throughout the time of the purification process.

At that time, James T. Rose was employed at the McDonnell Douglas Astronautics Company in St. Louis as the manager of space shuttle payload development for research and commercial applications of space. In that capacity, he applied his talent and skill toward utilizing the nation's space shuttle system for commercial advancement. Rose had instigated the privately financed EOS, which was a payload project aboard space shuttles via the first joint-endeavor agreement between industry and NASA to bring space commercialization into reality. After Walker's second flight aboard the shuttle *Discovery* on STS-51D, Rose said, "The product this time has been very clean. We reduced contamination tenfold. We were able to do this by using a stronger sterilizing solution in cleaning the machine and by keeping our test material cold almost all the time, thus preventing bacterial growth. We learned in the latest flight that we could run the machine for two hundred hours without a flaw [and] that we could do a batch of material and bring it back."

In a Johnson Space Center Oral History interview in 2006, Charlie Walker spoke about his work colleague and backup engineer Robert Wood and the larger EOS unit, which was to be flown on later missions. Meanwhile, McDonnell Douglas decided they needed to select a backup engineer who could also fly with and operate the unit.

So anyway, the company then went through that selection process internally for somebody that they brought forward to NASA as the second McDonnell Douglas electrophoresis operations in space payload specialist candidate. Robert Wood was the individual's name. We would call him an IT [information technology] expert today, but he was one of the computer gurus in our project at the time back in St. Louis.

The EOS-I was a five-thousand-pound, across-the-cargo-bay system. It was equal to twenty-four chambers, electrophoresis chambers; I think there were six of them. They were twenty-four times the capability of an individual electrophoresis chamber that I was flying in the middeck, [with] advanced electronics, advanced monitoring and control systems, as well as all the necessary support structure, insulation, and volumetric capacity for the fluids and the liquids, so that it could run out in the open cargo bay and run for a seven-day mission almost continuously, producing large quantities of purified pharmaceutical-grade material.

In March 1985 Wood was designated a payload specialist candidate. However, his excitement at being selected was not immediately shared at home when he broke the news to his wife. Alicia revealed,

When he told me, I have to admit I was very upset. I wasn't aware that this might happen, and my first reaction was that it was not only very dangerous and he was putting himself at risk, but by now we had a four-year-old child and an infant, and we should have talked it over instead of him deciding and then announcing it to me like that. But that was it; I felt it was something terribly dangerous, although everyone else we spoke to said it was exciting and I was just being silly. Anyway, that was Robert all the way; he wanted to seize on to any opportunity that came his way and give it his very best shot.

Wood's training involved numerous trips down to Houston, and one aspect of his training involved dizzying parabolic flights aboard NASA's KC-135 aircraft, during which participants would experience a number of periods of weightlessness. It was good fun, but the aircraft was not known as the "Vomit Comet" without good reason, as most of the participants had to fight bouts of extreme nausea, often unsuccessfully. Prior to the daunting flights, those taking part were offered Dramamine tablets, an antihistamine used to prevent the onset of nausea, vomiting, and dizziness caused by motion sickness. As Alicia recalled, however, her husband decided he would forgo any medication. It was a mistake. "Typically, Robert wanted to gauge what his parameters were, but he ended up vomiting all the time during the flight. He would have got a lot more out of the experience if he had just taken the Dramamine."

Following his period of training, Wood served as the backup or alternate crewmember to Charlie Walker for the STS-61B mission, this time aboard shuttle orbiter *Atlantis*, launched on 26 November 1985. Eventually, he was designated to operate as McDonnell Douglas's second corporate payload specialist astronaut on a later EOS flight. As Walker recalled,

> *I was training Robert in the interface with NASA and in what I had learned about the Flight Operations regime, working with NASA, the Missions Operations Directorate, and the Astronaut Office. At the same time, I was continuing to do my laboratory research and development for the project in St. Louis and spreading myself between the prospect of at least one more middeck experiment—which I would kind of be the lead PI on that, even if I didn't fly with it—and working with the engineers and the biomedical folks, the microbiologists and biologists in our team that were helping to develop the product that would fly as EOS-1, the automated production system, for its R&D flight, first one expected in '86.*
>
> *With regard to Robert, it was officially expected that [he] would, in fact, fly as the payload specialist and was being manifested as the payload specialist for that EOS-1 flight in mid-1986, and I would be his backup for that flight.*

Wood finally received his first flight assignment in that capacity when he was listed with the crew of STS-61M, a five-day mission aboard the shuttle *Challenger*, with a planned 22 July 1986 launch. The payload on this flight was to have been EOS-1 and the third TDRS (tracking and data relay satellite), which would have been deployed atop an inertial upper-stage rocket and propelled into its planned high Earth orbit.

Wood's solo task would have been to operate the first commercial electrophoresis preproduction unit (EOS-1), a much larger, pallet-mounted payload bay version of the continuous flow experiment that had flown with Charlie Walker on his previous missions. Had the shuttle program con-

23. McDonnell Douglas payload specialists Robert J. Wood and Charles D. Walker. Courtesy NASA.

tinued as planned, the EOS-I and the TDRS-D were already manifested to fly again on *Challenger*'s seven-day STS-71D mission in February 1987—as was Robert Wood.

The STS-61M crew was certainly filled with a lot of spaceflight experience. Both the commander, Col. Loren Shriver (USAF), and the pilot, Col. Bryan O'Connor (USMC), would be making their second flights into space. Mission specialist Sally Ride, renowned as America's first woman in space, was down for her third spaceflight, while another mission specialist, Bill Fisher, would be on his second flight. The only space rookies scheduled aboard the flight were Robert Wood and mission specialist Mark Lee.

Beginning in 1985 the crew continued to train for the STS-61M mission until that tragic morning of 28 January 1986, when the veteran space shuttle *Challenger* and its crew of seven were lost seventy-three seconds after lift-off. "Robert was beyond devastated," Alicia reflected. "He would just walk around with this stunned expression on his face all the time. He knew all the crewmembers personally, had worked with them, and he loved them all."

The horrendous shuttle tragedy caused an immediate postponement

of all subsequent missions. Eventually, as part of the return-to-flight recommendations handed down to NASA, the commercial utilization of the
space shuttle was curtailed in the wake of the *Challenger* accident, and all
payload specialists were informed that their flights had been placed on an
indefinite hold.

As it turned out, neither Wood nor the payload bay EOS-I system would
ever fly into space. McDonnell Douglas later withdrew their EOS payloads
from the shuttle after both that restrictive policy and advances in ground-
based research that had achieved a significant amount of what they were
trying to do on orbit crippled the commercial business plan.

Wood remained with McDonnell Douglas (which merged with the Boeing Corporation in 1997, headquartered in Berkeley, a suburb of St. Louis),
although it was reported that he did try unsuccessfully to be selected for
NASA's group 13 astronaut selection in 1990. He later became manager of
accelerator software for the neutral particle beam integrated experiment
and then manager of air vehicle software for the National Aerospace Plane
program. He was also a systems engineer on Boeing's Joint Direct Attack
Munitions program and a program manager for the multipurpose universal gunner sight in the Combat Systems Division. By now, he and Alicia
were the parents of five children—Lucas, Marcus, Munro, Juliana, and
Laurence—and grandparents, through Juliana, of baby Addison.

It was 12:15 a.m. on the morning of Thursday, 19 February 2009, and Robert Wood was driving his 1990 Mercury Topaz toward his workplace at the
Boeing plant in Berkeley. Always a conservative driver, according to Alicia, he was traveling around the speed limit of sixty miles per hour in the
right lane, heading eastward along Interstate 70 near Bryan Road in Lake
St. Louis, Missouri, when a car traveling at around twice the speed limit
suddenly rammed him from behind. Wood's car careered off the highway and overturned. It was totaled, and despite wearing a seat belt, Robert Wood was later pronounced dead at the scene.

That morning, Alicia Wood heard a knock at the door. When she opened
it, a grim-looking state highway patrol officer was standing there and asked
if he could come in. Bewildered, she let him in. They both sat down, and
he said he had some bad news—her husband had been involved in a fatal
accident. "It was awful," she recalled. "I remember thinking to myself, 'Is

he trying to say my husband has killed somebody, or is he going to say my husband has been killed?' I asked him to clarify whatever he was trying to tell me, and he told me Robert had been killed. I was in shock and went into denial, telling the poor trooper that I didn't believe him. All he could say was, 'I'm sorry, ma'am.'"

Missouri Highway Patrol investigators eventually revealed the sad facts behind the fatal crash, during the December sentencing hearing of local man Chad E. Frazer, the driver of the other vehicle.

In the St. Charles courthouse, highway patrol trooper Ryan Vaughan provided receipts showing that Frazer, then twenty-nine, had been drinking at two bars in O'Fallon, Missouri, prior to the accident. Surveillance video from an adjacent gas station showed him performing a tire-screeching burnout from the parking lot of the second bar in his 1991 Ford Mustang. Another state trooper, Sgt. Alan Nothum, testified that Frazer was under the influence of alcohol at the time of the crash, and a reconstruction of the crash indicated that he was traveling anywhere between 100 and 120 miles per hour in the center lane just before the crash occurred. He had impatiently changed to the right-hand lane in order to pass a tractor trailer and in doing so had slammed into the rear end of Wood's automobile, forcing it off the highway.

Following the impact, Frazer's car traveled off the left side of the road and came to rest against a median wall. Suffering only relatively minor injuries, Frazer had clambered out through the roof of his Mustang, which was extensively damaged, and fled in panic from the scene into a subdivision south of I-70. He was later arrested about half a mile from the crash site and taken to the SSM St. Joseph Health Center in St. Charles, where he received treatment to his wounds.

Mandatory hospital tests showed Frazer's blood alcohol level was .277 percent, or more than three times the limit for driving. The following Thursday, he was being held in the St. Charles County jail in lieu of a $100,000 bond, with a charge of manslaughter in the first degree hanging over his head. It was a class B felony, punishable by up to fifteen years in prison, compounded by the fact that he had left the scene of the accident, which was punishable by four years in prison.

At the hearing, Wood's family said that through their Christian faith they had decided to forgive the man who had killed him in the high-speed drunken crash, but while Frazer had expressed his deep remorse, they still believed he should go to prison. Frazer's attorneys asked the judge to only impose a six-year sentence, introducing a recommendation from the state's Division of Probation and Parole, but assistant prosecutor John Bauer asked for a full fifteen-year sentence due to an earlier municipal DWI charge in 1998 and his later arrest for disorderly intoxication in Florida in 2004. "This isn't an accident," prosecutor Bauer insisted. "This is a set of choices the defendant made."

Circuit judge Ted House agreed with Bauer and sentenced Frazer to consecutive terms of twelve years for involuntary manslaughter and three years for leaving the scene. State law required that Frazer serve at least 85 percent of his sentence—about ten years—before he could begin serving his sentence for leaving the scene of an accident. "You are the face of terror," Judge House told Frazer. "To every husband, wife, brother, sister, son, and daughter, you are the greatest nightmare." And he added that the jail term was a way of keeping the public safe.

Following the sentencing of Frazer, Wood's son Luke, the oldest of his children, spoke on behalf of the family, categorically stating, "My family does not hate Chad Frazer. We do not seek retribution against Chad Frazer. But no one should have to go through what we had to endure, and that's why consequences are necessary." Several months after the hearing, Wood's daughter, Juliana, also wrote on the matter, saying,

> No one can understand the grief and loss of losing a family member in this manner unless it has occurred to you. My family and I included in our victim's impact statement our feelings of forgiveness. We understand that it was his choice to drive drunk, and he was ultimately responsible for my father's death, yet it was not a deliberate act. We are grateful that justice was served, and believe that he deserves to be in prison, but we do not bear ill will towards him, nor wish for any type of vengeance. We certainly have a huge amount of compassion towards Chad and his family, because Chad and his family were also victims of his poor choices.

A service for Robert Jackson Wood had been held on the morning of 21 February 2009 at the Chapel of the Lake in Lake St. Louis, and he was laid to rest in the Wright City Cemetery, Warren County, Missouri. At the time of the service, he was survived by his wife, Alicia; his mother, Dorothy; his sisters, Leslie and Diane; his sons, Lucas, Marcus, Munro, and Laurence; his daughter, Juliana; and his granddaughter, Addison.

Luke Wood retains many fond memories of his father and also remembers his fiercely competitive nature, which spurred him on to achieve new goals and ambitions. He would doubtless have made the most of the experience had he been allowed to fly into space. Luke stated,

> I was very young when my father was training to be an astronaut. I remember him being gone for days at a time while undergoing training. Whenever he came home, he would always bring flowers for my mom and a toy for me. I loved the little Hot Wheels jets, and he usually got me one of those.
>
> He was often invited to go talk to the Boy Scouts, and he would always take me. On these excursions he would wear his baby-blue astronaut uniform, which was covered in patches and had a Velcro name tag on it, which said WOOD. He always showed the same video of astronauts in orbit. It had informational stuff, mixed with some funny spaceman moments, like an astronaut who wasn't like the rest of us because he put his pants on two legs at a time. My dad had to explain that one to me.
>
> After the Challenger blew up, my dad was transferred into the shadow works dept. He still was asked to speak by the Boy Scouts, and he would talk to them a little about his new project, the Rockwell X-30, or NASP (National AeroSpace Plane). He couldn't say much, and I used to harangue him to tell me about it, because six-year-old boys hate secrets. NASP was a single-stage exit and reentry vehicle, and one day he drew a triangle with wings and a cockpit as a crude picture for one of his speeches for the scouts. I was very excited and asked him if that was what the NASP looked like. He laughed at me and said, "That would never get off the ground."
>
> My dad had several lifelong hobbies: cycling, soccer, chess, guitar, and singing. He taught me soccer before I could walk by rolling a little ball to me in my baby swing. He taught me chess at age four. I was fourteen years old before I was good enough to beat him a single time in either game.
>
> Which brings me to his competitive nature. He was highly competitive in a quiet, brilliant way. He did not trash talk or boast; rather, he would simply dismantle you as an opponent with little fanfare or celebration. When he did lose, it vexed him greatly. He would start talking to himself

under his breath, and a look of deep consternation would fight its way to the surface of his face, which he would struggle mightily to control. The last Christmas we spent with him before he died, he called us all ahead of time and told us that he was imposing a video game ban during the holidays and that we would be focusing on family games. When I arrived home, he had the chessboard out in the living room. We sat down to a game, and since I had been playing Chessmaster religiously every night at work, I was able to beat him rather handily. He asked for another game, and I beat him again. By this time, he was quite vexed with himself; losing two chess games in a row to me was not a thing he did. Shortly after, my brother Marcus walked in with a hearty, "Hi, guys." Straightaway my father snapped, "Sit down." They played, and my dad won. He was in a much better mood after that.

When my dad took up a new task or hobby, he was a perfectionist about it. He would study compulsively and make sure he had the best equipment for the task. That was always his way—precision and perfection.

A couple of weeks after his headstone went up, I found a little toy space shuttle in a local store. I bought it, and we took it out and placed it on his stone. We think it is the perfect token for the man who taught us how to be men.

14. Argentina's Only Astronaut

Fernando (Frank) Caldeiro

It's not where your dreams take you;
it's where you take your dreams.

—Maya Angelou

When an apprehensive Fernando Caldeiro Cainzos arrived in the bustling city of New York from Buenos Aires in March 1974, the fifteen-year-old Argentinian could not speak English. His inability to comprehend the language was exacerbated by the streets crowded with people who always seemed to be in a hurry. It was a daunting prospect for the young student and his family. Enrolled as a freshman at W. C. Bryant High School in Long Island City, he was noticeably silent in class, which initially led school officials to believe that he might have a hearing impairment. They arranged for a visit to a doctor to have his hearing checked. "It wasn't that I was deaf," Caldeiro later recalled with a laugh. "It's just that I couldn't understand a word of what anyone was saying!" Twenty-two years after his family settled in New York, he proved that anyone from any background could achieve a great American dream, when he was selected as a NASA mission specialist astronaut. In fact, he was the first—and so far only—astronaut born in Argentina.

Fernando, who became better known to his friends in the United States as Frank, was the son of Spanish parents Carmen Doris (née Cainzos) and Jose Antonio Caldeiro. Hearkening back a couple of generations, his maternal grandmother was born in the southern Spanish region of Andalucia; and his paternal grandmother, in Asturias, located in the northwestern region of the country. His grandfathers on both sides were also from northwestern Spain, both born in the Galicia region. Fernando's mother, Carmen, came from the city of Leon, the capital of the province of Leon, and his father, Jose, from the Bercian town of Toral de los Vados.

Following World War II, Jose Caldeiro decided to emigrate to Argentina in search of a better life and settled in Ituzaingó in the province of Buenos Aires, sometime around 1950. His bride would follow some time later, as explained by their first child, Ana Marie.

My father was living in Argentina and had already met my mother in Spain through a friend of his from his time in the army, who happened to be a neighbor of my mother. As my father would not make the expensive trip to Spain just to marry, he issued a document at the Spanish Consulate in Buenos Aires allowing "a representative" of his to stand in his place and sign in his name throughout the civil wedding ceremony. So my mother has wedding pictures with her family, but her husband is not there. I believe this was not unusual at that time in Europe. My mother then left for Buenos Aires by boat on a two-week transatlantic trip and joined her husband sometime around 1952.

In Ituzaingó they set up home in a modest white tiled house with purely decorative bars on the windows, while their front garden was comprised of a rose bush and a huge jasmine shrub. Their daughter, Ana Maria, entered the world in August 1955, and three years later, on 12 June 1958, Fernando was born, completing the family.

While Ana attended a girls' school run by Catholic nuns, Fernando took his early education at Paul Groussac School No. 12, situated on Haiti and Columbia Streets in Ituzaingó. Fernando grew up fascinated by airplanes, helicopters, and gliders under tow, all of which regularly flew over his home. His childhood ambition to fly took root when one of his father's cousins, an Argentine army captain, allowed him to sit in the cockpit of a Gloster Meteor jet and run his hands over the unfamiliar controls and instruments during a festival in nearby El Palomar.

When Fernando was fifteen years old, his father, who worked for an electrical company, received a temporary work transfer to New York City. "It was supposed to be just for three months," Caldeiro reflected, "but it was extended to six months and then more."

In November 1973, by which time Caldeiro had just completed the third year of industrial school in Argentina, his parents agreed that it was difficult trying to make ends meet in Argentina. With the happy prospect of regular employment for Jose, they decided to move permanently to New York City in March of the following year, taking up residence in the borough of Queens. It was there that Fernando continued his secondary studies at W. C. Bryant High School, while at the same time learning the English language. He graduated in 1976.

As his sister, Ana, recalls, "I often think about that time and the hurdles we all overcame: new country, language, and customs; financial duress; irrational ideas of how we were fitting in. After all, if your first language was Spanish, you were Latino, along with all that this encompasses."

Nevertheless, life moved on for the Caldeiro family, and young Fernando still harbored a cherished boyhood dream that he had nurtured back in Argentina. "One thing that I always knew was that I've always wanted to fly," he once revealed to a reporter. Two years after graduating from W. C. Bryant High School, he earned an associate's degree in applied science in aerospace technology from the State University of New York in Farmingdale.

Caldeiro then decided to move to Arizona to continue his collegiate education. He was quite open in discussing this decision. "I just wanted to get out of New York City," he declared. At first, he enrolled at Arizona State University, but he later transferred to the University of Arizona in Tucson. In 1984 he was awarded his bachelor of science degree in mechanical engineering and also earned his pilot's license.

From 1985 to 1988 Caldeiro was employed by Rockwell International as an internal flight engineer and, later, as test director in the b-1b bomber program at Palmdale, California. In 1988, after the one hundredth b-1b had been delivered, Rockwell's Space System Division transferred him to the Kennedy Space Center in Florida to act as a specialist in the space shuttle's main propulsion system. Here he was appointed the representative of the Rockwell Design Center for ground processing and launch of the shuttle *Discovery* in 1991. NASA recognized his substantial talents in this effort and hired him to remain at the Kennedy Space Center as an expert in cryogenics and propulsion systems as a lead engineer within the space agency's Office of Safety and Mission Assurance.

While working at the cape and living at nearby Merritt Island, Caldeiro began dating Donna Marie Emero from Huntington Beach, who was employed by an independent contractor carrying out important work for NASA. Her father, Donald, also worked in the space industry, as vice president of space shuttle engineering for Rockwell's Space Systems Division. The young couple would marry and later have two daughters, Annie Aurora and Michelle Carmen.

A member of the Experimental Aircraft Association, the Aircraft Owners and Pilots Association, and the National Rifle Association, Caldeiro was known to enjoy flying and racing the bright-yellow two-seat Rutan Long-EZ experimental composite aircraft he had patiently built over seven years from plans and raw materials, in which he eventually logged over five hundred hours.

In explaining why he painted his airplane a vivid yellow, Caldeiro said that at one time, he had received an unexpected visit from a federal agent, who demanded to know if he owned an airplane with the registration November Foxtrot Charlie (NFC). When he confirmed this, the agent stunned him by saying, "Well, we have your airplane here in Chicago, loaded with drugs." A shocked Caldeiro responded, "That's impossible; my airplane is in my garage. I haven't even completed building it yet!" After inspecting the partially built small airplane, the agent was satisfied, and the matter was officially closed. Caldeiro later learned that a commonly used ploy of the Colombian drug cartels was to repaint an airplane white with a Federal Aviation Administration aircraft registration number that belonged to another plane. He subsequently added a number to his aircraft's registration, which now read N9FC. With the situation finally sorted out, he decided to make his little airplane far more distinctive to avoid the same situation happening, and when it was finally assembled, he painted his Long-EZ bright yellow. After proudly viewing the results, he affectionately named it *Bumblebee*.

Wes Lineberry from Clermont, Florida, was an engineer working on the space shuttle main propulsion system (MPS)—essentially all the plumbing between the external tank and the three main engines—when he got to know Frank Caldeiro.

I was originally working for Rockwell until the shuttle-processing contract was turned over to Lockheed. My supervisor, Steve Coester, stayed with Rockwell at [the Kennedy Space Center], while I accepted a position with

Lockheed. Shortly after the transition, Frank accepted a transfer from the concluding Rockwell B1 bomber flight test program to Steve Coester's group. This group was responsible for coordinating Lockheed MPS issues with the Rockwell Design Center in Downey, California. Our Lockheed group worked closely with Coester's Rockwell group.

During this time, I became a very good friend of Frank's, as we shared a common bond of aviation. Frank was building a Rutan Long-EZ airplane, while I was busy flying my sailplane. We frequently exchanged comments about our progress. After Frank's airplane was painted, he highly recommended an aircraft painting shop at the Merritt Island Airport, where I sent my sailplane. Incidentally, my sailplane received rave reviews for its unusual off-white color. Frank was later convinced that his experience in building his Long-EZ helped him win a position as an astronaut. He had always wanted me to fly with him in his Long-EZ, but that never happened. Then our correspondence slowed dramatically, although I knew he was flying in NASA's WB-57 weather-tracking aircraft. After I retired, I traveled to Houston once or twice per year. We tried to get together when I was there, but our schedules never meshed.

Jason Yokubaitis from Humble, Texas, knew that Long-EZ airplane well: "I think what I remember most about Frank is his yellow airplane. I grew up two doors down from the Caldeiros, and he used to fly over our house every week it seemed. He would fly around and around in circles until somebody came out and waved at him. Then he'd rock the wings side to side as he flew away to wave back."

In 1995, under a NASA grant, Caldeiro was awarded his master of science degree in engineering management from the University of Central Florida (UCF) in Orlando. He first came in contact with UCF while working as a project director at the Kennedy Space Center. "There was this program that UCF had with NASA [Kennedy Space Center] where you could get your master's degree at the cape," he once explained. "You didn't have to go to the campus; it could all be done after work hours." His timing was perfect; he now had the right qualifications to take a giant leap into the future. And fate complied. "All of a sudden [NASA] opened up applications for the astronaut program," Caldeiro recalled, "and if you didn't have a master's, then don't bother to apply."

With the encouragement of JoAnn Morgan, the director of Safety and Mission Assurance, as well as his coworkers, he decided to apply for the astronaut corps as a mission specialist. Despite their enthusiasm, he was unsure if he met the necessary qualifications imposed by the space agency. He would later learn that 2,432 applications had been received, from which number only a pool of 122 were subsequently invited to Houston in February 1996 for a series of personal (and probing) tests and interviews with the Astronaut Selection Committee. He did keep a diary of what he and some other hopefuls went through, extracts of which were recorded by the late former flight director James A. (Gene) Thomas in his book *Some Trust in Chariots.*

Day Three: Noon time at the psychological ward . . . They gave an 1100 question quiz. Questions such as "Do you hear voices? Do animals talk to you? Do you like your friends?" I'm glad that I can laugh at it now that it's all over and don't feel like screaming, "Say what?"

Day Four: Musculoskeletal exam, the neatest test of them all measures your body and skeletal dimension and determines if you will fit into a Russian Soyuz seat. (The requirement is because the Soyuz is the emergency return from orbit for crewmen manning the Russian space station, MIR). You are then strapped to a machine that tests your muscular outputs against a resisting arm monitored and measured by computer.

That day I also got the ophthalmology exam which was very thorough except the dilation process decreases your vision to nothing. Luckily, someone took us to dinner and read the menu to those of us who had dilated eyes.

After a day of recording my heart activity on an electronic monitor, on Day 5 we were given the neurology exam to check our reflexes. "Follow my finger, can you feel this?" Rubber hammer bang here, bang there, on the knee! Slap on the face! "Follow my finger!" I comically named it the Curly, Larry and Moe Test. "Follow my finger" . . . Whack!

Day Six: I received the echocardiogram test where heart status is measured by sound and you are able to hear and observe the muscular and blood flow activities of your own heart. What a mighty, regular organ the heart is!

Then I had the interview of a lifetime. I was asked to write an essay on why I wanted to become an astronaut. John Young asked me about the B-1 bomber that I had worked on. Bob Cabana, chief of the astronaut corps, asked about the experimental aircraft I had built and flown.

That evening we were cordially entertained at a traditional astronaut gathering place, a Cajun BBQ house, by Young, Cabana, and George Abbey, the [Johnson Space Center] Director. What a thrill to be encouraged by these top [Johnson Space Center] officials and to be told by Mr. Abbey we would probably fly in 1998 if we were selected.

Last day: We were debriefed on the physical and psychiatric test results. I guess I'm an ordinary Joe like most of the applicants. I still didn't hear any voices while in Houston! And to top off the long week, the plane I flew home on got hit by lightning about 70 miles out of Orlando!

By February the 122 candidates had been whittled down even further in number, and Caldeiro was surprised but delighted to know that he had made the cut. At this stage of the selection process, the remaining names were handed over to the U.S. Office of Personnel Management. Their responsibility was to pick up their phones and start calling everybody associated with each potential astronaut; their family, friends, coworkers, university lecturers, high school teachers, and others who had come in contact with them over the years, seeking personal references and noting down any potential problem areas.

On 22 April 1996, while clearing up some paperwork in his office, Caldeiro received a phone call from the Astronaut Office at the Johnson Space Center in Texas. He had spent an anxious six weeks following his interviews with the selection committee and had no idea what was in store when the caller identified himself as David Leestma, NASA's director of astronaut candidate training at the Johnson Space Center.

"When I heard [Leestma's] voice, I knew I was about five seconds away from coming back to normal life. . . . I was about to find out what I was going to be doing one way or another, and that was what I was looking for—relief. I was asked if I wanted to move to Houston," he said. "I asked why, and then I was asked, 'You *do* want to be an astronaut, don't you?'" Caldeiro was completely dumbfounded, and all he could think to say was, "You've got to be kidding!" Then he blurted out, "Count me in!"

He was elated—he had made it and was now officially an astronaut candidate in waiting and in line for a possible future assignment as a mission specialist. The caller asked him to report to Houston on 12 August as part of the group 16 contingent, where he would begin a two-year period of training and evaluation. He later discovered he was one of thirty-five successful candidates—the largest astronaut candidate group since the same number had been selected in group 8 back in 1978.

Group 16, which he had now joined, comprised ten pilots and twenty-five mission specialists, selected from more than 2,400 applicants. It's little wonder that with such a large number joining the astronaut corps, they were—by tradition—endowed by the previous astronaut group with an unofficial and humorous nickname. Due to the size of the group, they found themselves saddled with the name "the Sardines."

The ten pilots chosen in group 16 were Duane Carey, Stephen Frick, Charles Hobaugh, James Kelly, Mark Kelly, Scott Kelly (the latter two being twin brothers but no relation to James Kelly), Paul Lockhart, Christopher Loria, William McCool, and Mark Polansky. Apart from Frank Caldeiro, the other twenty-four mission specialists were David Brown, Daniel Burbank, Yvonne Cagle, Charles Camarda, Laurel Clark, Michael Fincke, Patrick Forrester, John Herrington, Joan Higginbotham, Sandra Magnus, Michael Massimino, Richard Mastracchio, Lee Morin, Lisa Nowak, Donald Pettit, John Phillips, Paul Richards, Piers Sellers, Heidemarie Stefanyshyn-Piper, Daniel Tani, Rex Walheim, Peggy Whitson, Jeffrey Williams, and Stephanie Wilson.

For their ASCAN training, they were later joined by a cadre of nine international candidates representing the Canadian, Japanese, Italian, French, German, and European Space Agencies, making forty-four trainees in all. The international group comprised Pedro Duque (Spain), Christer Fuglesang (Sweden), Umberto Guidoni (Italy), Steven MacLean (Canada), Mamoru Mohri (Japan), Soichi Noguchi (Japan), Julie Payette (Canada), Philippe Perrin (France), and Gerhard Thiele (Germany).

Ana remembered,

When Fernando was called in by NASA, our family was indeed very proud of him. His accomplishments and sacrifices paid off big time in that he achieved his lifelong dream. So here he was, a newly minted astronaut living his dream.

We followed as best as we could in all his experiences in this new world of shuttle vehicles, nongravity living, and technical manuals the size of Texas. We saw from the inside how he behaved toward the Argentinian and Spanish press tripping over each other to secure a visit to such and

24. NASA mission specialist astronaut Fernando (Frank) Caldeiro. Courtesy NASA.

such museum or an interview for television. Fernando was proud of his accomplishments, but I believe he was really in awe of how far he had come. To the press, he always emphasized "hard work, ethics, and studying till you cannot study anymore." Those were the home values we grew up in, and they served us quite well.

He used to say, "I cannot yet believe what I am doing, and they pay me for it." True indeed, he really loved it.

Danny Fitzgerald from the Kennedy Space Center was also excited to see his friend make the astronaut corps: "I met Frank for the first time when he came to [the Kennedy Space Center] from Palmdale, California. What a great sense of humor. He was always laughing and joking and frequently had me in stitches. It was also fun to see Frank get fired up. His eyebrows would raise as his eyes widened, and he would become very animated. The man had conviction. We were all very proud when he was selected to join the ranks in the Astronaut Office."

Being an astronaut in training was not all fun and games; it was tough going, as Caldeiro recalled: "Basically, they started feeding us through a fire hose. It was unbelievable the amount of work."

Following a full year of evaluation and shuttle training, each of the new astronauts received technical assignments within the Astronaut Office to further prepare them for future shuttle missions. They also received their silver astronaut wings, signifying the successful completion of their ASCAN training. Once they had made their first spaceflight, they would trade these with pride for the gold wings of a flown astronaut.

Two of his fellow Sardines would never fly into space. Christopher Loria was scheduled to fly as mission pilot on STS-113 but suffered a severe back injury and was grounded. Yvonne Cagle, although still listed over the years as an active astronaut, eventually went on to other duties with NASA. Another three, pilot Willie McCool and mission specialists Dave Brown and Laurel Clark, died in the *Columbia* disaster. Lisa Nowak would be summarily dismissed from the astronaut corps and reassigned to the U.S. Navy after being arrested and charged following a dramatic and well-publicized cross-country confrontation with a woman involved in a love triangle with another astronaut.

Nevertheless, there were also good stories to come out of the ranks of the group 16 astronauts, particularly that of twin brothers Mark and Scott Kelly, who made it into space a combined seven times.

Although chosen for astronaut training in 1996 and having qualified to go into space, Frank Caldeiro knew his first mission might still be a couple of years away and began working key roles in technical support. Among his contributions, he "flew" fifty-two space shuttle missions in a life-size shuttle simulator, nicknamed the "ghost orbiter," to assure NASA that each of their $1 billion space missions would run flawlessly. In these training exercises, carried out under the careful watch of a devious bunch of test controllers, he would be unexpectedly confronted with one technical problem after another that he had to solve quickly and satisfactorily. In this way, the astronauts became familiar with most of the problems they might face, including emergency contingencies, and how they could be overcome.

Caldeiro continually studied and revised the space shuttle systems, but one of his greatest joys as a proficient pilot was flying cross-country to attend meetings with contractors, visit factories, and give talks to audiences at different institutions. These flights were carried out using NASA's fleet of supersonic T-38 jets, although he told one reporter he frankly preferred trips in the little airplane he had built himself. "The Long-EZ is fun and relaxing," he remarked with pride. "It beats the T-38 hands down." In addition, he completed the EVA course covering space walk techniques, which required spending one hundred hours of practice inside a cumbersome EVA space suit while immersed in the simulation pool at the Johnson Space Center.

Later, in the possible event of being launched aboard a Soyuz spacecraft bound for the ISS, he also practiced similar EVA techniques for twelve hours while kitted out in a Soviet space suit in the pool at the Yuri Gagarin Cosmonaut Training Center in Russia's Star City. If he thought that learning English as a youth was a challenge, he now had to learn how to read and converse in the Russian language.

Finally, he completed more than half the classes necessary to become a functioning crewmember aboard a Soyuz spacecraft. He later described the Soyuz craft as "very reliable" but added that "it's very cramped in there, and uncomfortable, but it *is* reliable."

Back at the Johnson Space Center, Caldeiro became the lead astronaut working on ISS life-support systems, the robotics viewing port, and shuttle-lofted cargo carriers. His experiments included finding ways to filter out the potentially deadly carbon dioxide that the crew exhaled as they went about their normal duties.

As he continued to work on the shuttle systems, Caldeiro began to hear indications of his first possible mission assignment as a member of a shuttle flight to the ISS. Then in February 2003 a terrible tragedy struck, with the

25. Frank Caldeiro poses in front of shuttle orbiter *Discovery* in 1998. Courtesy NASA.

loss of the shuttle *Columbia* and its crew as the veteran orbiter descended at high speed through the atmosphere over Texas.

"I was scheduled [for a spaceflight] next year," he later explained, "but with the *Columbia* disaster, I don't know now." He added that morale in the astronaut corps seemed to suffer after the loss of *Columbia*, but it was not due to the tragedy itself or to the shuttle program. "It's that we lost personal friends," he said, "[but] you have to keep going."

The shuttle *Columbia* suffered significant damage on mission STS-107 when a piece of insulating foam broke off from the external fuel tank and struck the leading edge of the orbiter's left wing soon after liftoff on 16 January 2003. The resultant breach went undiscovered during the nearly sixteen days of the flight. Being a science mission, it did not rendezvous with the ISS, as most shuttle flights did at that time. If it had, the problem would have been noticed following the docking, and a contingency plan would have been initiated. Instead, the ferocious heat of reentry tore through the breach, causing the inner structure of the damaged wing to overheat and melt as the orbiter was on descent over Texas. The seven astronauts on board died when *Columbia* broke up and disintegrated, including McCool, Brown, and Clark from Caldeiro's group 16 Sardines.

Reassigned to Houston's nearby Ellington Field, Caldeiro now directed the high-altitude atmospheric research experiment program carried aboard NASA's WB-57 aircraft, which could achieve altitudes exceeding sixty thousand feet. While waiting for a shuttle flight assignment, he was responsible for supervising missions on the WB-57 that included atmospheric and earth science experiments, mapping, and collection of cosmic dust.

In 2004 he made a guest appearance in "My Favorite Sesame Street Moment" for the much-loved children's television program, which was celebrating its thirty-fifth season. On the show, he described how his family came to New York from Argentina and how he first began to learn English by watching *Sesame Street*.

From June 2005 until December 2006 Caldeiro served as the lead astronaut in charge of shuttle software testing at the Johnson Space Center's Shuttle Avionics Integration Laboratory, testing in-flight maintenance procedures.

"Frank knew the shuttle main engines like most of us know our children," said Mark Kelly, a member of Caldeiro's astronaut training class and a later veteran of four shuttle missions. Another classmate, Lee Morin, recalls, "Frank was very upbeat, reaching out to people in an uplifting way. He built his own airplanes, and he really knew the space shuttle engines and rocket propulsion systems."

In 2006 Caldeiro was interviewed for the *Orlando Sentinel* newspaper. "Flying in space, to me, has become more like, well, you know, you can't chase something so much that you run it over," he said. "You can be obsessed by it and be miserable or you can say, 'Well, this is an opportunity; I'm first in line in front of 350 million other people.'"

Then another, far more personal tragedy struck for the Argentinian astronaut. As he was driving home from work one day, he noticed that his peripheral vision seemed to be failing. Concerned, he consulted a doctor, and following a battery of tests, he was given the terrible news that he had been diagnosed with a brain tumor—glioblastoma type 4. These types of cancerous tumors emerge from what are called astrocytes—the star-shaped cells that make up the glue-like supportive tissue of the brain. Generally, they are highly malignant, as the cells reproduce quickly and are supported by a large network of blood vessels.

Following surgery to remove the tumor, Caldeiro was subjected to follow-up radiation treatment and a course of preventative medications. CAT scans were carried out periodically to see if he remained free of the cancer. Then, as he expected—but to his extreme disappointment—he was grounded from flying, which he hoped was temporary.

In a filmed interview in April 2008 he was quite open but optimistic about his prognosis for the future.

> *In my job and flying and all that, I always thought I was going to end up on the side of a hill at six hundred miles an hour, and now I have something that is lurking, looking at me very slow, so it's a different approach kind of thing.*
>
> *When I had radiation, it was very targeted, so in half of my head I went bald. In the old days I think they just put you in a machine and they just blasted away. Now it is very targeted, which is good. So half of my head has got hair, the other half . . . supposedly someday it will grow. I'm not too worried about it. It feels kind of alright, and it's in fashion now to be bald. So it's the new look, and if I don't like it, I just put a hat on!*

Then he became serious again.

It's tough when you've flown all your life and all of a sudden you're grounded, but it's part of the game. You know, I received a lot of training here in the NASA astronaut program in survival and all that, and dealing with emergencies, and this has helped me a lot, too. . . . My training has been great to cope with all of this—high-stress situations—and I'm trying to use it all and put it together, and we'll see what happens.

So I'm like living one day at a time and trying to enjoy it. It's not easy—sometimes I feel down and other times I feel great. I'm trying to keep on the great side, so there's not much of a rollercoaster like it could be.

Following his surgery and initial treatment, Caldeiro eventually returned to his astronaut duties, but without the flying, focusing each day on watching his health and maintaining a positive outlook. He was still working on those duties even as he underwent further treatment for the malevolent cancer that would eventually claim his life. He lost his brave, two-and-a-half-year battle with the disease on 3 October 2009, at the age of fifty-one.

A funeral service was held for the late astronaut at St. Mary's Catholic Church in League City, Texas, on Tuesday, 6 October 2009, followed that evening by a funeral mass in nearby Webster. At his funeral service, a family approached his sister, Ana. "They said, 'We lived down the block from him and have known the family since they moved there in 1996, and we never knew he was an astronaut. We always saw him mowing the garden or putting the garbage out for collection.'" It surprised Ana at the time. "For that split second, I did not know what to respond, and after the usual 'Thank you for your kind words,' I told them, 'Yes, that was him—not bragging about himself, humble and casual and doing everyday chores.' Fernando would greet everyone at work wherever he was, from the janitor mopping the hallway floors at the Johnson Space Center to the lady tending the cash register at McDonald's. He always said that you never know how hard they struggled to be there, just as he did!"

In his eighteen years of service with NASA, Caldeiro received nine different achievement awards. These included the Rockwell International Corporation Certificate of Commendation, the Kennedy Space Center Technical Leadership Certificate, the Kennedy Space Center Director Round Table Award, and two Kennedy Space Center Superior Performance Awards. He also received a Kennedy Space Center Public Affairs Certificate of Appreciation for Service, became a University of Central Florida Distinguished Alumni, and was announced as Tampa's Museum of Science and Industry Hispanic Scientist of the Year. In 2002 President George W. Bush appointed him to serve in the President's Advisory Commission on Educational Excellence for Hispanic Americans, under the No Child Left Behind Act.

"Frank was a valued member of the astronaut corps and the Flight Crew Operations team," said astronaut Brent Jett, at that time the director of Flight Crew Operations. "He provided a wealth of experience and made significant contributions to the success of both the WB-57 project and the space shuttle program. He will be missed by all those who knew him at NASA. Our hearts go out to his family."

Adding to the sadness of the Caldeiro family, Frank's beloved wife, Donna, who loved to host Bible studies at her home, passed away in League City, Texas, on 27 January 2012, at just fifty-two years of age. In her obituary it stated that "Donna had a passion for her family, her country and her faith."

"We like to say that it's better to be down here on Earth wishing you were up there, than up there and wishing you were down here."

Fernando (Frank) Caldeiro (1958–2009), NASA mission specialist

Epilogue

A Personal Reflection

The telephone rang in our darkened Sydney home just after 3:30 a.m. on the morning of 2 February 2003. My wife, Pat, reached out, and after a groggy "Hello?" she listened, said I was right there, and passed the receiver to me, wearily saying, "It's someone from the *Sunrise* show for you." Inwardly, I groaned. I had recently returned from a flight to Los Angeles and felt sure it was someone I had met there who had not factored in the time difference between California and east coast Australia.

However, the voice on the other end had an urgent edge to it. "Mr. Burgess," he began, "what have you heard about *Columbia*?" I was confused and about to respond that I had never been to that country but instead mumbled something like, "I'm sorry, but what is this about?" He then introduced himself as a producer from a Sydney television station and gave me the devastating news that the space shuttle *Columbia* and its crew had been lost when the orbiter broke up over Texas a few hours earlier. He asked if I could come straight to the station's studio to discuss the tragedy on air. Shortly after, still in a state of mild shock over the news, I drove to the station, where I would join live, on-air discussions on probable causes of the tragedy with Australian-born payload specialist Paul Scully-Power.

There was still very little to go on as to the cause of the accident, but even as that terrible morning wore on without any conclusive evidence to explain the breakup and loss of *Columbia* just sixteen minutes before the scheduled touchdown, one potent memory stayed with me. Five years earlier, in October 1998, I was at the Kennedy Space Center at the kind invitation of crewmember Scott Parazynski to attend the STS-95 launch of former Mercury astronaut and U.S. senator John Glenn and the crew of the shuttle *Discovery*. On arrival at the cape's VIP reception area I received a joyful greeting and warm hug from a surprised astronaut Laurel Clark, a med-

ical doctor from the U.S. Navy. We knew each other through our correspondence following her selection as a mission specialist in NASA's group
16 two years earlier, and my trip to view the shuttle launch had been made
in haste. She could not believe I had flown all the way from Australia to be
there and said it was wonderful to finally meet me. Almost five years later,
on 1 February 2003, Laurel was returning home from space in triumph
with her crew after their highly successful science mission. Then, tragically,
they all lost their lives when *Columbia* broke up over Texas during reentry.

Laurel, along with three of her STS-107 crewmates, pilot Willie McCool
and fellow mission specialists David Brown and Ilan Ramon from Israel,
were on their first mission into space. For close to sixteen days they had
been realizing and sharing a long-held dream of flying into space and were
returning home after living and working as a team aboard the shuttle *Columbia*. The first space-rated orbiter in NASA's shuttle fleet, *Columbia* had successfully completed the first operational spaceflight in the shuttle program,
STS-1, back in April 1981, and twenty-seven orbital missions overall. That
morning, the reality of what had happened hours earlier hit me hard, as it
involved an astronaut with whom I not only had shared correspondence
but had also met under such unforgettably happy circumstances.

Sadly, like the shuttle *Challenger* some seventeen years earlier, *Columbia* and its crew of seven never made it home. As astrophysicist and author
Carl Sagan once said of space travel, "If we are to send people, it must be
for a very good reason—and with a realistic understanding that almost certainly we will lose lives. Astronauts and cosmonauts have always understood
this. Nevertheless, there has been and will be no shortage of volunteers."

The fact that Laurel and many others have actually succeeded over the
years in achieving their long-held dream of spaceflight is perhaps of some
consolation as we recall the sudden and tragic end of a number of space
travelers. However, as Carl Sagan suggested, the catastrophic loss of those
two shuttle crews will always serve to remind us of the extraordinary per-
ils associated with that outward urge that impels human beings to want to
ride those mammoth, fuel-engorged rockets into space.

If the *Challenger* and *Columbia* tragedies had not occurred, many of
those whose stories are now told in this book would have finally realized
their ambition of flying into space. Nevertheless, history is history, and the
disappointments and disasters of the past should not discourage or dismay

present and future generations of those adventurers filled with determination and with stars in their eyes who seek to go on a journey of discovery and realize the fulfilment of a long-held dream.

In the inspiring words of the great American essayist, poet, and philosopher Ralph Waldo Emerson, "Dare to live the life you have dreamed for yourself. Go forward and make your dreams come true."

Sources

Books

Burgess, Colin. *Australia's Astronauts: Countdown to a Spaceflight Dream.* Berowra NSW: Communications Agency, 2009.

——. *Oceans to Orbit: The Story of Australia's First Man in Space, Dr. Paul Scully-Power.* Sydney NSW: Playright Publishing, 1995.

Burgess, Colin, and Rex Hall. *The First Soviet Cosmonaut Team: Their Lives, Legacies, and Historical Impact.* New York: Springer-Praxis Books, 2008.

Cassutt, Michael. *Who's Who in Space: The International Space Station Edition.* New York: Macmillan, 1999.

Cernan, Eugene, and Don Davis. *The Last Man on the Moon: Astronaut Eugene Cernan and America's Race in Space.* New York: St. Martin's Press, 1999.

Cunningham, Walter. *The All-American Boys: An Insider's Look at the U.S. Space Program.* New York: Macmillan, 1977.

DeGroot, Gerard J. *Dark Side of the Moon: The Magnificent Madness of the American Lunar Quest.* New York: New York University Press, 2006.

Ellis, Frank D. *No Man Walks Alone.* Old Tappan NJ: Revell, 1968.

French, Francis, and Colin Burgess. *In the Shadow of the Moon: A Challenging Journey to Tranquility, 1965–1969.* Lincoln: University of Nebraska Press, 2007.

——. *Into That Silent Sea: Trailblazers of the Space Era, 1961–1965.* Lincoln: University of Nebraska Press, 2007.

Graveline, Duane, MD. *Surly Bonds.* Self-published, Amazon Digital Services, 2010.

Graveline, Duane, MD, and Fred Kelly, MD. *From Laika with Love: Secret Soviet Gifts to Apollo.* Merritt Island FL: Self-published, Spacedoc Media, 2007.

Hawthorne, Douglas B. *Men and Women of Space.* San Diego CA: Univeld, 1992.

Hooper, Gordon R. *The Soviet Cosmonaut Team: A Comprehensive Guide to the Men and Women of the Soviet Manned Space Programme.* Suffolk, UK: GRH Publications, 1986.

Irwin, James B., and William A. Emerson Jr. *To Rule the Night: The Discovery Voyage of Astronaut Jim Irwin.* Nashville TN: Holman Bible Publishers, 1973.

Kelly, Fred, MD. *America's Astronauts and Their Indestructible Spirit*. Glendale CA: TAB Aero Books, 1986.

Rosholt, Robert L. *An Administrative History of NASA, 1958–1963*. NASA Special Publication SP-4101. Washington DC: NASA, 1966.

Shayler, David J., and Colin Burgess. *The Last of NASA's Original Pilot Astronauts: Expanding the Space Frontier in the Late Sixties*. New York: Springer-Praxis Books, 2017.

———. *NASA's Scientist-Astronauts*. New York: Springer-Praxis Books, 2006.

Slayton, Donald K., and Michael Cassutt. *Deke! U.S. Manned Space from Mercury to the Space Shuttle*. New York: Forge Books, 1994.

Tucker, Tom. *Touchdown: The Development of Propulsion Controlled Aircraft*. NASA Monographs in Aerospace History 16. Edwards Air Force Base CA: NASA Dryden Flight Research Center, 1999.

Periodicals and Online Articles

Amos, Jonathan. "When Britain Had a Small Astronaut Corps." *Spaceman* (blog), 19 March 2010. http://www.bbc.co.uk/blogs/thereporters/jonathanamos/2010/03/when-britain-had-a-small-astro.shtml.

Anderson, William. "Navy Amputee's Aim Is to Be an Astronaut." *Chicago Tribune*, 28 June 1964.

"Anderson Astronaut Felt Challenger's Disaster Firsthand." *Anderson (SC) Independent*, 16 February 1986.

"Anderson Native, NASA Pilot Killed in Pitts Crash." *Palmetto Aviation* (SC), 1 July 1986.

Anthony, Shane. "Man Gets 15-Year Sentence in Fatal DWI Crash on I-70." *St. Louis Post-Dispatch*, 5 December 2009. http://www.stltoday.com/news/man-gets—year-sentence-in-fatal-dwi-crash-on/article_a2c3926f-c0de-5135-9408-5a84e11d3b57.html.

"Astronaut John Bull Leaves Space Program." *Victoria (TX) Advocate*, 17 July 1968.

Bell, Kim. "Wright City Man Killed When His Car Is Rear-Ended on Interstate 70 in St. Charles County." *St. Louis Post-Dispatch*, 19 February 2009. https://doctorbulldog.wordpress.com/2009/02/20/in-memory-of-robert-wood.

Berger, Eric. "Argentinian Astronaut Dies of Brain Tumor." *Houston Chronicle*, 7 October 2009.

Biondo, Steve. "He Dared to Dream." *Anderson (SC) Independent-Mail*, 30 May 1986.

Burgess, Colin, and Kate Doolan. "Apollo: The Lost Flights." *Spaceflight* 42, no. 9 (1970): 387–92.

Burns, Greg. "From Hanna to Heavens." *Anderson (SC) Independent-Mail*, 13 June 1985.

"Cernan Defends Scientist-Astronaut Crewmate." *The Eagle* (Bryan TX), 20 August 1971.

Chapman, Philip K. "The Failure of NASA: And a Way Out." *Space Daily*, 30 May 2003. http://www.spacedaily.com/news/oped-03zn1.html.

"Dawning of a New Space Age." *Melbourne Herald Sun*, 17 July 1999.

"Death of Top Army Signals Expert and Intelligence Officer." *Courier and Advertiser* (Scotland), 26 December 2011.

Ellis, Frank. "No Man Walks Alone." *Foundation*, Spring 1996, 56–67.

Engle, Eloise. "He Fights for the Right to Serve His Country." *Listen* 17, no. 5 (1964): 17–19.

"First Such Switch: Britain to Use Ariane Instead of U.S. Shuttle." *Los Angeles Times*, 29 May 1986.

"Frank King Ellis." *Pensacola (FL) News Journal*, 1 January 2017.

Goldin, Daniel S., and John Murtha. Letter to the editor. *Indiana (PA) Gazette*, 28 June 1984.

Halvorson, Todd. "KSC Workers' Dreams Blast Off." *Florida Today*, 2 May 1996.

Hendrickx, Bart. "The Kamanin Diaries (1960–1963)." *Journal of the British Interplanetary Society* 50 (1997): 33–40.

Hengeveld, Ed. "Apollo Vacuum Chamber Tests: All Dressed Up and No Place to Go." *Spaceflight* 42, no. 4 (2000): 171–74.

Houston, Glenna. "Test Pilot's Life Full of Unknown Risks." *Anderson (SC) Independent-Mail*, 1983.

John S. Bull obituary. *San Jose Mercury News*, 29 August 2008.

Kersmarki, Michael. "200 Pay Tribute to Thorne." *Anderson (SC) Independent*, 2 June 1986.

Launius, Roger. "Exploding the Myth of Popular Support for Project Apollo." *Roger Launius's Blog* (blog), 16 August 2010. https://launiusr.wordpress.com /2010/08/16/exploding-the-myth-of-popular-support-for-project-apollo.

Lewis, Stephen. "The Fascinating Story of the York Man Who Should Have Been the First Briton in Space." *York Press* (UK), 10 May 2010. http://www .yorkpress.co.uk/news/8156108.The_fascinating_story_of_the_York_man _who_should_have_been_the_first_Briton_in_space/.

Logan, John S. "Duane Graveline, Doctor Who Was Forced Out as an Astronaut, Dies at 85." *New York Times*, 17 September 2016.

Manby, Christine. "Marina Popovich: Record-Breaking Soviet Aviator Who Highlighted UFO Sightings." *Independent* (UK), 17 December 2017.

Martin, David. "He Fights for a Chance to Fly." *Life*, 25 October 1963, 55–58.

Molina, David. "Astronaut Glides By." *Nogales (AZ) International*, 4 May 2003.

http://www.nogalesinternational.com/news/astronaut-glides-by/article
_705ab0cd-6c37-5d9c-99a3-3edf5d69fac8.html.

NASA, John F. Kennedy Space Center. "Two KSC Employees Named Astronaut
Candidates." *NASA Spaceport News* 35, no. 9 (1996): 1, 8.

NASA, Lyndon B. Johnson Space Center. "Astronaut John Sumter Bull (Ph.D.):
Biography Data." December 2008. www.jsc.nasa.gov/Bios/htmlbios/bull
-js.html.

———. "The Moon-Walker's New Clothes." *Space News Roundup*, 19 January 1968, 1.

———. "Stephen D. Thorne (Lieutenant Commander, USN)." November 1986.
https://www.jsc.nasa.gov/Bios/htmlbios/thorne.html.

———. "Two Die in Aircraft Crash." *Space News Roundup*, 30 May 1986, 2.

"NASA Names 19 New Astronauts." *Kingsport (TN) Times*, 5 April 1966.

Normyle, William J. "Major Decision on Space Near." *Aviation Week and Space
Technology* 93, no. 7 (1970): 14–15.

Paslay, Bob. "Anderson Man Trains for Shuttle Flight." *News Daily* (SC), 19
August 1985.

Pearlman, Robert Z. "Last Lunar Landing Launch 40 Years Ago Today." Col-
lectSPACE, December 7, 2012. http://www.collectspace.com/news/news
-120712a.html.

"Pocket Rockets." *Sydney Morning Herald*, 24 April 1999.

Ponche, Kalen. "Man Charged in Crash That Killed Wright City Triathlete."
St. Charles (MO) Post-Dispatch, 25 February 2009. http://www.stltoday
.com/suburban-journals/stcharles/news/crime/man-charged-in-crash
-that-killed-wright-city-triathlete/article_52210ce5-f3d7-5c42-9308
-fe3529a34230.html.

Quine, Tony. "Tereshkova's Secret Sisters." Pts. 1 and 2. *Spaceflight* 54, no. 6 (2012):
216–17; 54, no. 7 (2012): 266–67.

Sanford, Robert. "Mitsubishi to Aid McDonnell in Space Drug Development."
St. Louis Post-Dispatch, 6 May 1985.

Shok, Holly. "Patricia Robertson." Pennsylvania Center for the Book, Fall 2009.
https://pabook.libraries.psu.edu/literary-cultural-heritage-map-pa/bios
/Robertson__Patricia.

Shute, Joe. "Meet the 'Nearly Men' of Space." *Daily Telegraph* (London), 19
December 2015.

"Shuttle Hopefuls Named." *Flight International*, 24 March 1984, 734.

"Skynet IV: Passport to a UK Astronaut?" *Flight International*, 7 January 1984, 32.

Stevenson, Robert E. "The Energy of Carla." *Naval Research Reviews*, July 1963, 13–16.

Stevenson, Robert K. "Dr. Robert E. Stevenson: Father of Space Oceanography."
EIR Science and Technology, 2 November 2001, 42.

Ubell, Earl. "The Moon Is More of a Mystery Than Ever." *New York Times*, 16 April 1972.

"UK Astronaut Group Disbanded." *Flight International*, 28 June 1986, 52.

United Press International. "One of Four Candidates to Be Britain's First Man in Space." 14 June 1984. http://www.upi.com/Archives/1984/06/14/One-of -four-candidates-to-be-Britains-first-man/1172456033600.

———. "Plane Crash Kills Astronaut Trainee, NASA Controller." 24 May 1986. http://www.upi.com/Archives/1986/05/24/Plane-crash-kills-astronaut -trainee-NASA-controller/8682517291200/?spt=su.

Interviews and Personal Communications

Badillo, Ana (Caldeiro). Email correspondence with author, 7 July 2017–8 August 2017.

Bull, Scott. Email correspondence with author, 29 July 2011.

Burcham, Frank W. (Bill). Message relayed to author by Joseph J. Totah, 27 August 2011.

Carr, Jerry. Letter to Carlo Mikkelsen, 15 May 1996.

———. Letter to Francis French, n.d.

Chapman, Philip. Email attaching biographical information, 5 October 2002.

———. Email correspondence with author, 15 November 1997.

———. Interview conducted on Sydney radio station 2FC, broadcast 6 December 1970.

Farrimond, Richard. Email correspondence with author, 3–4 August 2017.

Ferrell, Jack. Email correspondence with author, 23 June 2016.

Fletcher, James C. Letter to Caspar Weinberger, 3 November 1971.

Gorie, Dominic. Email correspondence with author, 7 June 2017–29 August 2017.

Graveline, Duane, MD. Interviews with author, Merritt Island, Florida, 6–9 November 2006 and 18–19 October 2011.

Haise, Fred. Letter to author, 8 October 1996.

Kaneshige, John T. Message relayed to author by Joseph J. Totah, 27 August 2011.

Lineberry, Wes. Email correspondence with author, 11 September 2017.

Lousma, Jack. Letter to author, 6 January 1997.

Omelchenko, Svetlana. Letters to author, 16 September 2000–1 March 2001.

Popovich, Marina. Interview conducted by Rex Hall and Bert Vis, Star City, Moscow, 14 April 2007.

Quine, Tony. Email correspondence with author, 8–10 July 2017.

Robertson, Scott. Email correspondence with author, 14 April 2017–12 July 2017.

Schwarting, Sue (Thorne). Email correspondence with author, 5 May 2017–19 September 2017.

Stevenson, Robert E. Letter to Francis French, n.d.

Stevenson, Robert K. Email correspondence with author, 2 July 2017–30 July 2017.

———. Telephone interview with author, 1 July 2017.

Stumpf, Robert (Bob). Email correspondence with author, 25 July 2017.

Sudarmono, Pratiwi. Letter containing responses to author's questions, 18 October 1999.

Swenson, Harry N. Message relayed to author by Joseph J. Totah, 27 August 2011.

Taylor, Kevin. Email correspondence with author, 6 September 2016–15 July 2017.

Thorne, Melanie. Email correspondence with author, 25 July 2017–6 September 2017.

Thuot, Pierre. Tribute message via Melanie Thorne, 6 September 2017.

Totah, Joseph. Email correspondence with author, 27 August 2011.

Tuttle, Leslie. Email correspondence with author, 2 September 2017.

Walker, Charles D. Email correspondence with author, 13–18 August 2017.

———. JSC Oral History interview with Sandra Johnson, Springfield, Virginia, 7 November 2006.

Wood, Alicia. Email correspondence with author, 1–20 September 2017.

———. Telephone interview, 13 September 2017.

Wood, Lucas. Email correspondence with author, 17 September 2017–24 October 2017.

Wood, Nigel. Email correspondence with author, 20 May 2017–31 July 2017.

Worden, Al. Email message to author regarding John S. Bull, 9 August 2011.

Other Sources

Aviation Safety Network Archive. National Transportation Safety Board report on loss of Pitts S-2A aircraft, 24 May 1986. Flight Safety Foundation. Updated 21 December 2016. https://aviation-safety.net/wikibase/wiki.php?id=43235.

Cabana, Bob. Memorial service eulogy for Stephen Thorne, Houston, Texas, 4 June 1986. Melanie Thorne private collection.

Caldeiro, Frank. "Frank—Cancer Survivor." YouTube video, 2:46. 9 April 2008. https://www.youtube.com/watch?v=hoqJZ8c7MNE.

Cowan, Emery. "Profile: Frank Ellis." University of Colorado magazine archive, Boulder CO, 2016.

Department of the Navy—Naval Historical Center. "U.S.S. Little Rock Helo Pilot Lt. Leif A. Elstad." Online at "Awards, Citations and Recognition Earned by the U.S.S. Little Rock and Her Crew," USS Little Rock Association, http://www.usslittlerock.org/awards_and_recognition.html.

Ertel, Ivan D., and Roland W. Newkirk. *The Apollo Spacecraft: A Chronology*. Vol. 4. *January 21, 1966–July 13, 1974*. NASA SP-4009. Washington DC: NASA Scientific and Technical Information Office, 1978. https://history.nasa.gov/SP-4009vol4.pdf.

"Frank K. Ellis, Distinguished Flying Cross." Hall of Valor Project, January 1964. https://valor.militarytimes.com/hero/305209.

Harrison, Jim. "Maj James Ryan 'Jim' Simons." Find a Grave, 29 September 2011.

Memorial 77294292. https://www.findagrave.com/memorial/77294292 /james-ryan-simons.

Lechago, Juan. "Fernando Caldeiro (Astronauta Argentino) de la NASA." Obituary for NASA, JSC, Houston TX, 7 October 2009. http://www.taringa .net/posts/info/1991420/Fernando-Caldeiro-Astronauta-Argentino-de -la-Nasa.html.

"Marina Lavrentieva Popovich (Vasilyeva)." *ASTRONote Space Encyclopedia.* Last updated 12 January 2017. http://www.astronaut.ru/as_rusia/lady62/text /popovich.htm?reload_coolmenus.

NASA. "NASA Future Plans." Press conference transcript, 13 January 1970. Comment by Thomas O. Paine, 13 January 1970.

NASA *Astrogram,* NASA Ames Research Center. August 2008. https://www.nasa .gov/centers/ames/pdf/268983main_Aug.08.Astrogram.smallfile.pdf.

NASA Lyndon B. Johnson Space Center. "NASA Selects 13 Astronaut Candidates." News release, no. 85-023, 4 June 1985.

NASA Manned Spacecraft Center. "Flight Crews for Second and Third Flights." News release, MSC 67-67, 20 November 1967.

———. "Man Rating Apollo Suits." News release, MSC 67-69, 4 December 1967.

———. "Nineteen New Astronauts Named." News release, MSC 66-22, 4 April 1966.

Office of Naval Research. "Obituary Notice 'Father of Space Oceanography' Robert E. Stevenson." Scripps Institute of Oceanography, 15 August 2001. https://scripps.ucsd.edu/news/2728.

"Patricia Hilliard Robertson: A Tribute to IUP's Astronaut." Indiana University of Pennsylvania, Special Collections and University Archives, Indiana PA. http://www.iup.edu/archives/digital-projects-and-exhibits/patricia -hilliard-robertson.

Pearson, O. L., and P. R. Gauthier. *Manned Operations for the Apollo Lunar Module in a Simulated Space Environment.* NASA Technical Note TH D-5760. Washington DC: NASA, June 1970. This technical note includes the Lunar Module Test Article 8 (LTA-8).

Robertson, Patricia Hilliard. *Patricia Hilliard Robertson: A Tribute to IUP's Astronaut.* Memorial service eulogy to her father, 8 August 1999. Scrapbook sec. Indiana University of Pennsylvania, Special Collections and University Archives, Indiana PA. https://www.iup.edu/archives/digital-projects -and-exhibits/patricia-hilliard-robertson.

"Stephen Thorne '75." USNA Virtual Memorial Hall. https://usnamemorialhall.org /index.php/STEPHEN_D._THORNE,_LCDR,_USN.

Stevenson, Robert K. "Highlights of the Career of Dr. Robert E. Stevenson, 'The Father of Oceanography.'" Privately prepared unpublished and undated biography.

T. L. Hanna High School Guidance Department. "Scholarships." Last updated 8 April 2013. https://www.anderson5.net/cms/lib02/SC01001931/Centricity /Domain/875/20130408%20Scholarships.pdf.

U.S. Geological Survey. *Detailed Listing of Personnel Changes for the Branch of Astrogeology from 1960 through 1972.* USGS Open-File Report 2005-1190, Appendix B. https://pubs.usgs.gov/of/2005/1190/of2005-1190_appendix_b.pdf.

Index

CFES (continuous flow electrophoresis system), 218

Chaffee, Roger, 58

Challenger, 73, 117–19, 163, 218, 221

Challenger disaster: cause of, 139–40, 164; consequences of, 4–5, 7, 120, 140–41, 145, 164–65, 215, 222–23, 246; Ronald Reagan on, 99–100

Chapman, Colin Robison, 54

Chapman, Kristen de Querilleau, 62

Chapman, Pamela Gatenby, 57

Chapman, Peter Hume, 57

Chapman, Philip K., *61, 64*; in Antarctica, 56–57, 62; applying for astronaut position, 53, 59; background of, 54–55; becoming American, 57, 59; children of, 57, 62; on Deke Slayton, 66–68; divorce of, 71; education of, 54–55, 58; honors for, 58; marriages of, 57, 72; on NASA, 73; NASA career of, 63–66, 68–69, 69–71; as NASA civilian, 60–61; post-astronaut career of, 71–72; pre-astronaut career of, 55–57, 58; in retirement, 73; on Soviet space program, 63–65; in training, 60, 62

Chapman, Phyllis Kenyon, 54

Chappell, Charles, 53

Chawla, Kalpana, 205, 210

Chernyak, Lyudmilla, 81

Clark, Laurel, 210, 236, 238, 241, 245–46

Clarke, Arthur C.: *Interplanetary Flight*, 54–55

Coats, Michael, 144, 162

Coester, Steve, 232–33

Cold War, 64

Collins, Michael, 11, 128

Columbia, 31, 141–42, 144–45, 149, 152, 163, 201

Columbia disaster, 205, 210, 238, 239, 241, 245–47

Conrad, Charles (Pete), 22, 24, 65

continuous flow electrophoresis system (CFES), 218

Cooper, Gordon, 17, 18

cosmonauts, 1–4; accomplishments of, 58, 185; American astronauts and, 63–64, 169; female, 84, 189–92, 193–95; first group of, 188–89; living conditions of, 187–88; personal lives of, 196–97; as researchers, 81, 84; risks taken by, 196; secrecy surrounding, 188–89; in space disaster, 58

Crippen, Bob, 118, *121*, 152, 201

CSA (Canadian Space Agency), 8

Culbertson, Frank, 209, 210–11

Cunningham, Walt, 47

The Dark Side of Statins (Graveline), 50

Deke! (Slayton and Cassutt), 47

Delovoy Mir, 80, 85

Delta rockets, 145, 147, 148

Discovery, 142, 245

divorce, 35–36, 46–48, 52

DOSAAF (All-Union Voluntary Society for Assistance to the Army, Air Force, and Navy), 186, 187, 190

Dougherty, Sandy, 102

Duffy, Brian, 97

Duque, Pedro, 236

Dyson, Esther, 10

Eagle, 65

Eisele, Donn, 17–18

Electrophoresis Operations in Space (EOS), 218, 219–20, 221–22

Ellis, Christine Robarts, 170, 172–73, 183

Ellis, Dana Angela, 173, 183

Ellis, Daniel Andrew, 177, 183

Ellis, David Alan, 170, 183

Ellis, Debra Ann, 170, 183

Ellis, Frances King, 170

Ellis, Frank K., *178*; in accident, 170, 171–72; applying for astronaut position, 180–81; background of, 170; career of, 170–71, 182; character of, 171–72, 181–82; children of, 170, 173, 177; death of, 183; education of, 170, 179; honors for, 174; leg amputations of, 172–74; marriage of, 170; *No Man Walks Alone*, 181; and solo flight status, 174–79, 182

Ellis, James Delmont, 170

Emero, Donald, 232

England, Tony, 59, 68

Engle, Joe Henry, 15–16, *16*, 30–31

Enomoto, Daisuke, 10

Enos (chimpanzee), 43

EOS (Electrophoresis Operations in Space), 218, 219–20, 221–22

Evans, Ron, *16*

Evening Press, 161

Experimental Astronomy Laboratory, 57, 58

In the Outward Odyssey: A People's History of Spaceflight series

Into That Silent Sea: Trailblazers of the Space Era, 1961–1965
Francis French and Colin Burgess
Foreword by Paul Haney

In the Shadow of the Moon: A Challenging Journey to Tranquility, 1965–1969
Francis French and Colin Burgess
Foreword by Walter Cunningham

To a Distant Day: The Rocket Pioneers
Chris Gainor
Foreword by Alfred Worden

Homesteading Space: The Skylab Story
David Hitt, Owen Garriott, and Joe Kerwin
Foreword by Homer Hickam

Ambassadors from Earth: Pioneering Explorations with Unmanned Spacecraft
Jay Gallentine

Footprints in the Dust: The Epic Voyages of Apollo, 1969–1975
Edited by Colin Burgess
Foreword by Richard F. Gordon

Realizing Tomorrow: The Path to Private Spaceflight
Chris Dubbs and Emeline Paat-Dahlstrom
Foreword by Charles D. Walker

The X-15 Rocket Plane: Flying the First Wings into Space
Michelle Evans
Foreword by Joe H. Engle

Wheels Stop: The Tragedies and Triumphs of the Space Shuttle Program, 1986–2011
Rick Houston
Foreword by Jerry Ross

Bold They Rise
David Hitt and Heather R. Smith
Foreword by Bob Crippen

Go, Flight! The Unsung Heroes of Mission Control, 1965–1992
Rick Houston and Milt Heflin
Foreword by John Aaron

Infinity Beckoned: Adventuring Through the Inner Solar System, 1969–1989
Jay Gallentine
Foreword by Bobak Ferdowsi

Fallen Astronauts: Heroes Who Died Reaching for the Moon, Revised Edition
Colin Burgess and Kate Doolan with Bert Vis
Foreword by Eugene A. Cernan

Apollo Pilot: The Memoir of Astronaut Donn Eisele
Donn Eisele
Edited and with a foreword by Francis French
Afterword by Susie Eisele Black

Outposts on the Frontier: A Fifty-Year History of Space Stations
Jay Chladek
Foreword by Clayton C. Anderson

Come Fly with Us: NASA's Payload Specialist Program
Melvin Croft and John Youskauskas
Foreword by Don Thomas

Shattered Dreams: The Lost and Canceled Space Missions
Colin Burgess
Foreword by Don Thomas

To order or obtain more information on these or other University of Nebraska Press titles, visit nebraskapress.unl.edu.